Destined for Greatness

Destined for Greatness

Passions, Dreams, and Aspirations in a College Music Town

MICHAEL RAMIREZ

Rutgers University Press

New Brunswick, Camden, and Newark, New Jersey, and London

Library of Congress Cataloging-in-Publication Data

Names: Ramirez, Michael, 1976– author.
Title: Destined for greatness : passions, dreams, and aspirations in a college music town /
    Michael Ramirez.
Description: New Brunswick, New Jersey : Rutgers University Press, [2017] | Includes
    bibliographical references and index.
Identifiers: LCCN 2017033646 | ISBN 9780813588124 (cloth : alk. paper) |
    ISBN 9780813588117 (pbk. : alk. paper)
Subjects: LCSH: Rock musicians—Gerogia—Athens—Social conditions. | Rock music—
    Social aspects—Gerogia—Athens.
Classification: LCC ML3918.R63 R36 2017 | DDC 781.6609758/18—dc23
LC record available at https://lccn.loc.gov/2017033646

A British Cataloging-in-Publication record for this book is available from the British Library.

♾ The paper used in this publication meets the requirements of the American National Standard for Information Sciences—Permanence of Paper for Printed Library Materials, ANSI
Z39.48–1992.

www.rutgersuniversitypress.org

Manufactured in the United States of America

For Ashley, Brianna, and Sheila, my three dark-haired beauties.

Contents

Contents

Destined for Greatness

Introduction

●●●●●●●●●●●●●●●●●●●●●●

> I better have a good scar when this is
> all over.
> –Don Chambers, "Mountain"

I challenge you to think of a musician more impeccably feminine than Dolly Parton. Platinum blonde hair teased to the skies, famous buxom chest, and her immediately recognizable, high-pitched, sugary-sweet voice—her persona manifests what can only be described as an emphasized femininity (Connell 1987). Renowned for her songs of heartbreak and love gone wrong, Parton is femininity incarnate. One of the most telling songs in her catalog is "Jolene," originally released in 1973. In it, Parton pleads with the green-eyed, auburn-haired namesake to grant her the most important of favors: to not lure her man away. The story is one of fiction, but like many artists' songs, Parton admits that the song sprang from a real-life moment of fear—her reflecting on the possibility that another could tempt her partner away and the feelings of inadequacy such thoughts trigger.

Fast forward two and a half decades to the early 2000s. Rock duo the White Stripes—singer/guitarist Jack White and drummer Meg White—bathed in the blues tradition, begin including a cover of Parton's classic song in their repertoire. What is most surprising about the cover—in addition to the very idea of a garage rock band covering a country song, not as parody, but as an honorarium to the country icon—is the fact that the lyrics remain perfectly intact. White takes artistic liberty with the framework of the song—it's louder, faster, less melodic, a starker contrast in soft and loud—yet keeps the lyrics identical to Parton's original construction, leaving even the pronouns in place. Parton sings the song to Jolene, asking her to not tempt her man. White—presumably a straight, heteronormative man himself—sings the exact same words, begging Jolene to not tempt *his* man from him. It would have been simple to substitute alternate pronouns to make it a heteronormative story. The White Stripes' unaltered lyrics to "Jolene," however, add curious layers to the song. The gendered narrative of a woman pining for the forever with her man, through Jack White's filter twenty years later, now troubles gender. But troubling gender is not particularly new to Jack White (born John Gillis).

Despite intentional misleadings the band gave the press upon their celebrity, Jack and Meg are not siblings, but instead former lovers. Upon getting married, Jack Gillis took Meg's last name as his own, becoming Jack White.[1] At the demise of the relationship, the band continued, as did Jack's identity as Jack White, keeping her last name upon the dissolution of the marriage. Years later, upon falling in love with Karen Elson, the couple exchanged wedding vows. Jack, this time around, kept intact his surname as White. In 2006, the couple had their first child, Scarlett, and welcomed their second child, Henry, the following year. Interestingly enough, both children are christened with Jack's surname, thus sharing the last name not of their birth mother, but instead of Jack's ex-wife. Keeping the pronouns intact in his cover of Dolly Parton's song is only the tip of the gender-inverted iceberg in Jack White's history, whose life is peppered with troubling gender. The history of country cover songs and rock-and-roll surname etymologies is interesting in and of itself. But the relevance goes further than that, as these issues intersect with themes that are the focus of this book.

Music is culture incarnate. Music is central to many people's lives, young and old, as they move through childhood and adolescence to adulthood and beyond. Hit songs and popular artists over subsequent decades are part of what defines each generation as its own. Music has the power to stick with each generation, marking them in distinct and long-lasting ways (Kotarba 2013). Music is about identity: we are what we listen to, we are the concert T-shirt we decide to front. The genres and bands we follow presumably tell us something about who we are as individuals. Music is about aging. As we move through the life course, not only may people's musical tastes change, but the importance of music in their lives also tends to wax and wane. Music is—or *should* be—a leisure. As we move into adulthood, music should become less of a priority. And consequences abound to those for whom it does not.

Music is about inequality. The consumption of and participation in music is shaped by numerous dimensions of stratification. Those from the middle and upper classes not only have more resources to purchase music and attend musical performances, but they also are more likely to invest in the cultural capital of learning to play instruments. Music also tells a story about gender. Music genres, instruments, and even the experience of fandom bear on the social organization of gender.[2]

More than simply something people listen to, music is a barometer of our cultural landscape throughout history, marking what is valued, what is relevant, and what defines us as a nation. Music can literally be background music, whispering stories that are so nearly inaudible we fail to pick up on what they are telling us about our culture. Or we can figuratively boost the volume and be cognizant of the messages music is sharing with us about life in our world.

Music, Gender, and Aging

The history of rock music is a relatively short one, the genre being birthed in the early 1950s.[3] The icons of rock music who have emerged over the course of its short history can, however, certainly be characterized as diverse. Imagine them assembled side by side, a veritable line up of the icons of rock music culture.[4] At the helm of rock history are two icons: Chuck Berry and Elvis Presley, the latter singularly crowned the King of Rock Roll. Steeped in rhythm and blues, their reinvention of the style of the guitar and songwriting started the revolution of rock music in the 1950s. The Rolling Stones, the Beatles, and Jimi Hendrix were in their wake, defining the classic era of rock in the 1960s, along with folk hero Bob Dylan. The 1970s introduced David Bowie, Elvis Costello, Joan Jett, Bruce Springsteen, Heart, and seminal punk bands the Clash, the Sex Pistols, and the Ramones. 1980s rock changed direction with more introspective bands such as R.E.M. and The Police, while "cock rock" bands such as Guns N' Roses, Van Halen, and Mötley Crüe garnered massive followings as well. The 1990s birthed new trajectories of rock such as grunge, with Nirvana at the vanguard, and indie/college rock, including Pavement, the Flaming Lips, and Liz Phair.

What may at first stand out in this lineup of rock icons is their seeming diversity. These musicians and bands certainly sound distinct from one another, as the music they've created has little overlap other than the obligatory guitar and amplifier. They have unique presentations of self, each artist certainly inhabiting different styles and fashions. But, what is also hard to overlook is that these icons—nearly every last one of them—are virtually the same person in different clothing. Nearly all are men. Nearly all are white. Rock music has opened its figurative doors to women and people of color since the early 2000s, but they are few and far between. Rock music has, throughout its relatively short history, been a world populated by men.

One saving grace among the sea of men musicians in rock music is the range of masculinities they have inhabited. Whether intentionally or not, rock musicians, those discussed above and countless others over the genre's sixty-year history, have played with gender. Elvis was a consummate performer, his sexually suggestive body movements deemed too controversial for mainstream media during his era. Though a heartthrob with throngs of teenage girls pining for him, the press often described him in feminine terms in which he "embodied an underdeveloped masculinity" (Craig 2014: 85). David Bowie most profoundly toyed with gender: the concoction of his Ziggy Stardust stage persona was the immaculate blending of masculinity and femininity. Bruce Springsteen, in contrast, was the very definition of masculine Americana. Sprung from the salt of the earth, he has given voice to a population overlooked, silenced, and ignored: the working class. R.E.M., springing from the college music town that is the focus of this book, was in many ways the antithesis of rock culture. Far more melodic in nature, they also seemed less invested in fame, fortune, and the traditional rock masculinity.

All of this is to say that the history of rock music is in many ways a history of masculinity—the multitude of ways men have reconfigured the meanings and performances of what it means to be a man. The ladies' man, the everyman, the revolutionary, the working-class hero, and the introspective, softer man: despite the negligible variation in the gender composition in rock, it has witnessed a ceaseless wave after wave of change in masculinities over time.

Fortunately, music culture has become more inclusive in recent years. Women and people of color are increasingly represented in various subgenres within rock music worlds. The ideal type rock star is no longer necessarily a man, as women are not only entering but succeeding in the rock world. Likewise, backhanded "She's a good guitarist for a girl" compliments are waning, and women are increasingly ranked as rock's best musicians and accruing accolades in recent years. Girls and women are kindling interests in music at younger ages, and those pursuits are persisting into adulthood. Likewise, women are not only more invested in music as consumers and fans, but also as musicians themselves. Finally, and perhaps most importantly, girls and women are increasingly picking up instruments and forming bands of their own, reshaping the contours of gender in the rock musical landscape.[5] These issues ground the foundation of this book.

In this book, I examine the lives and aspirations of independent rock musicians in the college music town of Athens, Georgia. Independent (indie) rock is characterized by an anticommercial ethos, much like punk, in which bands use more limited resources in the performance and production of music. Unlike punk, however, indie rock typically embodies less macho, less aggressive masculinities with greater room for women and femininities. Nationally, the mid-2000s era of indie rock witnessed a return to a stripped-down "garage rock" sound. The scene in Athens mirrored this shift as well, along with a simultaneous nudging toward the pop end of the musical continuum. Scholars have examined other celebrated music scenes in the United States, especially those in Austin, Nashville, and Chicago (Grazian 2003; Shank 1994; Wynn 2015). These studies illustrate the extent to which culture and structure enable music scenes to thrive and musicians therein to persist. To be sure, the social structures of music scenes do more than allow for the cultural production of music. Just as importantly, they provide social space for opportunities for the

FIGURE 1 Caledonia Lounge, one of the many iconic music venues in
Athens, Georgia (Photo by Mike White, deadlydesigns.com)

construction of new identities (Shank 1994). Similarly, in this book, I attend
to issues of the context of the locale, particularly as prominent influences of
the opportunities and constraints that local musicians happen upon as they
forge musical careers. As a prominent college music town in the United States,
Athens shares some similarities with other influential music cities, such as Austin and Nashville (Shank 1994; Wynn 2015). Its size, locale, and culture, however, provide distinct and, for the most part, limited opportunities for local
musicians that are contextually important in this analysis.

The sociocultural context of Athens during this era informs the approach
to this book and the questions it answers. Within this framework, I focus on

the intersections of musical careers, gender, and adulthood among musicians active in the local music scene. My purpose is to examine the life course trajectories that allow for the pursuit of musical careers in a reputable college music scene, paying particular attention to the ways in which such aspirations are negotiated as women and men transition to adulthood within the contours of the culture's gendered landscape. Pursuing careers in rock music is seemingly open ended, insofar as musicians self-enter the world that has no "hard" requisites for admission. Yet, how open is access to the music world? And who is likely to succeed? Furthermore, as musicians increase their commitment to music during the all-important entry years of adulthood, what consequences does the pursuit of music have on the transition to adulthood?

In the coming chapters, I will trace the various life course pathways that lead women and men to pursue musical careers. Interests in music start out early in life for many musicians, and early events in the life course harbor great significance for their adult lives. For other musicians, more recent experiences in late adolescence and particularly the early adult years are more consequential. I also examine consequences pursuing musical careers has on multiple aspects of musicians' identities. Men and women who wholeheartedly devote their lives to music often have difficulty identifying as legitimate musicians. Despite their being in bands that tour and have garnered fans across the United States, they are often uncomfortable with claiming an authentic musician identity. The informality of the music world—the very aspect that should ease their entrance to the music world—paradoxically makes identifying as a musician more precarious. Gender is a centerpiece of musicians' experiences in the music world. Men's and women's life courses are similar in many respects, but diverge in key aspects that profoundly affect the likelihoods of making musical careers a reality. Men generally have an easier time entering the music world, while women often must negotiate their entrance with caution and additional effort.

I also assess persistence in musical careers. Not all musicians foresee a lifetime centered on music. Who remains most committed to music varies based on factors other than skill, fan base, and recognition in the music world. Despite their plans for the future, all of the musicians see their time in the music world as shaping their identities and life courses in profound ways, and as beneficial to their personal developments, as well as future careers, be they in music or elsewhere.

The Social Organization of Music, Careers, and the Life Course

Music, Culture, and (Shifting) Modes of Gender

Like numerous aspects of social life, gender is deeply embedded in rock music culture. In the first place, rock music is a cultural arena coded as masculine

(Cohen 1997; Frith and McRobbie 1990; Leblanc 1999; Leonard 2007). The rock attitude—tough, brash, defiant, and sexually indiscreet—is more closely aligned with traditional masculine gender norms than to femininity (Frith 1981). Moreover, rock instruments are catalogued as "men's" instruments (Clawson 1999). The guitar, the drum kit, the bass—all are heavy instruments, figuratively and literally, that are understood as masculine. Rock critics and fans rely upon Freudian imagery in discussing the guitar, which is often envisioned as a cultural extension of one's manhood (Frith and McRobbie 1990).

Second, rock music is structurally a male domain. By and large, musicianship is heavily stratified by gender, as a majority of musical performers are men (Bielby 2004; Frith 1981). Bands in various subgenres of rock are filled overwhelmingly with men, many of which were constructed with the explicit goal of the exclusion of women (Cohen 1997). Similarly, men's domination of music also takes the form of their overrepresentation in marketing roles of the music industry beyond musicianship. Men monopolize most business roles in the industry, filling a majority of production roles in recording and distribution companies. In contrast to women, men are also more likely to work in recording studios as producers and engineers. Men thus have substantial control over the products and images generated by performers of both genders in musical worlds. As a site of commercialized cultural production, the music industry is highly gender stratified. In sum, men—due to women's informal and formal exclusion from the arts—have long been the cultural producers of music—its primary musicians, songwriters, producers, and even critics. In this sense, the "art world" of music is one of masculinity (Becker 1982).

Despite the history of male domination of rock music culture, women are increasingly participating in music today as both fans and musicians. They do, however, continue to hold a limited presence within rock culture (Clawson 1999; Schilt and Giffort 2012). When they do participate in bands, women are likely to be backup singers in bands. They are often expected to "sing, not play" instruments (Groce and Cooper 1990: 224). In the instances when they do play instruments, they tend to hold less visible and less prestigious roles (Clawson 1999). For example, women are overrepresented among bass players, an instrument with modest status in rock culture. Furthermore, women musicians are apt to be sexualized, in terms of their appearances and expected behaviors. Women musicians often are hired for a limited and distinctive type of role within the bands. In general, women still hold token statuses as musical performers.

We can look early in the life course to understand symbolic reasons of women's limited instrumentation. One of the "first steps in learning the electric guitar force a young woman to break with one of the norms of traditional 'femininity': long, manicured, polished fingernails must be cut down" (Bayton 1997: 39). Another far more structural barrier to women's learning to play the guitar hinges on social networks, the medium through which the learning of rock music is often spread. Again, because rock is male dominated and children often self-segregate in their friendships by gender, girls are unlikely to be embedded in networks with other children who play the guitar and other rock instruments. As a result, boys learn how to play instruments from other boys and men in their social circles, while girls are excluded from such experiences.

Fandom in music takes a slightly different trajectory. While both genders participate in music culture as fans at approximately equal levels, their manifestations as fans contrast with one another.[6] When boys become fans, they want to become the rock stars they adore. Often in early adolescence, boys first play with their identities—dressing in ways that personify their fandom. They wear concert T-shirts, grow their hair out, and dress in clothing similar to their favorite bands. An American rite of passage is learning how to play the guitar, one that often stems from idolizing rock stars. By the high school years, many boys are learning rock instruments, spending countless hours holed up in their bedrooms attempting to master their favorite songs or perhaps even experimenting with writing original compositions of their own. Girls, on the other hand, engage in fandom in contrary ways. Upon discovering bands, girls are more likely to adore and pine for musicians in them (Coates 1997; Garratt 1990). Girls convert their rooms to shrines to their favorite music stars. Rarely do they choose (nor are they encouraged) to model the stars' behavior by learning instruments and becoming musicians themselves. Quite to the contrary, their fandom may center on connecting to musicians in other ways.[7] To participate in the rock music world means, for women and girls, to yearn for a romantic connection their heroes. Boys want to become their rock stars; girls want to marry them.[8]

Music has the power to reify normative conceptions of gender, as illustrated above, but has the power to challenge them at the same time. Take, for example, the case of punk. The 1970s witnessed the emergence of a genre that, from the onset, pushed music in new directions. Punk was founded on energy, on politics, and on a new (and lesser) requirement for the mastery of instruments. It was in many ways grounded on working-class foundations. To be punk, one did not need premium instruments, the highest skill, or the finest voice. Instead, a true punk needed, more than anything else, passion and ethos. Punk was heralded as the moment for women in music history, but it unfortunately never came (Reynolds and Press 1995). Despite its challenging inequalities and allowing a space for atypical musicians to participate in music, it relegated women to its outskirts—and literally to the back of the clubs. In the years since then, women have increasingly entered the punk scene. Seminal bands such as the Runaways, the Slits, and the Plasmatics, and the influx of women punk fans have shifted the punk scene since its inception. Women in punk scenes face a dual task, though. They must present themselves as legitimate punks and simultaneously as legitimate women (Leblanc 1999). These identities are difficult for women to balance, as the punk identity is the antithesis of femininity. Women have unmistakably carved a new space for themselves despite the culture of masculinity that imbues the scene. In so doing, they have disassembled and recreated femininity in punk subculture.

Punk is by no means the outlier when it comes to the embracement of women, though narrow it may be. Other scenes in the rock world have correspondingly carved more inclusive spaces for women, not to mention for men outside the bounds of hegemonic masculinity. Rock subgenres of late, particularly riot grrrl, straight edge, and indie rock, have veered major shifts in the structure and organization of music culture. Politics are a more critical centerpiece of rock microcosms today, and a culture of progressive politics has permeated contemporary scenes (Haenfler 2006; Monem 2007). Music culture is more inviting to women today, displayed by its subdued (though not entirely eradicated) misogyny and, in some cases, its heightened profeminist stance. Likewise, a culture of gender equality is increasingly informing behavior norms in contemporary rock (Schippers 2000, 2002). Contemporary music scenes, riot grrrl in particular, allow not simply for women's entrance to music worlds, but more fundamentally women's lifelong participation in music culture well into in the adult years (Giffort 2011; Schilt and Zobl 2008).

Of notable interest is the expanding genre of independent rock. Often noted for its "displaying a countercultural ethos of resistance to the market," indie rock also demonstrates a fluidity in the performance and enactment of gender (Bannister 2006: 57). For one, the image of the rock musician is less standardized within the genre. Cultural critics characterize indie rock as exhibiting a range of masculinities. Men in these bands "suggest a masculinity that is rather soft, vulnerable and less macho, less aggressive and assertive, less threatening or explicit than that promoted by many styles of heavy rock and metal, rap, or funk" (Cohen 1997: 29). Likewise, women are more regularly and widely visible in independent rock (Leonard 2007). In contrast to rock culture from years past, women are granted more autonomy, respect, and positive portrayals within the culture, due not solely to men granting it on their own, but more often to the history of women in music demanding equal treatment forthright (Monem 2007). By no means entirely balanced, women have made inroads into contemporary music worlds. Though more inviting to women today, problems persist, as women continue to have less status than men. Not only are women taken less seriously than men, but they also continue to be seen as peripheral members to the music world. Furthermore, the illusion of gender equality obscures the continued masculine organization by which access is structured. Music participants, by focusing on the "going rate" of sexism in music in other times and scenes, cast contemporary musical landscapes as inclusive, less sexist, and even equitable, while ignoring the continued dimensions that continue to privilege one group of men (Mullaney 2007).

Informal Careers

Music performance is simply a leisure activity for many people, but others, such as the men and women in this book, intend to pursue music more seriously as occupational endeavors. Scholars suggest that occupational aspirations are initially aroused through socialization within the context of the family (Clausen 1986). Family socialization and the exploration of interests, activities, academics, and extracurricular activities early in life expose youth to ideas as to what may be realized into aspirations later in life. The family's socioeconomic status acts as a key vehicle for children's aspirations (Lareau 2003; Wilson et al. 1993). Social class influences modes of parenting styles, which in turn can influence children's occupational aspirations (Kohn 1969). Middle- and upper-class families have more resources available to allow their children easier access and heightened opportunities to explore a more diverse range of activities and hobbies, from athletics to the arts. Such experiences can simply be diversions for some children, but others may develop heightened interests that can lead to occupational aspirations in related fields later in life. At the same time, sociologists are attentive to other powerful forces in play as occupational aspirations unfold, paying attention to both the agency that individuals enact as they choose particular occupational pathways while remaining attentive to structural forces that constrain those choices (Hamilton and Hamilton 2006).

Scholars have noted significant shifts in the occupational aspirations of contemporary generations. First, young adults today are not only optimistic about their future working lives but also suggest a wide array of career interests in which they are interested in pursuing. One important innovation among young adults is the generational shift in pursuing meaningful work rather than explicitly high-paying occupations. They increasingly define successful careers as those that reflect their personal interests, values, and priorities. Work is now more clearly focused on "self-growth and a personal quest for meaning and fulfillment" (Swartz et al. 2011: 72). As such, young adults are increasingly pursuing careers that they see as positively impacting the world and allowing for the expression of creativity. These shifts are particularly aligned with passions for musical careers for some.

Second, occupational pathways of today's young adults are characterized by "drift." Greater numbers of young men and women's lives are marked by multiple shifts from one occupational interest to another. Schneider and Stevenson (1999) have described young adults as ambitious and motivated, yet directionless. Others have characterized these trends as a "floundering" period of bouncing from job to job and one career interest to the next (Hamilton 2006). While some construe of this tendency as young adults' unwillingness to settle down, others see it as a "distinctly American pattern" in which they are not floundering per se, but instead are searching for the right job match, one that many will eventually attain (Hamilton 2006: 265; Heckman 1994). A growing number of young adults, similar to the ones in this book, are increasingly considering careers in the arts in their explorations for their right career. Nonstandard careers, those involving music performance in particular, are distinct in telling ways. In general, nonstandard careers are those often housed outside normative workplaces and institutions. They tend not to have simple, recurring patterns in their organization, but more typically are characterized by unusual sequences that are difficult to anticipate. These careers are often highly satisfying, yet may require a lengthier timeline to succeed in, thereby making them stressful in qualitatively different ways than are pathways to normative careers.

Scholars have described such career aspirations in two ways. A "subjective career" is understood as a self-defined line of activity (not necessarily regarded as work by the participants themselves) that is independent of external gauges of success and is not always visible (Evetts 1996; Stalp 2006; Stebbins 1979). "Serious leisure," in contrast, refers to the "systematic pursuit of an amateur, hobbyist, or volunteer core activity that is highly substantial, interesting, and fulfilling [in which] participants find a career in acquiring and expressing a combination of its special skills, knowledge, and experience" (Stebbins 1992: 3). Musicians do of course share some territory with both concepts. However, both are riddled with limitations that do not capture the working lives of musicians in their entirety.

Hence, I frame the musicians' engagement in music as "informal work." I suggest musical careers share qualities with similar nonstandard work and leisure pursuits explored and developed elsewhere, but are unique in critical aspects. I conceptualize informal work as characterized by the following dimensions. It is outside the standard structure and formal organizations and institutions of work. It includes no structured pathways to necessarily develop a career. Entrance is largely self-directed, requires no formal credentials or training, and is free from gatekeepers. Finally, it is not necessarily enjoyable or a leisure activity *per se* for participants. This precise conceptualization of informal work, as will be illustrated, goes beyond dimensions ignored by other theorists and is more aligned to individuals in nonstandard lines of work, of which musicians are one category.

Life Course Perspectives and the Social Construction of Aging

While aging of course has a biological basis, social scientists are more attentive to the social dimensions of aging. Sociologists in particular construe the life course as a patterned progression of social experiences as individuals age (Clausen 1986; Holstein and Gubrium 2003). Sociological life course perspectives allow us to grasp the interplay between individual life experiences and structure (Sackmann and Wingens 2003). They bring "an awareness of connections between widely separated events and transitions" over the course of one's life (Elder 1985: 34). Two distinct yet interrelated concepts, transitions and trajectories, comprise the central components of the life course. Transitions are the short-term experiences that mark and shape specific points as people age. They may have different meanings and consequences depending on when experienced and can have long-term implications for trajectories. Trajectories, in contrast, are the long, overarching pathways people move along on as they age. Finally, the life course is marked by turning points, times in life where trajectories make major and presumably permanent shifts.[9]

Sociological conceptions of aging allow for more precise readings of the nuances of the life course. While prior theories posed the aging process as rigid, unidirectional, and restrictive, sociological life course theorists suggest instead that the life course is far more variable (Ryff 1985). Likewise, in opposition to early theorists suggesting a universal unfolding of development, regardless of time, context, and identity, sociologists are attentive to variations in aging by culture, generation, gender, race, and social class. Finally, in contrast to early theories of aging, sociological perspectives grant people considerable agency in constructing the life course (Elder, Johnson, and Crosnoe 2003). People do not simply passively accept experiences as they experience them, but instead often respond in innovative ways, creating opportunities where constraints may exist (Brandtstädter 2006; Settersten 1999).

Sociological theories of the life course conceive of aging to be culturally constructed—the social meanings of age are fluid and prone to shift over time. Understandings and criteria as to what constitutes young, old, and variations in between have carried wavering consistency. What's more, people increasingly give precedence to their subjective age identities—the age they feel they are regardless of chronological age (Johnson et al. 2007; Kotarba 2013; Shanahan et al. 2005).[10] Despite the fluidity of people's subjective age identities, normative timetables function as social clocks that continue to be important in individuals' gauging their progression through the life course. Cultural milestones often key people in as to whether they are on time in meeting tasks for their respective life phases (DeMichele 2009; Neugarten et al. 1965; Settersten and Hagestad 1996). While age timetables are simply estimates as to where one should be by a particular age, they are often felt—even internalized—as expectations. Age expectations may concern relatively minor issues, such as one's leisure pursuits or style of dress, but they may also involve issues much more pressing, such as decisions on family and career.

Individuals who achieve tasks at culturally appropriate times are considered "on time." For instance, completing one's education, building a career, getting married, and starting a family at the "right" time (and in the "right" sequence) encourage individuals to feel more fully adult without tension. In contrast, individuals who stray from the expected times at which particular tasks should be met risk feeling "off time" in their lives (Hagestad 1990; Pickett, Greenley, and Greenberg 1995). They may be in jeopardy of being framed as immature and subsequently internalize such suspicions. Men and women may have off-time realizations through "age-clicks" moments in which they realize they are off course in comparison to their peers. Such realizations are not only personally troubling, but often require accounts and cover stories to salvage their stigmatized off-time identities (Laz 1998).

While many studies of aging concentrate exclusively on the later years, my approach begins far earlier in the life course. Consistent with sociological approaches to aging as a process, I am attentive to the lifelong social process of aging in the context of the music world as it impacts the lives of young adults. Most of the musicians in this book are young, yet are in a position in which they are beginning to feel the social effects of aging out of the culture in which they participate. In this analysis, I concentrate specifically on the influence aging has on musicians' lives as they are transitioning to the beginnings of adulthood. At the same time, I expand the notion of aging to include facing the potential end of one's musical career, regardless of one's chronological age.

The Wavering Criteria of Adulthood

For the past several generations, the attainment of adulthood has rested on securing key outcomes for a specific set of tasks (Arnett 1998; Levinson 1978; Shanahan 2000). First, individuals are expected to shed their adolescent self for a stable adult identity. Second, individuals must separate from the family of origin economically and residentially. Third, adulthood requires the building of a lifelong career. While cultivating a career is a lengthy process, what is imperative is taking the initial steps of structuring the foundation of one's career. Adults should, at the very least, have settled on suitable careers and be well on their way to building credentials, experience, and tenure in those lines. Fourth, traditional adulthood is marked by a change in family status, realized by entering marriage as well as parenthood. It is only after attaining these tasks that individuals have historically been recognized as having certifiable proof of becoming adult.

Of particular concern as of late, however, is the growing concern that recent cohorts of young adults are increasingly failing to meet the markers of adulthood. Cultural commentators lament the stagnant, self-indulged younger generations who have botched adulthood. Of central concern is the delay of entering the labor force, the postponing and avoidance of marriage and parenthood, and a general apathy among younger generations. Described as "postmodern postadolescents," these pseudoadults (or failed adults) are not only staggering, but have no interest in moving into true adulthood (Hymowitcz 1999). Postmodern postadolescents are those individuals who think only of themselves, act only for themselves, and cannot commit to anything: not a job, not a career, and certainly not a marriage partner. Scholars, however, have responded to such critiques by highlighting the ways in which every generation stumbles into the transition to adulthood, as well as the ways in which the social landscape has changed, making it more perilous to achieve traditional modes of adulthood.

Data clearly indicate trends signaling the "timing and sequencing of traditional markers of adulthood—leaving home, finishing school, starting work, getting married, and having children—are less predictable and more prolonged, diverse, and disordered" (Furstenberg et al. 2005: 5). By continuing to gauge the attainment of adulthood on traditional markers, few men and women in their twenties and thirties would qualify as adult (Fussell and Furstenberg 2005; Shanahan et al. 2005). Such is the case for many young adults today. It is the rare 18- to 25-year-old who self-identifies as a "complete" adult, due in large part to the traditional criteria of adulthood becoming less relevant to life in the twenty-first century (Arnett 1997 and 2001; Nelson and Barry 2005). Those life events simply do not cluster together in a short span of years as they once did for generations past.

In light of recent demographic shifts, a new understanding of adulthood is materializing among younger cohorts of adults in the United States. In place of the more objective (and ostensibly middle-class) markers of adulthood of the past, young adults today are making sense of the life course by substituting more subjective criteria for adulthood which resonate more soundly with their experiences of aging (Aronson 2008). They are marked by a growing "importance of individualistic criteria and the irrelevance of the demographic markers" of normative conceptions of adulthood (Shanahan et al. 2005: 230). In particular, growing numbers of younger cohorts center the attainment of adulthood on three criteria: attaining a sense of responsibility in day-to-day life, independent decision making, and financial independence (Arnett 2004).

Ultimately, the initial foray into adulthood is one of discovery. As many can attest, it is less typical for young people to enter and settle into long-term roles early in adulthood today. Instead, individuals more typically undergo periods of frequent change and exploration as they progress through the early adult years (Arnett 2000; Furstenberg et al. 2005). Testing various routes is not adolescent, nor is it poor decision making. Rather, it is a part of identity exploration. What was previously characterized as "false starts"—attempting something, then forsaking it for something else more suitable—may instead be a key task of contemporary adulthood.

A focal consequence of this new understanding of aging is the realization among recent theorists that these shifts do not simply suggest revised criteria for existing models of adulthood, but instead command a reconceptualization of life course models today. The reconceptualized period, coined "emerging adulthood," is a distinctly new, transitional time during which individuals have exited adolescence, yet are still exploring precisely what is to come in adulthood. Arnett (2006: 7) characterizes the five key features of emerging adulthood as the "age of identity explorations; age of instability; the most self-focused age of life; the age of feeling in-between; [and the] age of possibilities, when optimism is high and people have an unparalleled opportunity to transform their lives."

During this period of life, typically from age 18 to 25, many emerging adults may have few serious social obligations and commitments in the way of family, allowing them significant autonomy in exploring more options, particularly in their potential career interests. While the exploration component of emerging adulthood may partly be characterized by fun, it is also critical to attaining self-reliance and independence and understanding of self (Arnett 2006; Settersten 2011). Emerging adulthood may be the only time during life in which women and men can try out unusual work and educational possibilities, of which informal careers in music are one. Such experiences may be fun and exciting, but they are also undeniably serious endeavors. Reframing adulthood in this light grants more leeway in the diverse pathways that lead to adulthood, allows more agency to individuals carving out their life courses, and is more attentive to the cultural complexity as to what constitutes a "legitimate" adulthood for contemporary young people.

The individualistic turn adulthood has taken carries special meaning in terms of diverging demographics (Phinney 2006). Developing constructions of contemporary adulthood are implicitly organized by social class, race, and ethnicity and are centered on a white, middle-class standard. People of color from less-advantaged populations contend with the same challenges of adulthood as do their white, middle-class peers. However, their access to resources and corresponding responses are structured differently (Fussell and Furstenberg 2005; Mollenkopf et al. 2005). Adulthood is visibly shifting to allow for more open-ended outcomes, but seemingly for advantaged populations more than others.

Intersections of Music, Careers, and the Life Course

These issues, the social organization of music, informal careers, and the progression through the life course, inform the focus of this book. These matters intersect in compelling ways that sociologists have yet to examine. Individually, they each tell us about discrete aspects of social life, but, collectively, they illustrate the ways these factors mutually influence one another in the lives of musicians.

Music is viewed as leisure at best, and perhaps a privilege. Likewise, pursuing music seems not the best of choices. It is not aligned with adulthood and thus complicates securing an adult identity. In a more practical sense, it makes economic security a struggle. Why, then, do some men and women in early adulthood decide to proceed with their musical dreams? Why do some, but not all, persist? What opportunities allow some to do so and what constraints may pull others away from these pathways? As we hear the stories of musicians from Athens, we will come closer to understanding the answers to these questions, among others.

In this book, I bring into analytic focus the intersections of music culture, gender, and aging through the life course. I do so by compiling the stories and experiences of musicians themselves. In my interviews with the musicians, they would "talk about the passion"—as the famous R.E.M. lyric goes—that was ignited early in life and continues to burn in their devotion to their art. This book examines the ways in which adulthood is negotiated in the context of pursuing musical careers in a college music town. It simultaneously assesses both the structure of the music world and the agency musicians exhibit in challenging and reifying gender in their everyday lives.

Methods and Researcher Role

To answer the questions that are the core of this book, I interviewed 48 musicians living in Athens, Georgia. I conducted a majority of the interviews between March 2005 and May 2006, with additional and follow-up interviews from May 2007 through July 2007 and again from February 2008 through July 2008. The musicians ranged in age from 22 to 37, with a median age of 27. Fifteen of the musicians were women, and 33 were men. A majority of them were white, while only three identified as racial or ethnic minorities. In terms of social class, most musicians self-identified as coming from middle-class backgrounds. They were a well-educated group, as 31 had college degrees in hand at the time of the interviews (4 of whom had also attained graduate degrees), while another 5 were currently enrolled college students at the time I met them. Forty-five were employed in one of four different sectors.[11] Twenty-two held white-collar jobs. They worked in offices doing clerical work, either for local businesses or for offices on campus. Another 6 worked in sectors of the local music industry, often working for recording studios, record labels, or music promotion companies. The third segment, totaling 15 musicians, was employed in the service sector, often the food industry or in nightclubs as bartenders and/or bouncers. The remaining 2 worked manual labor jobs. Ten of the musicians were married (and 4 of these musicians' spouses were also their bandmates). Only 2 musicians were parents, both of whom were men.

I determined a set of strict selection criteria for those considered for inclusion in this study. I limited this study to musicians who had career aspirations to pursue music as a vocation, not those who simply participated in music as a temporary, short-term hobby. To be included in this study, musicians had to also meet at least four of the following criteria: be a member of their band for at least nine months, be a member of a band that rehearsed regularly (at least twice a month), be a member of a band that performed in public venues regularly (at least once every two months), be a member of a band that had gone on tour at least once, and/or have released at least one album.

The 48 musicians were members of 22 different bands. I attempted to interview multiple members of bands when possible, regardless of their instrument specialization, vocal contributions, and songwriting contributions. While the lead singers and primary songwriters were often the symbolic figureheads of the bands and were nearly always enthusiastic about participating in this study, I also vigorously recruited other members with less central roles in the bands. All in all, my sample comprises 21 singers, 23 guitarists, 11 bass players, 6 keyboardists, and 8 drummers.[12] The gender composition of instrumentation varied among some instruments. Each gender was about equally likely to contribute vocals and/or play the bass in their respective bands. A higher percentage of men played the guitar or drums in their bands. In no band in my sample did women play the drums. Women, however, were much more likely than men to play the keyboards and synthesizers in their bands.

Athens, Georgia, was an ideal research site due to its reputation as an iconic college music town. For one, Athens has a reputable music scene with an iconic history. The 1980s brought with it national recognition, due largely to local bands that developed international followings during that time period, especially R.E.M. and the B-52s. Athens's reputation continues to this day, as *Rolling Stone* recently ranked Athens as the top college music town in the United States, making it an excellent site for this study. Lastly, numerous bands make their home in Athens, many of whom strategically relocated to Athens specifically for its music scene and what they saw as opportunities to develop their musical careers. According to the Athens newsweekly publication, *Flagpole*, there were at least 250 bands whose home base was Athens at the time I collected my data.

I recruited participants using two main strategies. In the initial phase of my data collection, I reached out to musicians who fit the selection criteria by contacting them via their bands' self-administered websites. Since the bands were always responsible for maintaining their websites, I corresponded directly with the band members themselves. My second recruitment strategy was more personal, yet not nearly as successful. In these instances, I approached musicians after their public performances at music clubs in town. I would then briefly tell them about my study and ask their willingness to participate in it. When possible, I would exchange contact information with them to communicate about the interviews later, often within one to seven days after these initial acquaintances. While musicians contacted using both strategies expressed interest and enthusiasm in participating in this study, I had a significantly higher response rate from those musicians I contacted through their websites.

I was strict about scheduling interviews in a one-on-one format, even in instances in which the bands assumed I would interview the band collectively in one sitting (or requested such arrangements). The one-on-one interviews themselves lasted between 55 and 290 minutes each, with most averaging about 90 minutes. Being that I framed this study using a life course perspective, I chronicled the entirety of their musical lives, asking questions stemming from the musicians' early years in life all the way up to the present, as well as asking about their speculations on the future. I asked about the onset of their musical interest, the circumstances under which they learned instruments, and their experiences in bands. I also asked them about aspects of identity, particularly how they imagined music and their identities may have mutually influenced each other. I concluded the interviews by asking the musicians about their plans for future and the extent to which they imagined it may continue to include musical participation.

Identity matters in every sociological analysis, especially in terms of what the researcher brings to the research context. I was in a (mostly) advantaged position during my data collection for this book. First, I was relatively young when I started collecting data—in my late twenties—not much older than most of the musicians with whom I was in contact. Similarity in age often eases rapport, prompting participants to be more open and forthright.

My gender identity as a man was largely an advantage as well. As is often the case in interview contexts between interviewers and participants with a shared gender, men often felt an "instant" connection with me. While nearly every man I interviewed was respectful to women and did not embody a prototypical hegemonic masculinity, we still often connected via masculinity. They often engaged in masculine joking behaviors and discussed women, dating, and drinking, as well as other "guy talk" with me. The interviews often took an informal tone though mirroring patters of male friendships norms, factors that inadvertently boosted rapport with the men I interviewed (Brooks 2006).

With women, I did not necessarily feel my status as a man was a disadvantage in at least two respects. First, as musicians, the women with whom I spoke were embedded in a male-dominated music world. They were used to the scene—musicians, fans, and music journalists alike—being a world of men. Those who had previous experiences doing interviews with the music press stated they usually were interviewed by men. Second, I self-perceive my masculinity to be an inclusive one. While gender was salient to our interactions, as it is in most interactions in our gendered world, I was not necessarily in the powerful position due to my being a man. Quite to the contrary, I felt as if I was the powerless one in nearly every interview and interaction with musicians of either gender. Their social status stemming from their standing in the local music scene far outweighed any status I brought to the interviews.

My ethnic and social class identities, though less pronounced, no doubt mattered as well. As a Mexican-American man, I was a minority in Athens and the music world itself. Racial and ethnic issues only rarely surfaced in interviews, however. Typically, when such issues did emerge, it was with musicians of color. Most musicians were attentive to the lack of racial and ethnic diversity in the music scene, but people of color often had more to say about those constraints. My middle-class status—I was enrolled in graduate school at the time and lived quite the privileged life as one (student debt notwithstanding)—was aligned with the social class backgrounds of nearly all musicians. It was only the rare musicians who did not come from nor currently identify as middle class.

I am also a former musician myself, though I hesitate to use the term "musician" in reference to my limited participation in the music world. Like a number of adolescents in the United States, I grew up listening to rock music, begged my parents to buy me a guitar, and started the stereotypical garage band with friends in high school. (I even continue my pseudomusician status today as a member of a rock band with colleagues from the university at which I work.) Unlike the musicians in this book, however, I have limited experience performing in music clubs, and no experience recording or touring. I generally understood the world of musicians and was similarly familiar with the lexicon they used in terms of music gear and theory.

In sum, I felt that I was similar enough to the musicians to allow for their acceptance and entrée to their world as a researcher. I was far different, however, in that I was seen as an outsider, a status I saw an advantageous, as it allowed me to ask explicit questions and numerous follow-up questions. Some musicians even acted as tour guides, taking me through the history of the music scene and introducing me to additional musicians without my even making such requests. I was the nebulous "outsider-within" in that I was straddling both worlds: the music world as a fan and an outsider as my primary "home" was academic (Collins 1986).[13]

Outline of the Book

This book follows the life course trajectories of independent rock musicians as they grow into the early part of adulthood. My aim is to illustrate how lives are meticulously planned for some, while they take unexpected turns for others; how early experiences persist with individuals well later into life, how others break with their past to create novel futures, and how still others recollect their pasts to make sense of their present; and how, despite our best intentions, the social identities over which we have no control can advantage some and constrain others. To let this story unfold, I attempt to keep the voices of the musicians at the forefront. This is their world, these are their experiences; as such, I will let them tell the story as much as is possible.

In Chapter 1, I examine musicians' retrospective accounts of early events in life that initiated their musical pathways. Nearly every musician had memories of events in early childhood that nudged them in the direction of music. Their motivations to initially explore music were wide ranging, from the family to peers to exposure to bands of the day. I then examine musicians' learning their first musical instruments. I pay particular attention to the varied age at which musicians first learn their instruments and factors that influence the timing of those introductions. I examine their eventual learning of rock instruments, often accomplished through a lengthy negotiation with parents. Finally, I trace musicians' introductions to their first rock bands. I also examine other nonmusical trajectories in the early part of the life course—specifically other extracurricular activities in which they were invested, as well as their early career aspirations.

Chapter 2 continues tracing the musicians' life courses by examining the transition to adulthood. It begins with the decisions musicians made upon high school graduation. Many decided to extend their education and attend college, while at the same time continuing their explorations in music, something accomplished with little difficulty and little tension. Upon college graduation and/or the entrance to young adulthood in their mid-twenties, however, musicians felt forced to make a decision. The remainder of the chapter examines the two pathways they weighed: pursuing music wholeheartedly or putting music in the backseat in their life priorities and aspirations. The musicians' stories emphasize the extent to which the hallmarks of adulthood bear on their decisions to persist or not.

In Chapter 3, I examine the development of the musician identity and the extent to which the women and men internalize identities as musicians. I compare the varying ages at which and processes through which they are able to successfully and comfortably self-identify as "true" musicians. In particular, I examine the criteria they construct that qualify one as a musician, only some of which are tied to music itself. Many of the musician identities are marked by hesitation, due ultimately to the informal nature of this music sector. I then examine other aspects of their lives that contribute to their identities, the bands themselves and the culture of the town in which they live. Finally, I examine the work settings and situations that ease the internalization of the musician identity and others that complicate it.

Chapter 4 is the first of two chapters that explicitly examines gender over the life course, the focus of this chapter being men's lives. While Chapters 1 and 2 in many ways were the "general" patterns for musicians, I highlight in Chapter 4 the experiences and factors that were particular to men as they aged from childhood to adulthood. Men's lives are generally advantageous and more easily aligned to allow for their entry into the music world. They do, however, experience some disadvantages in their musical life courses, specifically in terms of the challenges to normative masculinities they face by virtue of pursuing nonprofessional careers in music. At the same time, the men ultimately reconstruct new masculinities in their lives, some of which reify existing normative conceptions, and others of which challenge them. All in all, multiple aspects of men's life courses are generally structured to advantage them over women in the music scene, a key factor that explains their overrepresentation in the rock world.

Chapter 5 shifts focus to women's experiences over the life course. In contrast to men, women face delayed starting points in both learning instruments and joining bands. A defining point in women's musical trajectories is focused on men, as their musical mentors are often men to whom they are connected. Once they do enter the music world, women self-impose shorter timelines for success and feel like impostors to the world. I then continue examining women's various speculations as to the origin of the gender imbalance in the music scene. In general, women's experiences in music are complicated, marked by constraints that are absent from men's experiences and thus relegate them to the fringes of the music world.

In Chapter 6, I consider two issues: commitment to music and anticipated futures. I begin by comparing musicians' thoughts on the role of music as they begin moving into the next stage of their lives. While all musicians initially moved into adulthood with desires to pursue musical careers, not all maintained those commitments. I contrast those musicians who imagine music as a bona fide career interest to which they foresee themselves being committed for the remainder of their adult lives with others who see it alternatively as an important, yet temporary leisure pursuit that may fade over time as they move into new ventures. All musicians recognize the consequences this phase of life will have to their futures. This chapter ends with the musicians' speculations of how their lives would have turned out had music not played such a central role in them. As the musicians peer into their alternate universes without music, they are consistent in the power music had in shaping their lives in one fashion or another.

The book concludes with contributions to sociological understandings of gender, work, and the life course. I emphasize the extent to which pathways to adulthood are less linear than previous models suggest. The "messier" life course pathways of young adults are not necessarily false starts, but instead are more convoluted pathways that nonetheless lead to successful attainments of adulthood. I also demonstrate a deeper understanding of the gendered life course that differentially opens up and constrains pathways for women and men. At the same time, I illustrate the extent to which women and men challenge and reconfigure gender in their cultural milieu. I also speak to the understandings of informal work sectors beyond the world of music. Informal careers are somewhat open ended but paradoxically generate particular obstacles that are typically not shared by more formal career paths and career patterns. I conclude by posing practical understandings of how contemporary young adults negotiate the transition to adulthood in world unlike that experienced by previous generations.

Ultimately, this is a story about the unfolding of life. A good number of us, musicians or otherwise, feel that we were put on this planet to do something worthwhile and to leave a mark on the world during the short time we are here. A good number of us feel we are, in a word, destined for something. We strive for greatness. It is our life's work. This book reveals how destiny and the pursuit of greatness unfold for musicians in one small college music town.

1

First Hearing the Sounds

•••••••••••••••••••••

Coming of Age and
the Discovery of Music

At age fourteen, a young Robert Zimmerman happened upon "Mystery Train," one of Elvis Presley's early recordings. It immediately struck him, so much in fact, that it fed his musical ambitions and career trajectories. "When I first heard Elvis's voice I just knew that I wasn't going to work for anybody, and nobody was going to be my boss. Hearing him for the first time was like busting out of jail," recalls Zimmerman. He is by no means alone in his perspective. The early adolescent years—particularly age fourteen—is a "sort of magic age for the development of musical tastes" (Hajdu 2011). Adolescence is a critical time, both physiologically and socially, for identity development and discovery. It also feels serendipitous. By sheer chance, Zimmerman came of age at the point of Presley's introduction to American culture. By sheer chance, he discovered "Mystery Train" at a point in life in which culture, art, and music tend to exert a heavier influence on life and identity. His life would never be the same. His identity would dramatically shift—he would literally adopt another name—as he moved into a musical identity. Several decades later, Zimmerman, now better known as Bob Dylan, cites his discovering Elvis as a critical moment, a turning point in his life. Given the power he cites in his musical development during adolescence, it is possible Bob Dylan would have never existed were it not for his chance stumbling upon Presley's music early in life.

While it feels like our music culture hit the jackpot with the auspicious chance convergence of Dylan discovering Elvis and subsequently shifting his life direction, there are larger social forces at play here. It is not simply luck that Bob Dylan, the musical icon, was spawned on that fateful day in his adolescent life. It was instead due to the complex interplay of culture, age, peer culture, gender, and motivation that led to the fortuitous creation of Bob Dylan.

For most people, Bob Dylan notwithstanding, life unfolds in unanticipated ways. The human condition is to plan for the future, to work our way towards specific life goals. But the reality is that such blueprints rarely go as planned. A good many of us end up in places entirely unanticipated later in life. Others end up slightly off target from their presumed goals set early in life. It is not that most people demonstrate bad judgment in planning their futures. Instead, it is perhaps something more universal: life intervenes in our plans.

In this chapter, I examine musicians' retrospective accounts of their early lives, moments they remember as influential, leading them to their career trajectories as musicians much later in adulthood.[1] I begin by examining the musicians' recollections of the time in life during which their interests in music were first triggered. I then review the musicians' histories of learning their first musical instruments and introductions to rock instruments. Following this, I trace a key moment in musicians' musical trajectories—their joining their first rock bands. I conclude by examining the musicians' retrospective accounts of their early aspirations in life. Those who did envision musical careers were the rare cases, as musicians typically imagined pursuing other, often more standardized, lines of work. As we will see, nearly all the musicians felt as if events early in life—those music related, but also those outside the milieu of music—set the stage for their ultimate pursuit of musical careers in adulthood.

Introductions to and Interests in Music

Many life course trajectories have objective starting points: educational trajectories begin with one's entrance to the school system; family trajectories may start with engagements, marriages, or births of children; and work trajectories may begin with securing credentials for the labor market or landing one's first "real" job. Musical life course trajectories, in contrast, are more fluid in their inceptions. Each individual musical life course—more often than not far less structured than educational, family, and work trajectories—essentially begins when musicians deem them to start. To capture this self-defined starting point, I began interviews by asking musicians when they remember first developing an interest in music. Many of them remember these moments as occurring very early in childhood. For seven of the musicians, all of whom were men, the toddler years were the point at which they first discovered the significance of music in their lives. They all had clear memories of their parents playing music in the house or on road trips—music that stuck with them and precipitated their appreciation of music. These memories were sometimes enhanced by other "proof": photographs of their childhood in which they were sitting in front of their parents' record player with headphones on or stories their parents shared with them later in life regarding their early interest in music. These musicians, however, have clear memories of these events themselves as well; they are not simply dictated by their parents' memories alone. Dean had strong memories of music early in life:

DEAN: You know, it's hard to say [when I first became interested in music] because it was so long ago. I remember some of my earliest, really vivid memories—you have a lot of memories temporarily when you're a kid, but some stick with you more than others. And I think some of the earliest memories I have—I couldn't tell you what age I was, but I remember just falling asleep in the back of my dad's car on car trips. We would drive a lot from Atlanta to Kentucky, where I'm from, listening to *Dark Side of the Moon* and *The Wall* by Pink Floyd. And at that time, I was pretty sure that that was the definitive music. I wanted to do stuff like that, too, but I just didn't really understand it. I really liked Elton John a lot when I was a little kid, too. I couldn't really grasp the concept of what it meant to be a musician because it seemed like those guys were making, I don't know, they had some sort of otherworldly gift to make music, whereas I did not. So I couldn't understand it. I was pretty obsessed, though.

MR: So being in your dad's car listening to music, was that when you were in elementary school, do you think?

DEAN: I was, well, in pre-elementary school. I mean, I really have those memories. I said that they were vivid memories, but they're not. They're really just kinda like nebulous, like I just filed that away somewhere like that. I can remember being really mesmerized by listening to [certain music], specifically *Dark Side of the Moon*. We always listened to that on car trips, and tucking my head away in the corner and falling asleep listening to it in the car. There was always music playing in the house and in the car and stuff like that, but that music particularly really moves me for whatever reason. I thought it was great.

The memories of developing interests in music early in life are a combination of the musicians' own memories fused with those of their parents or other documentation such as photos or home movies.[2] Nonetheless, the musicians are steadfast that music was a constant in their lives since their earliest memories. Some of them spoke of music being innate—a core aspect of their identity from early in life. While other memories of their toddler years were often fuzzy, their memories of music emerging during that time were sharp and less ambiguous.

FIGURE 2 Athfest, a three-day music and arts festival held each summer in Athens (Photo by Mike White, deadlydesigns.com)

Over two-thirds of the musicians (33 of 48), however, did not remember their interest in music being sparked until the early childhood years.[3] Many musicians cited age five, in particular, as the year at which they started on their musical pathways.

> ANDREW: Growing up, I was exposed to music by my parents and obviously my surroundings. But I think what I really initially latched onto was the Beatles, Creedence [Clearwater Revival], Michael Jackson even, [and] Genesis's *The Invisible Touch* record. But at the same time, the first time I heard classical works like Bach, I was immediately drawn to that just the same. There was an immediate interest I feel like.
>
> MR: Was this in elementary school or middle school?
>
> ANDREW: Oh man, all the way back to when I was in primary school. I went to the symphony with either my parents or some of my buddies' parents or something. In North Carolina, the symphony orchestra played a Christmas concert, and just seeing that for the first time for me, it was like, "This is awesome." I was really into it.

Some of the memories are a bit fuzzy, as are the details of some of the events (or the people with whom they shared them), but what remains clear is the feeling of awe that music instilled in them immediately upon discovering the sounds of music. The musicians cited their musical memories in early childhood as clear and the definitive start of their moving toward musical life course trajectories.

The remaining eight musicians with delayed starts remembered their musical trajectories beginning in the preadolescent years. They cited a particular and powerful influence in their social networks during the middle school years as sparking their musical interests. Abby, for instance, had two older brothers who were invested in music, one of whom was in a punk band when she was in middle school. For Abby and others in similar situations, music grew to be more interesting as they were embedded in contexts in which others intensely valued music and the arts. The mere presence of individuals who centered their lives on music had a rub-off effect on them.

The three musicians who had the latest start on their musical pathways cited more concrete issues of identity exploration, in line with traditional theorists such as Erikson (1950), as the conduit for their discovering music. Seth, for instance, felt that his enthusiasm for athletics was waning and music provided an alternate path as he continued exploring who he "really" was. His devotion to baseball was not giving him the anchor in life it had in early years, and he began exploring music instead. With that shift, he began to develop a new sense of who he was and where his true talents and passion lay. These musicians suggested it was more than age itself that prompts youth to delve into culture, be it music or otherwise. It is moving into one's own self-constructed identity that can prompt searching for music.

Objectively, these moments may appear insignificant. Symbolically, however, these moments are incredibly important. Musicians, with little prodding, were easily able to return to key memories in their early lives in which music took center stage or, at the very least, where the context in which other important childhood events took place. Musicians easily and in great detail remember particulars about music early in life. Furthermore, they internalized these musical moments as life-shifting moments in their early lives.

Musical Influences in Early Life

The musicians did not magically develop an interest in music from out of nowhere. Instead, they often cited the context of the family as sparking their interests in music early in life. In particular, parents' interests in music often shaped their children's music appreciation. One or both of their parents was often a "music lover" and, as such, music was a bridge connecting parents to children early in life (Kotarba 2013). Parents often purchased, shared, and played music in the home, thus socializing their children to appreciate and genuinely love music. They played a clear role in their children's musical development, often acting as an agent of socialization for musical interests, whether they intended to or not. Roger remembered the dual impact both parents had on his musical development.

> Well, [music] became interesting to me when my parents—I guess I was like five or six, they went to New York for the first time in their lives. I didn't go, but they went to New York City, and they saw two or three Broadway shows. They came home and they had all the soundtracks. They bought the original cast recording of those particular shows, like *Phantom of the Opera*, *Into the Woods*, and *Will Rogers Follies*. My earliest memory of loving music is me singing along with my mom. She'd do the female part and I'd do the male part, singing along to the songs. And then my dad was really into classic rock. He liked, you know, the big names: the Beatles, Rolling Stones, stuff like that. Those are like the two sides of me. Both of my parents were really into music. My mom was really into show tunes and light rock. My dad was really into classic rock. They played music a lot, and by proxy I listened to music a lot.

The parents' collective musical influence was not always focused on rock music per se. They often instilled a more general appreciation of numerous styles and genres of music, as well as an appreciation of the arts in general. The influence is more than just familial socialization—it is the influence of a certain *kind* of family, namely, those in which music, art, and culture are valued by parents and instilled in their children early in life. Musicians overwhelmingly came from middle-class backgrounds, the context of which allows more opportunities for potential musical and creative development. Parents spent resources of time and money on music and embedded those values in the development of their children.

Fathers were somewhat more likely than mothers to influence the musicians' interest in rock music. The musicians, both women and men, had particular memories of enjoying rock music with their fathers. They often specified that "listening to rock and roll with dad" tended to occur in contexts in which the mothers were away, either temporarily, such as when dad took them on car rides, or permanently, via postdivorce living arrangements. A number of musicians cited one-on-one time with fathers as the moments during which they began exploring music by virtue of their fathers' love of music. As such, they often cited their fathers as having a particular influence on their attraction to rock music (Kotarba 2013). Julia said her diverse music interests began through her relationship with her father: "I'd say probably when I was six or seven, [music] really began taking hold of me. Most of it came from my father. He was really cool. On Sunday afternoons, he would pull up all the windows in the house and blast the stereo, and we'd run around and dance. I thought it was really cool. He had a convertible. He would drive us around town and blast the stereo. He was just a lot of fun. He really brought music into our lives."

Similarly, Stewart said:

To me, that turning point when I realized [music] was something that I was really into was probably fourth or fifth grade, because my dad at that point had separated from my mom, so I got to hang out with him on weekends and we would always be driving around, and he would always have music on in the car. And I think he didn't play as much [music] at home when they were married, but when they were separated he could listen to his own music, so I really got a taste of that. He listened to a lot of Jimi Hendrix, Jethro Tull, progressive stuff like [Pink] Floyd, Yes. They are still some of my favorite bands. They are what started me.

Music served a dual purpose in musicians' early lives. Rock music was one way that musicians forged deeper relationships with their fathers early in life.[4] It was also a time in life that fueled their future career trajectories, as they would later come to realize.

Fathers were the consummate rock-and-roll fans. The musicians lovingly referred to their fathers as "music geeks," highlighting their intense love—nearly obsession—with rock music. Similar to many musicians, Damien specified that his dad was "not a musician or anything, [but] would always go around, excited and singing songs, though not too well." Some fathers owned guitars and "would goof around [on it] a little bit, but never really [learned how to] play it," as Roman described his father. As such, fathers were not necessarily musically inclined. Their love of music was passed on to their children and was one of many influences that would prompt the musicians to one day take up music themselves.

Other musicians cited their mothers as a stronger influence in their burgeoning appreciation of music during the early years of life. Mothers' influences seemed to emerge in ways different from those of fathers. Kayla said: "My mom, when she was in college, she ran her own radio show. And she and my aunt would do duets a lot and play guitar and had a little group. My aunt was in a group with Paul Simon's brother. They were always doing [musical] stuff like that [throughout] their lives. She was always musical, and she passed it on to me." Like fathers, mothers were of course often deep fans of music. However, mothers were often true musicians as well, having spent part of their lives not only playing instruments, but also performing music in some context. Sometimes they hosted radio shows, as was the case with Kayla's mother; other times they were in folk bands; and still other times they were active in church choirs. Their active involvement in music beyond fandom was a trait that they often, intentionally or not, passed on to their children. A few of the men had mothers who not only participated in music as a leisure pursuit, but also had initiated career avenues focused on music. Owen said: "My mom was a soprano in the opera. I saw my mom perform a lot when I was a kid. Music was always playing in the house. My mom gave up the opera as a profession shortly after my brother and I were born. . . . My dad was in Vietnam at the time. She couldn't continue to do artistic stuff [after becoming a mother]."

Mothers, as these musicians suggest, often had a substantial, though peppered, history with musical performance. In contrast to fathers, mothers were generally more artistic and creative in their passions and hobbies. Instead of being simply music fans, as was typically the case with fathers, mothers were often musical performers themselves. Many of the musicians' mothers played the piano, guitar, and/or were trained singers. As the above musicians suggest, their mothers had lengthy histories playing instruments or singing, some of whom having ventured into musical careers earlier in life. Some musicians, such as Owen, recognized that their mothers' musical dreams were deferred because of family responsibilities, often initiated after the birth of children. They sacrificed musical passions for the family, although they ended up passing on their creativity and musical interests down to their children.

Perhaps the most surprising commonality among the musicians was the influence of the family's religiosity. About a third (15 out of 48) of the musicians cited the church as a driving influence of their musical interests. Culturally, we tend to place rock music and religion in opposition. The church has long battled music (and other media) as a negative influence in youth's lives. Rock has borne the brunt of the blame for youth's experimentation with drugs and sex, with their propensity for delinquency, and even for mass murders and school shootings (Roberts and Christenson 2000; Roberts et al. 2003; Schudson 1989). "The devil made me do it." "The music made me do it." These are frequent charges that echo in our cultural conversation about music's influence on adolescent delinquency. However, for many women and men, musical interests were not driven purely by the secular world, but inspired by religious contexts. Take, for instance, Nate's experience: "When I was real little and I used to go to a Baptist church, and they would sing all those old hymnals. And I just remember being really small and really loving those hymnals. I think that's when I started liking the idea [of music]. It used to seem like this weird magic thing—making a song—like all those hymnals. How did somebody come up with that? That's when I started thinking about it."

The musicians did not necessarily come from "holy roller" families that were devoutly involved in the church. Instead, church attendance was part of their family Sunday routine, but not quite a defining centerpiece of their family lives. Lilly's early interest in music stemmed from the musical aspect of religious services as well: "I remember going to church. My parents took us to church and there are a lot of things about church that I didn't really enjoy, but I liked the hymns. I looked forward every Sunday going to church and singing the hymns."

A number of other musicians shared similar sentiments. Music worked in tandem with religion for some to discover something bigger than themselves—both the afterlife and the power of music. Looking back, what the musicians often remembered most (and sometimes valued the most) about their religious upbringing was the opportunity to get to hear live music every week: the interplay of instruments and especially the layering of a multitude of voices in harmony was what mesmerized them the most. It was also the first time they began to discover the magic of music.

Learning First Instruments

Some musicians, at an early age, craved more than the pleasure that came from simply listening to music and developed a more active curiosity and yearning to learn how to play instruments of their own as well. Many of them first began exploring and learning to play musical instruments at presumably the earliest point in life possible—early childhood. During the elementary school years, the musicians (sometimes at the urging of their parents) began learning instruments. Exactly half of the musicians (24 of 48) did so by age 8. Boys had a bit of a head start in comparison to girls, with 17 of them picking up their instruments at age 5, whereas the earliest age at which girls remembered learning to play instruments was two years later.

During this time period, the musicians overwhelmingly started, with rare exception, on the same instrument: the piano. For most of them, it was at the prodding of their parents.

ADRIAN: My mom started teaching me piano when I was five. I started taking lessons, private piano lessons when I was maybe seven, but I didn't really quite feel the fire [and quit]. I'm kind of sad I didn't stick with the piano now.
MR: Were you interested in it on your own or did [your mom] push it on you?
ADRIAN: It was her influence. She's definitely been a big inspiration in my life. Music was always around. She definitely nurtured that side of me.

Like Adrian, Heath's taking up the piano was more the choice of his parents.

MR: Is there a reason they enrolled you in piano lessons?
HEATH: It was just the thing that happened once you got to a certain age in my family. "We're gonna send you to take piano." My parents wanted to well-round their children.

Nearly all of the musicians who started on the piano described it as a rite of passage: it was something everyone in the family or their neighborhood did early in childhood. Not all of them necessarily dreaded it, but had their parents not suggested the piano, a clear majority did not imagine the idea would have ever come to mind on their own.

The piano—their introduction to music, the thing they would come to love and center their lives on—was by no means a consistently enjoyable experience. Even those musicians who love music with every fiber of their body did not always have fond recollections of their experiences with the instrument.

> HEATH: Everybody in my family, my parents sent my brother, sister, and I to piano lessons and stuff, but I was never really into that aspect of it at all, playing music because it was way too academic, too much studying required.
>
> MR: About how old were you when they enrolled you in piano lessons?
>
> HEATH: Probably seven, eight years old.
>
> MR: Was the piano the first instrument you learned how to play?
>
> HEATH: The first instrument I was *supposed* to learn how to play.
>
> MR: [laughs] How long did that last?
>
> HEATH: Probably about a year of lessons. It seems like forever though when you're a kid. It seemed like a long time.

For some, this was due to their being forced to learn the instrument. Typical of the middle-class family experience, many musicians were enrolled in piano lessons much to their dismay because of their parents' wishes for them to become well-rounded children. "Good" middle-class parenting consists of encouraging one's children to try out a number of extracurricular activities, in hopes of honing their interests, discovering their talents, and ultimately allowing the children to discover exactly who they are. This "concerted cultivation" model of parenting suggests an active prodding at the hands of parents to encourage—even actively push—their children to discover new things and develop a broad range of interests and skills (Lareau 2003). In contrast, the typical working-class "natural growth" model of parenting is one in which children are responsible for self-exploration, entertaining themselves, and organizing their informal leisure activities without the instruction of adults (Lareau 2003).

For others, especially those who were interested in music and had a drive to learn instruments, their dissatisfaction with the piano in early childhood was explicitly tied to their not having the power to decide which instrument they would start learning (Wagner 2015). Very few musicians asked to learn the piano in particular. Instead, they often wanted to enroll in guitar or drum lessons. Parents, during the early childhood years, never allowed their children to do so. The children, already learning the lessons of their middle-class socialization, attempted to negotiate with their parents as to which instrument would be appropriate for them. Adrian was a bit atypical in that his negotiated instrument was the classical guitar—an instrument quite similar to his preferred instrument of choice, the electric guitar:

> MR: So when you were ten years old and you started playing guitar, the classical guitar, was that something you sought out on your own as well or was it the influence of your school or your parents or anyone?
>
> ADRIAN: I just decided that I want to play the guitar. And Mom was like, "Well, maybe you can take classical guitar lessons and just get a foundation from there. And [then] we can see about this rock-and-roll thing."

Getting parents to agree to one's preferred instrument of choice was a negotiation, often with varying success. Children had ample opportunities to learn new musical instruments, though not always the ones they felt passionate about or keenly interested in themselves.

The musicians' tenure on their introductory instrument of the piano varied. Most of the men quit the piano after several weeks (and none continued with it for more than a year) for various reasons. The men who quit the piano after a few weeks typically did so due to their dislike of the instrument. Some men "remembered hating it and not wanting to do it" and had parents who acquiesced to their desires to quit. Brandon had clear memories of the conclusion of his time with the piano: "I took a couple of piano lessons, maybe two months, when I was six or seven. But I *hated* it. This is why. It's a neat story, if I can tell you about it. I hated it because, if the beat of the song was [traditional], I would be [instead] play it [in the style of country music]. And that would be a problem. The teachers would say, 'It's not written that way. It's written this way.' But I would be like, 'But it sounds better this way.' So that was kind of the end of my piano lessons."

Formal instruction required adherence to norms of learning the instrument the "right" way, an additional factor that men used to push themselves away from the piano. For the men who played the piano for up a year, however, the strongest factor that prompted them to abandon the piano was the opportunity to learn a new instrument, primarily the guitar:

> MR: And once you got your guitar, did you just pretty much ditch the piano and say, "Forget this"?
>
> AARON: Yeah, yeah. I think I may have played it for another year or so, just privately from some lady who lived in the neighborhood. And then I just went, "Fuck it, I've got to do this [the guitar]." My entire focus was on [the guitar].

The typical truncated time with the piano is tied to the fact that the instrument was almost always the suggestion of the parents. Boys were not hesitant about informing their parents that they did not enjoy the instrument and wished to quit or, more often than not, switch to another one. Parents would often concede to their children's wishes to get a different instrument given they demonstrated their commitment to the first instrument for a suitable period of time. In general, this trend was gendered. The men were more likely to seek out new instruments on their own, instruments their parents often wanted to stall. However, coupled with their learning a new instrument was the tendency to completely abandon the piano upon taking up the preferred instrument.

Women, in contrast, typically had a lengthier commitment to the piano. Women who played the piano as a child had a significantly longer span of years mastering the instrument, as they often spent the entirety of their childhood taking lessons. Beth said: "I played piano. At first, I took lessons from my aunt that weren't extremely serious for about three years. I learned to read music, but I didn't really excel very well at piano. And then I got a better teacher, a high school piano teacher, and took lessons until I was probably eighteen. Then I quit lessons and then went on to learn more [on my own] about equipment and keyboards and dealing with sounds instead of dealing with [music theory] and stuff like that."

Women's devotion to the piano aided them later in life and was key to their securing spots in rock bands in the future, as will be discussed in Chapter 5. Childhood gender norms may be at play here. Boys were more likely to abandon the piano due to sheer frustration or simply preferring more "masculine" instruments. Girls persisted with the piano perhaps due to its being a more gender-appropriate instrument that was attuned to femininity.

Other musicians (17 of 48) had later starts in developing musical interests in their learning their first instruments during the middle school years. Unlike the musicians who began learning their first instruments in elementary school—nearly always the piano—these musicians had a wider range of instruments on which they started. Some did begin on the piano, but the more common introductory instrument during this period was the saxophone, clarinet, trumpet, or trombone, as well as the drums and guitar for a select few. With the exception of the latter two, these instruments were part of the middle school band curriculum, the primary context in which students began exploring musical performance during the preadolescent years.

These musicians showed considerably more agency in that they independently decided on exploring instruments on their own, largely without the guidance of their parents. Some of them, of course, were inspired by the peer culture in which they were embedded: their friends and classmates were learning instruments during this time frame, sparking those ideas in them as well. More significant turning points, however, occurred in the context of academic settings.

JACOB: I joined the middle school band in sixth grade and started playing trumpet. I'm not exactly sure why I picked trumpet, but I know why I joined the band. The year before in fifth grade, everybody from the elementary school went to [visit] the middle school. They had some sort of orientation there, and the [middle school] band performed for all of the fifth grade students that were coming in. And the thing that really got me—they started playing this song, which I thought it was the coolest song I'd ever heard in my life. And they played the scales and the arpeggios, and I had no idea what that was. I was like, "That's the coolest thing ever. I wanna do that."

CLIFF: I remember specifically what catapulted me into getting into it. I remember, in seventh grade, my homeroom teacher brought his guitar [to class]. It was the last day of school, and he was wanting to play songs for the kids. It was an electric guitar, and I was like, "Yeah, that's pretty cool." You hear it, you see somebody playing it, what they're able to do. You're like, "Man, that's pretty amazing. That's pretty cool." Then you realize, "Yeah, I could do that. Maybe I can try to do that." So it was right then, I saw somebody brought a guitar to school and, within the year, I started. That's when I started learning how to play an instrument. I grabbed my dad's old guitar out of the box and just started basically teaching myself.

In contrast to the first population who learned how to play instruments in early childhood, these musicians are different in two respects: they seemed to have greater intrinsic enjoyment and a more self-motivated interest in their instruments. All of the musicians who took on their first instrument during the middle school years suggested that they selected their instruments of choice themselves. They were drawn to particular instruments for specific reasons. Their parents were of course supportive of their exploring musical instruments, but unlike their younger counterparts, these musicians were not pushed to try out particular instruments at the suggestion of their parents. This was a primary reason for which their tenure with their instruments was typically lengthier—they had more satisfaction and higher drive for the instrument, propelling their commitment to it for several years.

Still other musicians—those often self-described as "late bloomers"—did not pick up instruments until well into adolescence or the post–high school years. What is most noteworthy about this group is the extent to which this group is marked by gender. The late bloomers are predominantly women. This was not necessarily the typical experience for women, as only about one-quarter of them (4 of 15) fit this tendency, but, in contrast, less than 10 percent of the men (3 of 33) picked up their first instruments this late in life. The men with the latest start to learning instruments began in high school, whereas the women with the latest start were beyond high school, often in college. The three men who learned their first instrument in high school did so only after they abandoned what was their lifelong passion up to that point in life: athletics. As their participation in school-structured sports dwindled, they took on a more concentrated interest in rock music and correspondingly began learning the guitar and drums. As they disengaged from sports, their peer group shifted away from athletes and toward the "metal heads"—an additional influence that prompted their taking up rock instruments.

The women did not necessarily suggest other activities or interests detouring them from the potential opportunities to learn instruments earlier in life. Instead, they found themselves generating increased interest in music in the years following high school. Also in contrast to men, the women were typically beyond the high school years when music became a growing priority in their lives. During their early twenties, the idea "finally dawned on [them] to learn the guitar" or other instruments. They felt far behind their peers, especially men, who had a much longer tenure with their instruments. Nikki jokingly said: "I started with the guitar I think at twenty [years old]. I got one and just kind of tried to play it. I tried. I really tried. I stared at it a lot. And cried a lot [laughs]."

Though spoken in jest, her late start illustrates her frustration in her pressure to learn and gain comfort with the instrument as quickly as possible. The late bloomers, both women and men, felt more pressure to learn the instrument in a shorter time span, something they framed as a disadvantage to starting much later than what they imagined to be the "average" age of musical starts. At the same, however, they also described themselves as having the advantaged mindset of a more mature commitment to learning instruments due to their self-motivation to test the musical waters.

The First Rock Instrument

A clear turning point that paves the way for possibilities to participate in rock bands is the requisite learning of rock instruments. The musicians easily recollected the contexts—and struggles therein—that accompanied their obtaining and learning their first rock instruments. For most musicians, it was a long process of negotiation with their parents. Many musicians yearned to play rock instruments, especially the guitar, at early ages, much to the dismay of their parents. After demonstrating commitment to an "appropriate" instrument such as the piano, coupled with the increased interest in rock music during the teenage years, some of the musicians were at long last able to convince their parents to allow them to learn an additional instrument of the rock variety, such as the guitar and drums. Jack remembered: "The reason I quit piano lessons is because I got into [grunge] music. I went on a school trip. . . . I had [just] bought Nirvana's *In Utero* and *Nevermind*, Pearl Jam's *Vs.* and *Ten*, and

Stone Temple Pilot's *Core*. Those five tapes. I went on a school trip and me and my friends just listened to them [nonstop]. We thought they were the coolest things you ever heard. So I came home and immediately was just like, 'I want a guitar. I don't want to take piano anymore.' I continued the piano for six months and finally just lost all interest."

This negotiation of sorts was only acceptable to the parents upon children proving their commitment to classical instruments early in life. Furthermore, this typically happened during the adolescent years, well after the musicians had devoted a few to several years on the previous instrument.

Children, of course, acted with agency in beseeching their parents' approval to allow them to obtain rock instruments. Again, such processes of negotiation may be indicative of the children's socialization, as they learn at an early age to negotiate with parents and adults alike. The children's debates were ultimately successful, as all of the parents eventually agreed to a compromise. Some of the musicians remember the process being a long, almost painful wait, though one that was ultimately worthwhile, as they were eventually rewarded with their instruments of choice.

Musicians typically had to prove their dedication to the classical instruments for the span of two to five years before upgrading to other instruments. During this time, the musicians were often enrolled in private music lessons, and some performed in public recitals. To be sure, some of the musicians did intrinsically enjoy these instruments. Upon reaching adulthood, as I discuss in the next chapter, they would be grateful for their parents "forcing" them to endure the pains of the piano for years on end during their childhood, as they recognized its positive, though unintended, consequences later in life. One valuable latent function of their less-than-enthusiastic dedication to the piano and other classical instruments was the ease at which they could adapt their musical talents to new instruments. Many of the musicians felt that learning additional instruments was somewhat easier after mastering the piano. "Once you know how to play the piano, everything else comes easy," was a common sentiment shared by many musicians. They were able to translate the skills, ideas, and lessons to other instruments, particularly the guitar. As such, their frustrations with learning rock instruments were minimal in contrast to their peers who were not obligated to start their musical trajectories on the piano.

Although women and men first learned to play instruments at about the same point in life, they differed in when they learned to play their first central "rock" instrument. While all of the men and most of the women had learned their first instrument by the end of middle school, and while many men were able to negotiate their first rock instrument in the years after that, often by the middle school years, many women, in contrast, did not pick up their first rock instruments that early in life. Jen had only been playing her rock instrument, the bass, for a year and a half before joining her current band in her early twenties. She often felt behind the learning curve: "I wish I had started earlier. I wish I had taken piano lessons or played an instrument as a kid. I just wasn't able to do those things. I wish I had learned [music] theory. It's one of those things. I'm still trying to better myself, but it's hard and I don't have a whole lot of time to dedicate to it. But I *really* wish I had taken piano. [laughs]"

Part of her laughter was due to her acknowledgment that most kids, as discussed earlier, loathed being forced into piano at early ages. Granted, she imagines she may have been fussy at the time had she had been forced into the instrument, but she would have been in a more advantageous place in music today had she had that experience. Furthermore, like Jen, these late bloomers who began playing their first rock instrument in the beginnings of adulthood more often than not selected the bass guitar. They suggested that the bass was their strategic choice, as they imagined it would be the one instrument easier to learn, particularly "this late in the game."[5]

Nonmusical Extracurricular Interests

Though music was important to a vast majority of the musicians during their formative years, their early lives were not characterized solely by music. Most of them participated in various extracurricular activities from childhood through adolescence. The typical experience for men and women was characterized by an exploratory interest and participation in organized sports. Both had experience participating in basketball, track and field, golf, and soccer. Men often had experience in football, baseball, wrestling, and (rarely) gymnastics. Women, in contrast, were involved in softball, tennis, and cheerleading.

Sports are a rite of passage in US culture, as discussed by both the women and men with whom I spoke. Men suggested it was a near requisite for a suitable adolescent masculinity (Messner 1990). Warren was one musician in particular who had extensive participation in a range of sports:

> WARREN: I played sports my whole life: baseball, basketball, football in junior high. I was pretty involved in other things besides music.
> MR: Did all that continue into high school too?
> WARREN: Yeah, it did. I liked those things, and I played them, but it wasn't too much of an option really. Once I got to a certain age, you were kind of expected to play freshman year basketball and things like that. I think even if I didn't want to do it, I would have been sucked into it.

Warren suggests that sports are a typical rite of passage for adolescent boys (Connell 1990; Messner 1992). He suspects that he would have participated in them regardless of his personal interest in trying them out. While he does not suggest who would have "sucked [him] into it," other research suggests it could be his father, siblings, friends, or other peers (Stuij 2015) His discussion implies that athletics are a typical way to adhere to normative masculinity during adolescence. Even nonathletic men suggest this was the case as well in their discussions of not being a "normal kid" due to their not participating in sports during their adolescence. Sports, as others suggest, are one key way to attain a suitable masculine gender identity for boys (Messner 1990). However, other activities allowed adolescent boys to secure a masculine gender identity, though perhaps one less valued than the sports-centered version.

Women in my sample who came of age during the 1990s and early 2000s expressed similar but slightly diluted sentiments that sports were perhaps important, but not necessarily "required" to the extent they were for boys. They did, however, suggest they felt some pressure to explore athletics to some extent. Sports were also a conduit for a suitable adolescent femininity, though this was the case for some sports more than others (Ezzell 2009). Basketball, tennis, track and field—and especially cheerleading—were more easily aligned with normative femininity, while golf and, to a lesser degree, softball lent themselves to a less valued feminine gender identity (Cahn 1993).

During this general time period, girls and boys also explored music-centered extracurricular activities, often times while simultaneously participating in athletics. Many of the school-organized music activities were the contexts in which the musicians began investing more heavily in classical instruments. After taking substantial years of private one-on-one music lessons, the next step for many was enrolling in concert bands or community orchestras. The most common pathway to musical participation, however, was via the concert band, which became an extracurricular opportunity for most during the middle school years.

The music bug bit many of them early in life, as nearly all of their nonacademic time was consumed with various musical outlets. These musicians were intrinsically motivated to devote themselves to music. They consumed every musical opportunity that presented itself, learning every instrument they could, joining every activity that their parents (and hectic schedules) would allow. Many of them were active in the marching band and concert band, often playing the saxophone, clarinet, flute, or trumpet. Others were involved in higher-status jazz bands organized by their schools. Still others began participating in orchestras, often through community-based organizations. Finally, some, instead of learning instruments, focused on vocal performance and joined the choir or show choir. Boys had sketchier histories in choirs in comparison to their female counterparts. The rare man who had this musical experience in high school added the disclaimer, "I don't even know why I was in it, to tell you the truth." Without question, a greater proportion of students who focused on vocals were girls. This experience among girls mirrors their lesser and later likelihood of learning instruments early in life. In lieu of instrumentalization, some of them focus their musical participation and skill building on their vocal performance.[6] Many of them were pushed to pursue vocals, seemingly at the cost of exploring musical instruments, because of their "naturally" good singing voices, like Lilly: "I was in chorus from the fifth grade to the tenth grade. I liked being in the chorus. One time we performed Handel's *Messiah* from start to finish, which I thought was really neat. But I ended up stopping that in high school. The teacher couldn't really control the class. I kinda out grew it. And finally I said, 'This is just unpleasant. I am sick of this.'"

Many of the women began to find their voice during their years in the chorus and choir. They increasingly grew bored or frustrated with some aspect of the class, as was the case with Lilly. They incrementally drifted away from their commitment to the music program, ultimately quitting at some point during the high school years.

Participation in one of the above activities was by no means exclusive, as many juggled—even overcommitted themselves to—multiple musical extracurricular commitments. For instance, Vincent, though at the more overcommitted end of the spectrum, was typical in his interest in many musical outlets: "It was all basically everything surrounded around music. It just seemed like it was all [I did]. I mean, I was playing in the jazz band, I was in the chorus, I was in the symphony, [and I] had my garage band with my friends. [Music] took up so many afterschool hours."

Scholars have described individuals who consume both "high" and "low" culture—those who attend Tchaikovsky ballets one weekend and pop princess Britney Spears concerts the following—as "cultural omnivores" (Peterson 1992; Peterson and Simkus 1992). The musicians similarly were "musical omnivores," eating up every opportunity in music, both high- and low-brow that presented itself to them. Their passion for music was broad and would later unfold as important in their rock careers later in life.

Still other women and men opted for other pursuits during middle and high school. Broadly speaking, these individuals tried out activities in the "arts," broadly defined. They took classes or joined afterschool organizations that allowed them to explore art (such as painting, drawing, sculpting, or photography), drama, yearbook staff, and other previously unavailable opportunities. While the art students often described themselves as more introverted, the drama students were particularly drawn to the stage aspect of those extracurriculars, like Abby: "I was in the drama club, which I think is similar in a lot of ways to being in a [rock] band that performs. Both share similarities, like being onstage and kind of being the center of attention in a way." Nearly all of the students who pursued the arts in high school drew some relevance as to its later connection and significance to their future musically focused lives.

They more often explored these options well into adolescence, due to the mere fact that such options did not arise until high school. As Kinney (1993) has noted, the structural opportunities in high school settings in the United States are arranged to allow for more options for extracurricular activities, and hence allow for more identity exploration via those options. Nate, for instance, discovered acting midway through high school and enjoyed it, much to his surprise: "I was a drama nerd. I was my last two years of high school. Before that I was [insecure]. If it weren't for drama, I probably wouldn't have done the music thing because I was really insecure—I *still* am really insecure, but I was more so then. I had zero self-confidence [but] I started getting into drama and getting onstage and being in plays and started having more confidence. So I don't think that I could stand up in front of people and play right now if I hadn't done that." Similarly, Robert looked back on his drama experience as crucial for his musical development: "We had a drama team that I [participated] in, which became, unbeknownst to me, an influence on who I am right now. It paved the way for where I am now. I can get up on stage and dance around like a fucking fool. I dress up and these things don't really bother me. I've always thought it had some sort of influence [on me]."

Their participation in the arts did more than consume their time, give them a circle of friends, or provide an outlet for their creativity and expression. For some of them, though they did not realize it until years later, it was a testing ground for their future public performances on stage. In this sense, it contributed to the development of their musical possibilities in adulthood. The musicians often saw aspects of those extracurricular activities as providing informal training for music careers that would emerge in the future.

The First Rock Band

Early introductions to musical instruments set the stage for the founding of peer-organized rock bands. The first band was a significant turning point for nearly all of the musicians. It was an orientation of sorts to the worlds they would later enter at a more professional level. It was in the first band that a genuine commitment to music was often sparked. The intrinsic satisfaction became a driving force that set them more concretely on pathways toward musical futures (and *off* pathways for more normative adulthoods). These events correlated with the age at which they learned their first rock instruments, as those who started playing rock instruments earlier in the life course were likely to join bands at younger ages. Clear gender differences did emerge as well, as men on average played in their first rock bands far earlier in life in comparison to women.

The earliest time period during which musicians joined their first bands was in the middle school years. One-third of the men (11 of 33) but not one of the women started playing in bands during this time frame. Aaron's first experience playing in a band early was in his preteen years:

AARON: I knew that I wanted to start a band. Jimi Hendrix made me want to play guitar, but I was also really into skating. A lot of my [peers] were skaters and really into punk at the same time, so the first band that I ended up starting was punk. Punk rock is obviously easier for a beginner to play, so I did it with my best friend and a drummer friend who lived down the street from me . . . [They were] two really good friends. In the sixth grade we made a band together.

MR: That seems really early to start a band.

AARON: Yeah, yeah. We would even write songs together. We would write all our own songs. We never played anybody else's. And I think in sixth grade we played at some school function, maybe a dance or something. [We were] horribly mediocre back then. Then in seventh grade we did a talent show, and all the parents were supportive of it. So yeah, a really early start.

Looking back, Aaron realizes, perhaps in contrast to other musicians with whom he is acquainted, that he did have the earliest of starts in playing in a band as a child. Similar to other men's stories, Aaron's early inception into the world of rock was contingent on two aspects of his adolescent life. First, he began learning his first rock instrument, the guitar, at an early age. By the time he was in early middle school, he had mastered the instrument well enough to join a band and begin composing his own songs. Though Aaron remembers his first band as "horribly mediocre," he is among the musicians who had the earliest start in performing in bands. Furthermore, by the seventh grade, he had two public performances under his belt. Second, Aaron was involved in a network of peers who played rock instruments as well. Forming a band clearly necessitates the involvement in social networks with peers who play instruments themselves.

As they moved more fully into adolescence, a greater number of both the men and women found an upsurge of opportunities to join their first rock band. Over half of the men (18 of 33) and about a quarter of the women (4 of 15) joined their first band during high school. Warren said he was "around 14 or 15 when we started a band. It was like a neighborhood kind of thing. My friend lived next door and my other friend lived [nearby] too. One played bass, the other played guitar, and our other friend Dave played the drums. We tried to write our own songs, but we'd also play cover songs. We played one of our friends' fifteenth birthday party. We thought we were rock stars. Once we did that, started our band, pretty much that was when I really started getting into it all the time, constantly." Constructing the band was often a matter of convenience, as the boys often recruited others in their neighborhood who happened to play instruments themselves. Warren formed his first band with his close friends, but other men suggest that their first bands were composed of acquaintances, not necessarily friends to whom they were closely attached.

Similar to Lever's (1976) study of sex differences in childhood play, the adolescent boys in my study suggest that the structure of their leisure activities (in this case music) dictated that they broaden their social circles to include greater numbers of potential playmates to fill all requisite roles.

In looking back on these experiences, the musicians were hesitant to describe them as "real" bands. More often than not, the musicians, especially those who devoted a substantial portion of their high school years to rock, characterized their bands as "silly" or "time wasters." Isaac remembered his first band in high school as a fun but sloppy and amateurish activity:

> It was mainly just messing around. We didn't have any concept of how you get a band together, and then if you got a band together, how would you go about writing songs? And then if you wrote a song, how do you convey that information to the other people in the band? And then how do you practice the songs? And then how in the world would you call a club and get booked there? I mean, we knew that this sort of thing happened, but it wasn't going to happen to us. It just seemed like an impossibility—maybe later on down the road. I guess it was one of those things where we felt like we probably had to get better at playing our instruments before we could actually do anything like that. So the idea of playing in public was just kinda unimaginable really. We played for ourselves, and we would smoke pot in the basement and then record what we were doing, and then we would go back and listen to it, and smoke more pot. "Oh, did you hear that? That was so cool." So yeah. I guess we thought we had a band, but we it was more like a secret club really.

While not all of the teenage musicians were "that serious" about their rock bands in high school, many of them did have what amounts to a productive tenure with these early bands. Most of them began composing their first original songs during this time period with their bandmates. Surprisingly, over two-thirds of the musicians (33 of 48) had experience in rock bands by the end of adolescence. By high school graduation, twenty-nine of the men had been in at least one rock band, and over half had performed publicly at least once. In contrast, four of the women had been in a band and two had performed in public by the end of the high school years. Though they discount the talent and authenticity of their early rock bands, these "amateur" experiences were more professional than they may imagine and would later prove to set the stage for future and more professional opportunities in music in the future.

The remaining fifteen musicians (11 of whom were women and 4 of whom were men) did not join their first band until well after exiting adolescence and entering emerging adulthood. College was the setting that provided such opportunities for many of them. The combination of pursuing a postsecondary education and doing so in the context of a college music town was, for some, the perfect storm that led them to music's doorstep. Many believed that exploring their foray into rock bands could only happen when the "stars were aligned" upon their arrival to a college music town and befriending other musicians to prod them to invest more in music, thus prompting their growing internalization of the possibilities of musical participation and musical identities. These "late bloomers" were unique in that they discovered hidden interests and buried talents that they perhaps would have never discovered where it not for the context that is college life in Athens.

What is particularly relevant for this subgroup of musicians is the substantial boost in women's entrance to the musical world during this time frame—the largest proportion of women in my sample joined their first band during the years following the completion of high school. Clearly, postadolescent introductions to participation in rock bands are considerably marked by gender. Participation in inaugural rock bands post–high school was the norm for women. In stark contrast, only a minority of men (4 of 33) started their first band after high school.

The grounds for this gendered trend lay in social networks. Women do not have access to musical peer networks until well later in life, while boys' culture is saturated in music from an early age. Boys are embedded in those networks that ease their musical development and allow ample opportunities to try out rock music as early as the preadolescent years. However, girls are in entirely different networks during this time period. Their peer culture growing up, while sharing some overlap with boys', tends not to include the traditionally masculine pursuits of playing rock music. It is not necessarily due to boys' barring girls from their culture, although exclusion is a factor for some. Instead, girls' exemption stems from their interests in other activities, some of which are historically coded as masculine, such as sports. Girls' worlds growing up have broadened in comparison to earlier generations, evidenced by the increasing rates of girls' participation in once all-masculine milieu of sports, but musical participation has been slower to shift to encompass girls' coming of age.[7]

In general, the earlier that the musicians, both boys and girls, learned instruments, the younger they were when they were introduced to their first rock bands. An early start in learning instruments of course allows for additional years to master the instrument (or at the very least, improve one's playing), hone one's style, and ultimately mull over the idea of playing in a band before actually doing so. All of these advantages are more aligned with the boys' lives rather than girls', illustrating not only the importance of gendered peer cultures as influences for the future, but the extent to which the life course is organized differentially by gender.

The varying times at which the boys and girls began their first bands were also dependent on contexts that allow differential opportunities to such networks. First, the opportunities to participate in rock bands were informal. The bands were created and structured by the musicians themselves, unlike musical activities in which they were previously involved with in the church or the school band. In most of the stories I heard about the musicians' first rock bands, they portrayed these opportunities happening "by chance." They just happened to be in the same classrooms or friendship circles with peers who invited them to play music with them. The first bands by no means required a formal audition. In fact, when the youth would convene to play music, there was often no discussion of them "starting" a band. Instead, it was an activity that was for mere fun, enjoyment, and to pass the time during after school hours. Some of the musicians suggested they "accidentally" or unintentionally started bands—it was not until a few weeks of getting together with their friends that they realized they were a band. This is band creation in the most informal sense—they often did not realize they had started a band until weeks after the fact.

Second, the musicians acted with agency to create these opportunities. There were no academic rewards for joining bands. In fact, adults involved in the organization of school-structured extracurricular activities, be it in music or athletics, downplayed the value of informal music. They would even discourage some students from devoting "too much" time to these activities in fear they would take time away from the students' other interests. A few musicians had music teachers and coaches who warned that their potential futures in formal music or sports could be threatened were they to distract themselves with rock music. The musicians took their suggestions with a grain of salt and rarely heeded their warnings, thus demonstrating agency in the creation, maintenance, and devotion to their afterschool musical interests.

Early Aspirations: Perceived Futures during Adolescence

The late teen years are a typical time during which adolescents begin considering options for their futures, particularly in terms of career possibilities (Csikszentmihalyi and Schneider 2000; Osgood et al. 2005; Sandefur et al. 2005). The musicians were no different. Upon nearing high school graduation, they all had ideas in mind as to what would come next upon moving into the emerging adulthood years. Of course, their parents had ideas and hopes for their children's outcomes as well, and they were often quick to impart those ideas with their daughters and sons.

A majority of the musicians' parents imagined their children would follow their familial occupational and social class pathways and become upwardly mobile (or at the very least end up in a comparable position as the family of origin). The parents anticipated or, more to the point, *expected* their children to further their education post–high school and attend college. They anticipated their children to achieve professional occupations in engineering, journalism, business, law, medicine, or teaching. Very few parents suggested that their children model and pursue the very careers they had, but they nonetheless assumed their children would enter professional, high-status, and relatively high-paying careers. Julia's experience was typical:

> My mom was always [saying], "You should be a journalist or a writer." My dad was like, "You should go into engineering or pursue this archaeology that you've seemed somewhat fascinated with since you were a kid." And just that, "You can do this, or you can do this, or you can do this. Go to college, go through rush, and be in a sorority like your other friends. Make lots of money, be happy, whatever it takes." Just typical [parents] worrying about you, so they're gonna push you into their idea of the corner that you should be in. They just want you to be safe, so I [initially] tried to go within those guidelines.

The musicians had the typical middle-class experience of their parents pushing them not just to explore various extracurriculars during the middle school and high school years, but to also "aim high" and pursue the most lucrative and elite occupations in adulthood (Bozick et al. 2010; Hargrove et al. 2002; Schoon and Parsons 2002; Sewell and Hauser 1975). Their parents were unequivocally encouraging and supportive, wanting the best for their children. Parents' encouragement, however, was often loaded with middle-class expectations of pursuing high-status professional careers in the white-collar world.

In contrast, very few parents weighed the possibilities of their children pursuing careers in music or other arts. In the eyes of the parents, their children's histories and passion for music were a key part of their development, but not a rational occupational outcome. It shaped them into well-rounded young adults. It helped them appreciate the arts, and likewise contributed to their habitus to ensure their successful foray into upper-middle-class culture (Bourdieu 1984). But it was beyond the parents' thinking to imagine such interests could pan out to possible musical careers in adulthood. This is not to say parents never suspected their children would pursue music. For a handful of them, such was the case. Parents' conceiving of their children's pursuing a musical career in adulthood was a rare instance, and one that only emerged in the lives of men. Nevertheless, while their parents anticipated music in their sons' futures, they did not explicitly foresee their sons becoming rock stars per se.

And what about the musicians themselves? How did they foresee their futures during adolescence? They were generally a diverse group with diverse interests. They anticipated a range of possibilities for their adulthoods. For a vast majority of them, college was always on the horizon. The only musicians who did not suspect they would attend college were those from working-class backgrounds and/or those who had begun developing technical skills in working-class industries early in adolescence.

Given their social class upbringing coupled with their parents' expectations, it was no surprise that a solid majority of the musicians anticipated enrolling in college. About half of the men (15 of 33) and two-thirds of the women (10 of 15) were fairly certain they would attend college after high school graduation. The women anticipated studying education, medicine, veterinary medicine, and business. Men expressed early interests in similar fields of study, although some were also interested in formally studying music at the college level.

Furthermore, a higher proportion of men than women anticipated venturing into musical directions for their career. Among the men, a greater number foresaw musical careers over college and professional careers in their future. Over half of the men (17 of 33) and only a few women (3 of 15) had musical ambitions early in life. Musical plans were shared with parents when it focused on musical careers as in the classical music or orchestral world.

ADRIAN: It was there [at the magnet school] that I was able to start getting into the orchestra, the string program, which is what ultimately led me to [college] to study classical music.

MR: This was after you learned the guitar?

ADRIAN: Yeah. I was taking classical lessons with the guitar. That's what I auditioned with to go to this magnet school. That was seventh grade. The string teacher there was like, "You know what, I really need some bass players in the orchestra. The bass and the guitar go hand in hand." I was like, "Okay, I'll give it a shot." I started playing string bass. I kept the two going. I'll always love classical music. And for a while I thought I could do that professionally, but I think somewhere deep inside I always knew that I just wanted to play rock and roll.

MR: There was a time when you thought classical music was your future?

ADRIAN: Yeah, in college. That's what I studied. I studied double bass. . . . I thought, "Maybe I can do symphony work for a living." But it's such a cutthroat nature, playing in an orchestra. I don't think I would change anything because I learned a whole lot in music school that really helped me as far as like arranging goes and writing. I make money on the side playing for musical theaters now, in the pit orchestra. It goes on, that side of me, still.

Adrian's academic history in music clearly impacted his career in rock music. His music teacher encouraged him to learn and pursue classical music in high school. While he cites this aspect of his history as influential to his development as a musician in his rock band, he simultaneously regards the decision to pursue a career in the classical music world as more "cutthroat."[8] His parents were aware of his initial plans and unequivocally supportive. Classical musicians, though not part of the normative world of the middle and upper middle class, still maintain a status consistent with middle- and upper-class backgrounds.

In contrast, those musicians who dreamed of informal musical careers in rock often kept such plans covert, as parents were typically not aware of these plans their children were making. Similar to those with aspirations for careers in professional music worlds, a higher proportion of men than women anticipated from a very young age that they would pursue rock later in life, like Vincent: "But I think it was the teenage years when I knew I wanted to play in a band. I was always playing in a band for school talent shows and stuff like that. I think by thirteen or fourteen there was no question I wanted to be in a band either playing guitar or singing." Furthermore, pursuing music and furthering one's education were not mutually exclusive choices, for the men at least. Often unbeknownst to their parents, they had inklings of plans to pursue both higher education and music simultaneously. They ultimately not only had to share their covert musical dreams with their family, but would also have to make the painstakingly difficult choice between the two options in the coming years, as will be discussed in the coming chapters.

Conclusion

The early years in life were influential in shaping the musicians' life course trajectories, in terms of music and their educational and extracurricular pursuits. What is particularly insightful is the extent to which the musicians themselves could easily reminisce on and perceive the influence moments early in life had on their positions to come much later in adulthood. The musicians did not magically develop interest in music from out of nowhere. Their musical participation was often due to parents' interests in music, highlighting the particular ways in which the family exacerbated musical development, often through moments as simple as turning up the radio on weekends with their children or attending concerts or symphonies as family events. The family's love of music was almost contagious during the early years. The development of musical interests hinged on opportunities and socialization patterns available in predominantly middle-class contexts. Other institutional contexts in which the musicians found themselves, such as the church, nudged them to develop deeper interests in music, particularly music performance.

During the early years in life, the musicians came of age in the context of a range of activities and interests. Some were persuaded by adults and parents, while others' musical interests arose through self-motivations. Though they would later focus on music, their early years were punctuated by other activities beyond music, such as other arts and athletics. These activities, whether taken on for a few weeks or several years, allowed for presumably the first opportunities for the musicians to try out different identities via their leisure pursuits. Different rewards and consequences stemmed from these experimentations. Perhaps more importantly, discoveries were made—and early in life, no less—offering the potential for new possible pathways to be more actively undertaken upon moving into the emerging adult years. Men's experiences in extracurricular pursuits while growing up were diverse, but narrower than the range of activities in which the women participated. These differential experiences illustrate both the gendered patterns of the life course that emerge early on, as well as the gendered consequences of pursuing particular activities.

Ultimately, what triggers women and men to pursue music is not simply the age at which they pick up instruments, join bands, and otherwise undergo socialization for such informal careers, although these factors clearly set the stage for such possibilities. There are, no doubt, a good many boys and girls who come of age in the United States with similar experiences and interests in music who never contemplate careers in music. It takes more than experiencing those moments or feeling passionate for music to push one to make those leaps. What matters more in nudging musicians toward the pursuit of musical careers are the contexts in which women and men find themselves in the emerging adulthood years and the opportunities (and constraints) that develop postadolescence, allowing some to close their eyes, imagine their possible futures, and see music. These issues are the focus of the next chapter.

2

First Making the Sounds
• •

Negotiating Adulthood
in a Musical World

In Richard Linklater's 2003 film, *School of Rock*, Dewey Finn, played by Jack Black, one of the lone adults in the story, is anything but adult in his behaviors. The narrative critiques Dewey's character: he's unemployed, he's a couch surfer, he fakes his way into employment, and he's not even that great a musician to boot. But the biggest critique is his failing to be a true adult. Beside the fact that he steals a friend's identity to secure a job at a prep school, exploits the students' talents, and undermines their education, the "big" problem is that Dewey refuses to let go of his dreams of rock and roll. While everything ultimately turns out fine (this is Hollywood, after all), the storyline implicitly focuses on Dewey's struggle to become adult while keeping music at the center point of his life. He is the consummate manboy, technically an adult, yet refusing to accept the responsibilities of the adulthood and happily stunted in an adolescent lifestyle.

Such is the narrative our culture presents in examining adults who cling to adolescent pipedreams of music. The rock band, we are told, is a fine way to spend one's leisure time during the teenage years. However, once the threshold of adulthood is upon men and women, music is presumed to take a back seat in life. It is time, both figuratively and literally, to put the guitar down.

In this chapter, I follow musicians' postadolescent life course trajectories as they move into the emerging adult years. I begin by examining the directions musicians took immediately after high school graduation, whether focused explicitly on music or not. I then trace the decisions and factors that prompted the musicians to move to a college music town, only one factor of which was college itself. As they transition more fully into adulthood, they face numerous tasks and challenges of adulthood, as do all adults coming of age in the United States. As I will illustrate, the dilemmas of adulthood are additionally compounded for those pursuing musical careers. Multiple aspects of their identities are in conflict with one another, making the adult identity far less comfortable and less attainable for them. I unpack the tensions of aging musicians face, and conclude by comparing the strategies they use to reconcile adulthood with musical aspirations.

Launching into Adulthood: High School Graduation and Postadolescent Plans

After the culmination of adolescence and the symbolically important rite of passage of high school graduation, musicians began considering options for the future. The late teenage years were far too early for a number of musicians to know precisely what the future had in store for them, much less what initial directions they wanted to take in this new phase of life. For most musicians, the entrance into the postadolescent years was informative to their identities, and likewise enlightening in terms of finding their way, but most did not characterize those years as intensely stressful in terms of feeling pressure to "figure life out." Many of them were still contemplating their futures and simultaneously continuing to sculpt their interest in music. They did feel some pressure—often self-inflicted—to figure out precisely in what direction they would go next. For many of the musicians, the ideas they fashioned for their postadolescent years were nebulous.

A good number of them foresaw entering standardized professions: teaching, architecture, journalism, law, or medicine. A few imagined they would pursue artistic careers, either formal or not. And some, of course, anticipated forging musical careers. Some musicians, like Adrian, saw their futures in teaching music or performing with orchestras. Others vaguely considered pursuing rock music, but these were often characterized as teenage daydreams. Regardless of their precise (or imprecise) ideas of their futures, their wandering and early aspirations are characterized by dual forces: exploration and hope.

Very few of the musicians felt pressure to decide on lifelong careers during this time period. Many were able to successfully defer such decisions because they were preparing for or were currently enrolled in college. College, while placing them on the normative pathway to adulthood, is a time of further exploration and discovery (Karp et al. 1998). Pursuing higher education allowed them to be seen as on the right track in their parents' eyes and was simultaneously a ticket to delay the full responsibilities of adulthood. The decision to go to college was not much of a decision per se, as most of the musicians came from middle-class backgrounds with at least one parent with a college degree, prompting higher education to be an assumed (and sometimes unspoken) lifelong expectation, one that was often internalized in the musicians themselves. The decision did not feel quite like a decision in the normative sense, but as the "next natural step" in life after high school graduation. Early in life, they knew they would one day go to college, many of them even knowing at an early age which particular college they would likely attend. Their thoughts and plans about majors they would pursue and careers they would enter after college were often described as improvisational, such as Eli's comment: "I thought I would be in college. I didn't really have any idea beyond that. Yeah, it's where I thought I would just be—I'll be in college and I'll figure it out there. I didn't put much thought in what I was gonna do exactly beyond [that]." Others, like Alicia, had fairly concrete and well-defined life plans that inevitably changed upon moving through the college trajectory:

> I always thought that I would go to college. I always wanted to be an English major, which is what I ended up doing. And then I kind of had this idea that I would go on and get my master's degree and then maybe get a PhD in English and teach or something like that. But then once I got to college, I realized that teaching was just about the last thing that I ever wanted to do. So I definitely didn't see myself doing what I'm doing now, but I really enjoy working at the library. It works out well with everything else that I'm interested in. It's not the kind of job where you go home and you have to think about it while you're at home or do anything on the weekends or whatever, so I have a lot of free time, and it's really good.

Some musicians, those from working-class backgrounds in particular, did not share such expectations. Instead, they imagined that they would perhaps learn a trade or start their careers upon high school graduation. Others were overtly encouraged by their parents to further their education for a better future. Lauren's working-class background posed some dilemmas in college.

> The one problem that I have with college actually is if you come from a small town, there are not a lot of opportunities to try stuff. And when you come to college, there's big emphasis to "pick something, pick something!" You don't really get to try things. And college is the first chance you have to try things. They sort of frown upon you changing your mind, but if you come from a small town where there's not a lot of opportunities, you now have a chance to try things, so why not? If you went to some urban school where they have a drama department and all different kinds of clubs, all different kinds of [extracurricular

activities] like photography or whatever that you could try out, maybe you'll have a better idea when you get in to college of what you want to do. But in my little town, there was hardly anything. . . . There just weren't a lot of opportunities because it's a small town.

One of the consequences of a working-class upbringing is the truncated opportunity to explore various activities to discover one's skills and interests while coming of age. This initially hindered those from working-class backgrounds who did not have the opportunities, much less the resources or cultural capital, to allow them to begin exploring options for the future early in life. Lauren's discussions of the limitations and the pressure to decide on one's future upon one's arrival to college highlights additional factors why working-class women and men may be less likely to pursue music: they have not been socialized to even consider such nontraditional options.

During the emerging adulthood years, musical careers were on the radar for some, but not many, musicians. To be sure, musical interests and leisure pursuits were characterized as important to many musicians, but only the rare musician felt music as a calling in the early transition to adulthood, such as James: "[After high school] I knew I would [pursue] music, but no, not necessarily as a career. I spent so much time playing in orchestras and bands, so I knew I wanted to [continue with] music somehow, but I never really thought of it in career [terms] . . . But I never really had all that much desire to pursue something else that I could do as a backup in place of music." James knew early on he would persist in his following music into adulthood. Other musicians were similar in forecasting such futures, but overall the conviction of music as one's destiny was rare. Many of them instead described their orientations for the future as "really kind of nebulous." Typical of most emerging adults, the musicians had many interests they were exploring simultaneously, but careers in music were not necessarily among them. Those interests would develop later once they found themselves in particular locales and embedded in particular social worlds in the coming years.

At first glance, the early part of musicians' adult lives seemed to not follow any discernable pattern that led them pointedly to the pursuit of musical careers. The musicians did share a general similarity, though, that was necessary for them to shift gears toward music: a majority of them did not end up where they initially imagined they would, similar to other studies of adulthood outcomes (Gerson 1985). Heath, for instance, revealed his unfulfilled dreams and aspirations in the arts:

HEATH: I thought I was going to be an artist. I wanted to be either a filmmaker or a fine artist, somebody doing gallery painting, really artsy stuff. That's where I saw myself.

MR: Is that something else that you hope to do [as a career]?

HEATH: Is this the point [in the interview] where everybody's like, "Damn, I sure as hell didn't do what I planned to!" [laughs] Is this the point where everybody gets depressed? "Damn, I missed my mark on that one!"

Unrequited dreams are, as strange as it may be, necessary for musicians to imagine other possibilities in life. Those musicians who were intensely focused on a particular career outcome early in life often felt shock at those plans being deferred, but there was also a newfound freedom that accompanied those disappointments: the freedom to imagine something new (Fornäs et al. 1995). Musical careers would fill those now open spaces for musicians' thoughts on their futures. The musicians all shared yet another similarity. They all would find themselves in Athens, Georgia, during their adult years for one reason or another, a situational factor that set the stage for their musical futures.

Moving to a College Music Town

Although every musician in my sample lived in Athens at the time at which I spoke with them, only a few were born and raised there. A clear majority of them made deliberate decisions that brought them to Athens: education and/ or music. A minority of the musicians (8 of 48) initially moved to Athens with full intentions to extend their education. These musicians moved to Athens to attend the University of Georgia. As the flagship university in the state, it was the institution a number of musicians grew up considering attending for various reasons. For some, it was for its reputation. They often had parents, siblings, and other family members who graduated from UGA. Others were familiar with the areas of study offered at the university and the reputable schools of journalism, business, and the arts. Initially focused on academics, they expressed sentiments similar to Jacob who stated, "I was just trying to get an education. I wasn't thinking about music at the time."

By far, the most frequent reason for relocating to Athens was due to its reputation as the music hub of the Southeast. Almost half of the men and women (21 of 48) cited moving to Athens precisely for the music scene itself. Long known for its supportive music scene and its encouraging atmosphere for culture and the arts, many musicians were tempted by the allure of Athens. Its mystique was mesmerizing to many of the musicians, drawing them to relocate to the small town in northeast Georgia.[1]

MR: Did you move to Athens for school or music?

BETH: It's really actually kind of cheesy once I think about it ... [A particular band from Athens] are really big in Salt Lake [City]. They came through town several times, and we just got to be friends, started talking. And they'd always say, "Yeah, Athens is really cool." They sang its praises and said how great it is for touring bands, for people that are interested in music, and how great the music is here, blah blah blah. So I applied through the national student exchange . . . It's a program where you go to another school for one semester and study, just on an exchange. I came up here and I was supposed to stay here for only one semester, but then I just really liked it here, so I stayed.

MR: You just stayed?

BETH: Yeah. I haven't been seriously focused on school since that first semester that I was here. I mean I tell people I came here because I was friends with [that band]. I really wouldn't have moved here if it weren't for those two. I just fell in love with the town because it's so great. It nurtures the arts, and not just music. It's just really easy to be an artist or musician here. I mean, it's not simple, but it's a lot easier than in any other city.

For Beth and a number of other musicians, the lore of Athens as a supportive and arts-friendly locale proved to be true. It tempted them to make the initial move, but, more importantly, their experiences once in Athens prompted them to stay. Hometown vicinity played a role as well, as some musicians came from nearby Atlanta or neighboring states, often the Carolinas or Florida. It was not unheard of, however, for some to come from as far away as Utah, Michigan, and New York. Paul discussed his move from the Midwest: "[My first band and I] lived in a pretty rural area in Michigan. There wasn't really any music scene, so we decided were gonna move to a bigger [music] city. That's how I ended up in Athens. We were serious [about pursuing music] . . . We knew about Athens. We were really big R.E.M. fans. So we decided really quickly that we'd move here. But it was really just for the music [scene]. We didn't have any real goal in mind." Paul's plans were somewhat tentative. Other musicians had similar stories, discussing how they moved to Athens on a whim to "test" it out. Many who initially had short-term plans stayed indefinitely. Still others had music contacts in Athens, giving them a foot in the door as well as access to insider knowledge regarding the town and music scene, not to mention the social support, comfort, and informal socialization for their budding careers.

Again, young adults with music orientations could have presumably moved to any host of music cities across the United States. Why Athens? While many did cite New York or Los Angeles (and sometimes, though less often, Nashville) as influential music cities, economics factored into their decisions as well. The low cost of living in a small college town in Georgia made the town a more attractive option, as Brandon explained: "Rent is cheap. You can get a [service-sector] job, and you can live for real cheap here. This is never-never land. And I've heard a lot of people refer to [Athens] as a time warp because we see people leave and come back and they look like they have aged. Because they have gone into the real world. Here, this isn't the real world. . . . You can work at a place like the Taco Stand and pay your rent and you can do that for years and you still have enough money to go drink."

Many others suggested that Athens was a prime venue to be able to pursue artistic careers without having the added burden of a taxing "side job" to pay the bills, like Julia: "For now Athens works. I don't see any need to move to New York because it just seems like you'd be struggling. You'd be putting so much more time and energy into just being able to live and pay your bills that it would take away [from the music]. It just seems like it'd be a lot more difficult because that's how it was when I lived in San Francisco. I couldn't even [pay my rent]. It was so expensive that I couldn't even find a place to live or pay my bills. And my whole time was spent on that and not on music. So, yeah, Athens works, and it's cool." Musicians suggested the culture of Athens promoted fewer stresses than would presumably be the case in other music scenes in bigger cities. Work was fairly easy to come by, and though the wages were not necessarily high, living expenses in Athens were modest. It was possible—with the right work hours and the right living arrangement—to make ends meet without overextending oneself to one's job.

Over a third of the musicians (19 of 48) had slightly different routes to Athens. They cited the twofold rationale of educational opportunities *and* the local music scene as prompting their move to Athens. Specifically, those musicians who were not too invested in college used UGA as a pretext for relocating to Athens. They enrolled in college, but anticipated their musical lives would flourish in Athens. For these musicians, their selecting UGA as their college of choice was tied more to the town itself, rather than the educational opportunities they could accrue. The musicians who anticipated pursuing music saw Athens as the ideal locale due to its having a good university as well as excellent musical culture. Ben recalls contemplating college his senior year of high school:

> I totally fell in love with Athens my senior year of high school. . . . My senior year I came up to see a Flaming Lips concert and I came up and saw a Ween concert. Those were the two concerts I saw. I went to the 40 Watt and the Georgia Theatre, and I saw where the dorms were, and the venues too. Everything was right here. All these great concerts. I didn't know anything about the local music scene at all. It was in my head that Athens had a great music scene. I was like, "Well, if I want to play in a band while I was in school, I want to move to Athens." I didn't even know what my major was going to be. I just checked something off on the application at that time. I definitely came here with the intention of knowing I can be in a band. As long as I do well in school, I can play music.

Alicia was attracted to UGA more for Athens's music scene than for any degree program offered by the school. She is convinced the town shaped her life choices:

ALICIA: I probably wouldn't have been in bands if I lived someplace other than Athens. I don't know for sure, I mean I haven't been to a lot of other college towns, so I don't really know what the music scene there is like, but I came here because I knew that there was a music scene and there were bands that I liked that were playing here at the time that I came to college.

MR: So you came so you could see these bands or because in the back of your mind you were thinking, "Well, maybe I could start a band too" and this would be the place to do it?

ALICIA: [laughs] I don't really remember if I actually thought that about it, but there were bands at the time that I really liked who were playing at the time that I came to college. . . . I didn't come here with that in mind, but I think that Athens is a really easy place to start a band because you just know so many people. Once you start playing music and you meet people who play music here also, it just seems like people are starting bands all the time. It's just really, really easy.

Like other musicians, Alicia believes she would not have pursued music had she moved to a town other than Athens. Charlie pointedly stated what influenced him to relocate to Athens after high school.

CHARLIE: The reason I came to UGA was because of Athens. . . . The reason that I'm here is because there are bands that play every night.

MR: That was part of the reason you applied to UGA?

CHARLIE: That was *the* reason. I had [full intention] to go to college and start a band.

As these musicians categorically indicate, the central reason many musicians applied to UGA was because of the music scene. And by so doing, musicians were able to incorporate music more easily into their lives: they satisfied their parents' wishes for them to attend college, and they were able to make music on the side. These musicians worked to negotiate appropriate life paths to satisfy simultaneously their own passion for music and the expectations of their parents that they pursue higher education. Their parents were delighted with their children's progression to college, while the musicians themselves were often more excited about the musical possibilities in Athens. Some of the musicians felt some guilt in fabricating their investment in college, but their being typically good, dedicated students assuaged any such feelings. Their performing well in college and making good grades was a bit of a ploy for some to ensure their continued enrollment in UGA and therefore their continued time in Athens.

In general, the grounds for moving to Athens varied by social class, as did the point in life at which they did so. Typically, middle-class men and women moved to Athens earlier in life, often at or around age eighteen. At the emerging part of adulthood, they were following the normative route to a middle-class adulthood via college, prompting their move to Athens immediately after high school graduation. Their focus only later shifted to prioritize music, as they initially moved to Athens for education. The culture of Athens progressively influenced their interests, diverting them to a new direction: one focused on musical participation. Similarly, those who had a dual focus of music and education arrived in Athens at similar times in life, if not at age eighteen, by the early twenties at the latest. Those men and women, however, who were not on the normative middle-class pathways to adulthood often did not move to Athens until later in adulthood. It was a longer, deliberate, and more calculated pathway that led them to Athens—one that required more planning and effort than the former group.

Transitions and Tensions in Emerging Adulthood

As other scholars have theorized, the move into adulthood is accompanied by one's contemplation of future career prospects (Levinson 1978). A majority, but not all, of the musicians with whom I spoke were enrolled in college in the time period during which they were transitioning to emerging adulthood. Of course, many of them envisioned careers that could stem from their education. At the same time, nearly all of them simultaneously contemplated pursuing music as a career. This push and pull incited an important development of distinct identities: they were college students, but they were also musicians. The two identities were not always entirely compatible with one another, but they felt very little tension between the two. It was fairly easy for them to reconcile both identities, as both were compatible with emerging adulthood (Ramirez 2013).

> MR: Is it hard, since you are still enrolled in school and taking classes, to still have time to devote to the band?
>
> STEWART: I don't think so. I was a really good multitasker. I'll admit, I would bring my laptop to school, and I would take care of all the press and e-mail for the shows and everything while I was in class. We played a lot of weekday drinking shows, so I had my share of hungover school days, but being in class definitely helped [the band]. I mean, handing people flyers in class—that was cool. It was nice because it was easier to meet people in your classes. You get to say you're in a band.

While some musicians admitted the toll music took on their academics, most were consistent with Stewart and were successfully able to balance college life with musical interests. Some, like Roman, admitted to not being an ideal student, but stressed that music was not to blame: "Right now it works out pretty well. Honestly, *I* distract myself more than the band does. At least when the band is doing stuff, it's focused. It's like, we are practicing from 7 to 10, and we have a show Friday. But in between those [time commitments], *I* am the one essentially that is slacking. If there's ever a time in school when I don't do well on a paper or an exam, it's not because of the band. It's because I didn't put in the right amount of time to do it."

The structure of their lives during college also lent itself to participation in music. First, they lived in a college music town. While football games, partying, Greek life, and barhopping are mainstays of contemporary college life, music was another principal centerpiece of college in Athens. College life entailed having multiple distracters outside of academics. They imagined if they were not in bands, other "time wasters" would have filled those hours. The musicians felt, in contrast to those "vices," they ultimately had something to show for their time devoted to musical participation. Second, they have fewer time constraints in comparison to other populations. College life can very well be demanding, but students often have tremendous leeway in time. Even taking a full course load and working part-time left significant chunks of time open for leisure—in their case, for music. College-enrolled musicians who had band members outside of college—those with full-time jobs in particular—had a clearer indication as to how much free time they had in contrast. Third, they fit the ideal type of both social categories of student and musician. The normative time at which to attend college is the early twenties, as is the most appropriate time to explore leisure pursuits in music. Likewise, it is not a stretch to do both simultaneously. Musicians typically felt little tension to be college students by day and moonlight as musicians in their extracurricular time. In this sense, both identities were compatible with one another.

However, as they gained experience in the music world and became more invested in their bands, tensions began arising that conflicted with their musical lives. Particularly as they neared college graduation, anxieties increased. Musicians felt a pressing need to decide to which path they should devote themselves. Warren admitted that his final year in college was stressful due to several factors, many of which hinged on music: "I think recently now I've been getting a little scared about graduating [from college] because now I'm like, 'Well, am I going to continue to do music or am I going to just try to get a job?' I'm just kind of waiting to [decide]."

Similarly, Jane recounted a similar period of anxiety during her emerging adulthood years: "After I graduated from my master's program, that was probably more of a time where I really did have to think, "Well, do I want to go out and get a job in my field since I'm probably going to have to move to a different town? Or do I want to concentrate on the music?" So I did have to make a decision. I've somehow been able to do a little bit of both, so I've sort of made it so that I've gotten the best of both worlds. But it's still this ongoing decision I'm having to make." As college life came to a close, musicians found balancing both the normative and the musician pathways more difficult. With graduation comes a mounting pressure as to whether to continue with music. Some, like Jane, are able to easily resolve the conflicts. For many other musicians, however, these tensions implicitly or explicitly attempted to pull them away from music and onto more traditional paths to adulthood.

Other normative aspects of adulthood were not particularly overwhelming to musicians in emerging adulthood. Tensions with family members were minimal, if present at all. Parents of musicians in emerging adulthood were often quite supportive of their children's musical endeavors; many even took pride knowing that their children were students by day and musicians by night. Similarly, tensions of starting a family via marriage and parenthood were not problematic issues in their lives. The men in emerging adulthood (all of whom were unmarried) rarely mentioned family issues as potentially problematic to their musical lives. This nonissue is perhaps tied to traditional assumptions that men's careers in any field are largely unaffected by the addition of children (Coltrane 2000; Hochschild 1989; Townsend 2002). Women, in contrast, did recognize that children would complicate life as a musician. However, all of the women with whom I spoke were either not interested in ever having children or did not plan to have them for several years. As such, the issue of having children was easily reconciled in their personal lives, in ways similar to some women in standardized careers (Gerson 1985).

Reconciling the Dilemmas of Emerging Adulthood

The "on-time" musicians were those in emerging adulthood (between the ages of 21 and 25 in my sample). These nineteen musicians were pursuing music in the earliest beginnings of adulthood, a time during which there was not much pressure to be fully adult (Arnett 2000; Furstenberg et al. 2005). Because music was not putting these musicians off-time with appropriate age expectations for emerging adults, they could easily pursue music without great tension (Ramirez 2013). Most peers in their cohort, whether they pursue music or not, are also similarly delaying the benchmarks of traditional adulthood: marriage, parenthood, and career (Shanahan et al. 2005).

During the college years, musicians were successful in balancing their educational lives with their musical interests. This was possible due not only to the degree of flexibility during the college years, but also because the musicians remained on-time in life while pursuing music at this age. Emerging adulthood allowed them to simultaneously explore two potential adulthood possibilities at the same time in the same locale: education and music. They were able to use the university as a cover story to their parents. They were unquestionably invested in their education, but music equaled if not surpassed it in priority. Being "good college students," however, provided them a safe haven to remain in Athens, at the very least, until graduation, at which point they would have to come to terms with their postcollege lives and the place music would fit into it.

The on-time musicians, however, still had to contend with the coming tensions of growing into adulthood. To do so, they often described their experiences of adulthood as one of an exploration of a range of opportunities, not all of which must necessarily lead to standardized careers (Arnett 2000). The musicians, particularly the women, stressed that having time to discover themselves through exploration was only truly possible without major outside commitments such as marriage and parenthood. Warren rationalized it this way: "You only live once. You should try it, if you have the resources and the ability. I'm just going to kick myself if I don't at least give it a shot."

Like other musicians in college, Warren had the resources, in terms of time, finances, and limited responsibility, to test out a career in music. While many musicians in their early twenties were steadfast to their musical commitment, Marcus was one of many musicians who had to explain and defend his decision to pursue music to his family: "The closest thing to a grilling I ever got was when we were on our first tour. We had a day off, so we went to Chapel Hill, [North Carolina], so I could go to my cousin's graduation party. My uncle who is a heart surgeon, also pushing for me to go to med school, asked, 'So what do you think you're going to do with this music?' And I said, 'Well, I'm in college now. I don't have any real responsibilities. This is my own time when I can have that sort of fun without any real consequences, so this is for me, for right now to have a good time.'" That's what I told him." Despite trends indicating that a number of young adults are delaying the traditional markers of adulthood, musicians often face the predicament of explaining their "arrested development" to their families. Marcus's circumstance exhibits a "now or never behavior"—engaging in an activity that may be lost upon entrance into adulthood (Ravert 2009). Marcus did not feel he was "off-time" or that his participation in music would negatively impact his future adult life, nor did he perceive of his life choices as delaying adulthood. His family, however, thought otherwise.

Similar to formally trained musicians studied by other researchers, rock musicians in my sample also revealed that their parents attempted to influence their opting out of music (Burland and Davidson 2002). They felt pressure to suspend their musical lives to fulfill their parents' wishes of their attaining a normative adulthood. Some emerging adults were veering off the musical career pathway because of their impressions that musical career trajectories would be daunting. This, coupled with the milestones they had reached with their bands, made the tail end of the emerging adult years seem a suitable stopping point. Ben said: "I know I'm only twenty-three, but it's out of my system to an extent. If it does work out, I'd love to keep doing it. At the same time, I got to accomplish all the goals I wanted to accomplish, and a lot more. I never expected multiple tours and multiple records. It's already gone beyond what I would've ever imagined."

Like other musicians who didn't "entertain the notion of becoming a professional musician," Ben was fulfilled with his tenure in the music scene. The sense of accomplishment was a suitable foray into the next phase of life. In sum, the emerging adulthood years were characterized as fostering their increased participation in music culture. While emerging adults were able to reconcile many tensions successfully, other musicians—especially those in young adulthood—struggled to do so, as we will see next.

Transitions and Tensions in Young Adulthood

Musicians in the young adulthood years (ages 26 through 37) experienced aging as musicians in ways unique from the emerging adults. Though only a few years beyond the musicians in emerging adulthood, their experiences of aging in the music world included tensions creating deeper conflict in their identities, life choices, and life course pathways. The twenty-nine musicians in young adulthood discussed the extent to which their musician and adult identities conflicted with one another. They also cited the particular challenges with which they were dealing in negotiating their adult identities. These tensions, in comparison to those felt by emerging adults, were far more stressful and demanded stronger plans of action to reconcile.

Tensions with Parents

One of the central themes characterizing the early adult period is establishing an identity independent of one's family of origin (Arnett 1998; Furstenberg et al. 2005; Settersten 2011; Shanahan 2000). Middle-class men and women often remain financially if not emotionally dependent on their parents well into their twenties. This seems to be the case with the musicians as well. A few admitted that their parents would help them financially from time to time. As they moved into the young adult years however, they experienced two changes. First, parents began discussions of "cutting them off" financially. The college years were over, and it was time for their children to become entirely independent, economic and otherwise. Second, musicians began refusing economic assistance from parents themselves, even when life would be a struggle without their contributions. During this time period, the musicians felt the beginnings of an internalized adulthood—self-sufficiency, in particular (Arnett 1998).

Their foray into this new—and fuller—sense of adulthood was coupled with their parents' stronger and more overt expectations for them to start a legitimate career. Such was the case for Owen as he launched into adulthood:

MR: Early on when you were investing yourself in music, was your family telling you, "Don't count on it. Have a backup plan. What are you gonna do for the rest of your adult life?"

OWEN: My mom, when I quit school to play music, her response was, "Don't ask me for a damn thing." My dad was always sort of cautiously supportive. So I just had to strike out on my own because I couldn't *not* do it. There was a lot of, "When are you gonna get a real job? Why are you traveling? Why are you going all the way to Spokane to play music, don't they have any bands in Spokane?" [My previous band], in many ways, was able to sustain ourselves as musicians by sheer force of will because nobody really encouraged us, our families or our peer group. We were sort of an oddball band, so ambitious. That's one of the reasons I'm drawn to [my current band], because there's no lack of ambition. A really ruthlessly ambitious band.

Musicians in young adulthood faced more numerous and persistent tensions in their lives due in large part to cues suggesting they were becoming off-time in their life trajectories (Ramirez 2013). The most stressful pressure young adult musicians cited was that with their parents. While most parents were initially supportive of their children's participation in the music scene, the parents' outlook on their children's devotion to music waned over time, particularly as the musicians entered young adulthood. For some parents, it was due to their assumptions that musical participation was a leisure activity, something that was a temporary part of college life and would be abandoned upon graduation.

Even among musicians who persevere with their music careers, many discussed how one or both of their parents would regularly ask them when they were going to "ditch the music." Despite their parents' objections, they continued performing with their bands. Of course, these musicians were adults and were, by this time of life, independent of their parents' economic contributions—factors that facilitated their continuing with their career of choice. Still others' parents were somewhat less concerned about their children's vocational pursuits, so long as they were financially secure. Women musicians suggested their parents were more concerned about their futures than were men's parents. This trend is somewhat surprising given cultural assumptions of men's expectations for being the provider, but men seemed not to have parents who were overly concerned about their sons' futures. This, however, may be due to men's increased independence from and separation from their parents—yet another manifestation of masculinity.

No doubt, some musicians lost fellow band members due to the informal sanctions borne through parental conflicts. Every musician with whom I spoke had undergone changes in their band's lineup over the years. In some cases, it stemmed from creative differences, but it was more often due to band members abandoning music for other career possibilities. A majority of band members who left to pursue other options cited the regularity of parental tensions as central to these turning points. Lilly recounted the issues that led to a bandmate leaving the band: "Our first drummer, he was in his thirties, and his family constantly pushed him to have a career and stop this band stuff.... His parents were like, 'You need a career.' He got interested in [respiratory therapy] and decided that that would be a good career. But in order to go to school and become a respiratory therapist, he thought, 'I can't do the band. I have to focus on this.' It was completely amicable. He decided, 'I want to start doing this now,' so he left." Although he implied that his change of heart was his idea, his backstory suggests that the shift sprang from his parents' dissatisfaction with his life choices, as they initially planted the seed of a new potential career.

Parents prompt the avoidance of risky behaviors—in this case, musical participation—to allow for a straightforward entrance to adulthood (Ravert 2009). Of course, these musicians seem to have internalized a perspective that is not unique to their parents, but also in line with the broader cultural age norms of appropriate adulthood. Andrew lost a senior band member due to similar circumstances: "Erik's dad is an efficiency manager. Companies hire him to check the efficiency of the company. If people aren't pulling their weight or not worth it, he fires them. Erik's got that fella as a father. I don't think his dad will ever be supportive of something like this, honestly.... Erik's got it rough, no doubt about it, and I think it's a big reason why he's not in our band anymore."

Musicians, in discussing former band members, suggested that parents in middle-class, business-oriented professions were the ones most likely to discourage their children from music. Informal modes of social control, such as those experienced by Erik, are powerful, often acting to bring them "back in line" (Settersten 2003: 86). These experiences are consistent with other research that suggests parents may act as "'eliminators' that rule out future possibilities" for younger generations (Mortimer et al. 2002: 462). In general, parents were not reserved in hiding their aversion to their children's choosing music over other career prospects. They believed their children's education had "gone to waste" and that music was no means to a legitimate adulthood. In sum, they believed their children were further delaying and avoiding adulthood by continuing with music. Some musicians, in turn, internalized these ideas, prompting them to take action to resolve their anxieties.

Tensions with parents may be indicative of both micro- and macrolevel changes taking place in the larger context of the United States. On one hand, the rift may signal generational change in the transition to adulthood (Smith

2005). The cohort of musicians in young adulthood see this time period as an opportunity to explore options before settling on a lifelong career, while their parents view such life choices as irrational, problematic, and destructive. At the same time, larger forces may be at play in the shift in adulthood. A number of today's young workers experience frequent movement from one job to the next in the early part of their working lives (Hamilton and Hamilton 2006).

Tensions of Aging

A second anxiety musicians felt was that of aging itself. Though most musicians were in young adulthood, primarily in the latter twenties and early thirties, some musicians admitted to feeling older than they "really" were (Shanahan et al. 2005). By the time they reached their late twenties, musicians described themselves as the "geezers" of the music scene. Some questioned whether it was appropriate for someone in their thirties to be performing music or whether it should instead be reserved for the young. Israel said he first felt old "once [I] hit thirty in this town. Everyone [in this music scene] stays the same age, and you start feeling old. And just being in rock bands, when you see all the bands in magazines that are five years younger than you, I just remember always looking up to them, and now I'm just like, 'Oh my God, I'm on the other side of the fence.'"

Like other musicians beyond their mid- to late twenties, Israel wrestled with transitioning into a fully adult status and his identity as a musician. The factor most readily feeding his apprehension was the population of comparison in this musical context—the younger musicians newly entering the music scene. He was by no means alone in this feeling. Isaac said: "It's like that line from *Dazed and Confused* when the guy is like, 'I get older, and they stay the same age.' That's the way it is here. It's like you always have young kids who have their rock-and-roll pipedreams, and have electric guitars and drum sets and always will end up in town here. By the time they're 19 or 20 years old, they have a band put together and start playing shows. . . . It's like the University of Georgia is just a factory that pumps out bands. People always want to play music."

Independent rock musicians are in a setting with a high turnover rate. Most participants in the scene are in their early twenties, and many exit by their midtwenties. For music fans and musicians alike, this is primarily due to their graduating from college and moving on to careers in other cities. Participants in the music scene who age out are continuously replaced by new members (e.g., successive cohorts of college students). As a result, as the musicians age, the transient population of their audiences and musician peers consistently remains youthful in a context that musicians described as a "la la land."

Other musicians felt their aging identities when comparing themselves to their nonmusician peers, particularly those who have taken the normative pathways in life and are meeting the traditional benchmarks of adulthood. Dean left a decent job at a music promotion company for a job in the service sector and recognized the pros and cons:

> [The job with the music promotion company] was taxing, and I didn't wanna just go and jump into something else after that, so I've kinda just been on this like occupational vacation for about a year, which has been great, but at the same time I feel like I'm nineteen years old again, for better for worse. There's not a whole lot of responsibilities that are heaped on my shoulders, but at the same time, the bills get hard to pay sometimes. I think it's difficult when people play music in town and don't necessarily have that career occupation. You wanna leave things open a little bit so that you're able to do the things that you want to do, like maybe go out of town for a week to play some shows. But at the same time, you're kinda inhibiting yourself from actually having a real career, and I think for a lot of people—me included—it's difficult to justify that sometimes when you see that a lot of your friends are almost done with med school now and that kind of thing. It makes you question your worth as a human being and say, "Well, is it worth me just doing what I want and maybe not having some of the other luxuries that some of the other people that I know have?" And maybe being looked down upon, just kinda like, "Well, gosh, maybe I should be a banker or something like that, have a real job." But at the same time I have luxuries that other people will *never* have. I can go off and play in bands, and other people can't. They'll never have that ability. There's just not enough time in life—the way that other people have structured their lives to [not be able to] go off and do what they [really] want to do.

Musicians in young adulthood feel caught between two worlds. Yet it is more than simply a suspicion, as their feeling of limbo is not entirely inaccurate. They are, in many ways, living with a foot in two very different worlds. They recognize the benefit of exploring possibilities early in life, but do so at a cost. Those costs are readily apparent when they see their peers' lives and cannot help but compare themselves to their recognizable successes.

One consequence of aging was the growing premonition that the current band was a "make or break" situation. A number of musicians in their late twenties and beyond felt like their current band was their final chance in music. Jade had been performing music throughout her twenties, and anticipated her time remaining in the music world to be limited: "If for some reason [my band] did break up, I don't know if I'd be in another band. I think by the time that happens I'll definitely feel like I'm too old to play music in this capacity. I don't know how cool it would be to be an old, a really old lady playing [in a band]." In comparison to standardized lines of work, career timelines for musicians are truncated. Though Jade was speaking partly in jest, a musician beyond her late twenties is not the ideal type musician.

Musicians experienced the social aging process at a pace distinct from their nonmusical peers in more standardized careers and normative contexts. The musicians' subjective age identification—the age at which they "feel" in the social-psychological sense—was out of sync with their chronological age (Johnson et al. 2007; Settersten and Mayer 1997). While the musicians were certainly young in regard to their chronological ages, their relative age identification felt awry. This age disjuncture surfaced due to the external pressure they felt to be adult. In contrast to their same-aged nonmusician peers, the musicians—not to mention their parents—felt as though they had not met the traditional markers of adulthood. They were perceived as being economically and developmentally stunted, exemplified by their preoccupation with music. The musicians believed themselves to be appropriately aged, while their parents and other nonmusician peers evaluated them as behaving as juveniles. As a result, even the most committed musicians began contemplating their exit from music.

Reconciling the Dilemmas of Young Adulthood

The musicians in young adulthood received numerous cues—social, economic, and internal—that triggered their feeling off-time in life. They felt more pressure to conform to a traditionally adult status and often struggled to defend their life choices. They responded with two broad reactions to being off time. Those who less successfully overcame the dilemmas often opted out of musical performance for other activities. Others, however, who realigned music to make it compatible with adulthood remained persistent in their drive to pursue music.

Disengaging from Music

Leaving Music Behind. Some musicians reacted to the tensions of adulthood by starting the process of leaving the musician identity behind (Ramirez 2013). In most cases, it was to more fully secure a normative adult identity. Some were beginning to mute the musician identity, citing it as no longer central to their identities. They stressed that music was an important part of their transition to adulthood, but they were now moving on. The off-time musicians downplayed their identities as musicians, by disengaging from it in one of two ways. One response was to suspend their participation in music. Musicians such as Roger were beginning to feel the tensions of adulthood and recently began contemplating his future in music.

MR: Has there ever been a time when you were contemplating giving up music or at least making it less of a focus?

ROGER: Every single day. It stresses me out so much. I'm kept up at night sometimes thinking about a song or what people think about the band. Or when

FIGURE 3 Kay Stanton of Casper & the Cookies (Photo by Mike White, deadlydesigns.com)

we're recording, [I think about] how it could be better, what could be different. Or I'm thinking, "Is my band member going to be sober at the show tomorrow night?" It stresses me out so much. It's so much more stressful to me than being in school, which to me, convinces me that I care about it a lot, but at the same time, every single day, at some point I say, "What if I just quit? What if I just quit playing music and didn't have to worry about it anymore? Just went to my job and lived my life?" A lot of times my concerns are financial. I contributed X amount of dollars to the band this month. This is really putting a hurt on me and my living situation. If I wasn't in this band, all the money I was making, I could just spend on whatever. I could save money. Every day something crosses my mind: "God, it would be so nice to quit the band." But it's usually fleeting.

Mindsets such as these tempted Roger and others his age to disconnect from music during young adulthood. Some musicians suggested that by their mid-twenties, they had "gotten it out of [their] system." The economic toll of pursuing music is taxing. A number of musicians were experiencing the financial strains of musical pursuit in their young adult years. While the parsimonious lifestyle had been tolerable during the emerging adult years, it was becoming more and more burdensome as time went on. They suggested that musician-hood was incompatible with adulthood. These perceived incompatibilities were often powerful enough to drive musicians out of this once-important social milieu.[2]

Musicians are attentive to age-appropriate social roles and are made aware of being early, on time, or late in transitions to successful adulthood (Elder 1975). In general, the musicians are cognizant they are late in adopting an adult identity in comparison to many of their traditionally oriented peers. Work is a marker of where they *should* be. And since a number of musicians are far from being financially stable, they are feeling the stresses of an unattained aspect of traditional adulthood. As a result, some begin to abandon music.

Deemphasizing the Musician Status. Other off-time musicians were in the process of deemphasizing their statuses as musicians (Ramirez 2013). They dealt with dilemmas of aging by stressing that they intended to continue their participation in the music world, but in roles other than as musicians. Beyond the college years, they often had family pressures that shifted their expectations and dreams of musical perseverance. These musicians, a number of whom were men, were battling ideas of salary, family responsibility, and masculinity in their lives as musicians. For some musicians, like Aldo, it impacted their career aspirations:

MR: Ultimately, would you like to make a career out of music or is it a hobby?
ALDO: If you had asked me that question when I was [in my] late teens or early twenties, I would have definitely wanted to make it more of a career. Now that I'm married and have responsibilities and a job, it is probably more of a hobby . . . It's definitely a lot harder as you get older and you have more responsibilities: you're married or have a job or whatever. It's a lot different than when you're eighteen and you don't have a lot of responsibility. But if you really want it, you'll make sacrifices for it.

The added responsibilities that have arisen as he has further entered adulthood limited his interests in music to a hobby.

As some musicians began their subtle move away from careers in musical participation, they anticipated building more standardized careers in other sectors of the music industry. Typically, they were initiating careers in the production aspect of music as recording engineers, producers, or by starting record labels, while others ventured into the music business via music promotion companies. A few musicians were even at the point of running their own recording studios where many local bands recorded music. Musicians with similar plans emphasized that more stable income made these careers not only more promising, but also more in line with a normative adult identity. They consistently suggested these careers to be more realistic, professional, stable, and less stressful. In a word, these careers lend themselves to a more adult-like status by virtue of their being more closely aligned with traditional careers. Furthermore, they saw these skills they have picked up during their tenure in bands as marketable and in demand—much more so than their performance and songwriting skills. In these ways, they have maintained some semblance of their identities as centered in music, similar to formally trained musicians who abandon musical careers in adulthood (Burland and Davidson 2002; Wagner 2015). While they are moving away from the musician identity, they are keeping one foot in the music world while simultaneously moving to a more normative adulthood through honing their professional skills in the studio (Ramirez 2013). The musicians who have made such shifts suggested that these strategies encompass the ideal route for musicians to ultimately take in life. In discussing her early days in the music scene, Lilly emphasized the main lesson she learned from her mentor who ran a small record label herself: "I always admired her. She played in [a band] that had a great impact on me. . . . And I liked the fact that she also ran a [record] label. . . . One time when I helped her get a show here, she did say, 'The more realistic idea when it comes to music is that you will, through your contacts, find a career instead of being able to play music and tour and earn a living, which is really just not feasible.' You don't earn a living touring. You don't usually earn a living being in a band." Lilly learned that to be successful, she should use her band to network for a more promising career in another branch of the music business. Doing so will also help her to attain a more appropriate adult identity. By emphasizing the business skills they are developing through their experiences in bands, musicians began setting up their redefinition of adulthood.

In general, liminality is especially event among musicians contemplating their disengaging from musicianhood.[3] Music does not have to be temporary. Some individuals in music are able to successfully carve out lifelong participation in music culture in roles other than that of performer. Not only do they maintain connections to music cultures, but they also find new meaning in music as adults (Giffort 2011; Schilt and Zobl 2008). One bonus of these shifts they insinuate is the closer alignment those careers have with normative adulthood.

Persisting with Music

It is possible, of course, for women and men to successfully fit music into their adult lives, as Bennett (2013) and Kotarba (2013) suggest in their work on aging and music. The second group of musicians in my sample was not too different, as they genuinely envisioned themselves pursuing music throughout the remainder of their lives. These persistent musicians frequently forewent other opportunities in order to devote themselves completely to music. They were inventive in weaving music into the adult life phase and constructing valid adult identities. Jane, for instance, said: "I was offered a job recently—a full-time job—and I had to ask if I'd still be able to go on tour. I was told no, so I had to decline the job. And it would've been a cool job, but it was either [the job] or the band. That's the only [thing], like I said, weighing the two sides of my life: How am I responsible with how do I do this [musical] part of my life? Because ultimately music is what I really want to do."

The off-time musicians have essentially been forced to weigh the ramifications of their musical decisions. As such, they frame music as intentional decisions on which they have spent considerable time contemplating. They reconfigured the musician identity to make it compatible with an adult identity. Doing so allowed them to successfully continue pursuing music into adulthood. They accomplished this in three main ways.

Reconciling Age. "Rock and roll is for the young." "Hope I die before I get old." These and other clichés marking the "rock is youthful" conceptions of age complicate the responsibility required of participation in bands. For many musicians, music is not simply a fun endeavor. Rather, it is something they take incredibly seriously and therefore treat as others would a professional occupation. Commitment, responsibility, devotion, and hard work are required to make the band successful. These qualities, however, are not aligned with—and are often in opposition to—traditional notions of youth, not to mention embody the antithesis of rock culture. These qualities, however, help the women and men emphasize ways their identities as musician are comparable with their statuses as true adults.

For these musicians, their aging process in the perpetually young music world was one tension they needed to address. While they did make connections with their younger peers in the music world, problems did regularly arise. For one, musicians were forced to come to terms with the age division between them and their younger band members and audiences. They came to recognize and accept the generational differences that at times put them at odds with the younger cohorts in the music scene, while securing their positions in the social spaces they shared with them in the music world. Sometimes, however, they had no choice but to alter the band lineup, replacing youthful, irresponsible members with older, responsible members who treat the band seriously (i.e., in a way more consistent with adulthood). Lilly, recounting her experience with a former drummer in her band, said:

> He was in his early twenties, still sort of going through that—you know how in your early twenties you're not necessarily the most responsible person? You're very carefree. . . . He just lived this carefree lifestyle. And we were past that point. I think it was just a clash of ages. There's not really a huge difference in our ages, but where I was at in life, here I am playing in this band, I have this job that I could make into a career if I wanted to. I want to keep the one job as steady employment, at the time thinking about the possibility of eventually buying a house, which we now have. Partying was not really all that interesting to me. I

had sort of gotten past that, whereas he was still into the partying and lack of responsibility. And any time we would want to get more responsible actions out of him, he would lash out against that. . . . He didn't want any responsibility, I would say. So it just ended up being [a problem], it got unpleasant.

Maturity, as discussed by Lilly, was a recurring concern among young adult musicians. Though music was a leisure activity early in life, it was elevated to one of professionalism as musicians continued to pursue it in their young adult years. Having similarly minded bandmates helped confirm one's posture regarding music as an adult activity. The number of years between Lilly's age and that of her drummer was not great, but the social meanings of their ages were worlds apart. She embodied a more adult status (accompanied by stable employment and home ownership) while her drummer was adhering to a status closer to adolescence than adulthood. Their social age difference far exceeded their chronological age difference, making them incompatible with one another in the context of the band. Having a band member who embodied the party lifestyle distanced Lilly from the musician identity herself. She felt like a parent, rather than a bandmate, in her prodding more responsibility from him. Fortunately, her band found a replacement drummer who was more suitable for the band. Lilly described her new drummer, Aldo, as a perfect fit for the band, due not only to his skills on the drums but also to his heightened sense of responsibility: "He's older. He's married. His wife is a physician's assistant and has a career. They have a house. They have a responsible lifestyle, and it's more in line with us than with a carefree young twenty-year-old hormonal male. [laughs] I don't think there's anything wrong with that necessarily, but we're just sort of past the stay-out-late, pay-your-bills-late, and work-to-get-your-bills-paid-before-the-power's-cut-off [lifestyle]. We're not like that anymore, whereas [the former drummer] was on that mindset, the whole lack of responsibility."

In comparison to her previous drummer, Aldo is more suitable because he adheres to a normative adult identity. He is responsible, married, and less interested in the party atmosphere of the music scene. Jason, Lilly's bandmate and husband, corroborated the tensions in finding a permanent drummer. He too sees Aldo as the best drummer with whom he has ever worked, and, like Lilly, credits this partly to Aldo's dependability and adult status. Releasing the immature member from the band also helped Lilly to reaffirm the musician identity in herself, thus enabling her to persist with music.

Redefining Music as a Business. Musicians, particularly those in the young adulthood period, noted the internal tension that mounted from the conception of rock music being for the young.[4] This notion, as many musicians implied, was at odds with an adult status. Most successfully relieved this tension by virtue of their taking music seriously, reframing their informal career as a normative and professional occupation, and therefore challenging the notion of musical participation as a purely leisurely pastime. Attaining a moderate level of success also helped buttress their musician identities as congruent with adulthood, as it elevates their participation in music from a mere hobby to a legitimate career.

Some musicians enacted strategies to preserve their identities by reconfiguring the musician identity to complement their subjective identities as adults (Ramirez 2013). They reconstructed their identities as musicians as more in line with normative business culture. Rather than simply rock stars, the musicians saw themselves as skilled business people with legitimate expertise. In particular, they redefined musical participation as a business endeavor in which they invested significant personal effort (Stebbins 2009). The musicians with whom I spoke handled all of the business aspects of their bands themselves: they booked shows at venues, scheduled tours, promoted their bands, and made contacts with others in the music industry at both the local and national level. As such, some musicians saw themselves not only as musicians but also as savvy business entrepreneurs. Andrew, for instance, took the reins on the business side of his band: "As far as PR, booking shows, and where the band was going, I completely took over. I wanted to go balls out. I was like, now I can do all these things that I never thought I'd be able to do. Things I want. I [negotiated for] a CD with a jewel case and shrink wrap and a bar code on it. I want to play the [bigger clubs]. I want to go on tour. All the things that bands do."

Andrew and other musicians emphasized that musical talent was only one part of the formula for success. Bands need to tour and to market themselves to a wider audience. And to do so, they need to embody tactics of the business world. Furthermore, some of the musicians imagined that these skills could potentially be useful in any business setting, whether in the music world or elsewhere. As such, some suggested these skills are transferable to the traditional business world, were they to redirect their career options.

The Adult "Alter Ego" and Alternate Versions of Adulthood. Musicians are notorious for creating alter egos. Artists—from David Bowie to Marilyn Manson to Prince—have constructed distinct on-stage and off-stage personas. The lesser-known musicians with whom I spoke shared similar sentiments, though they specified their dual identities were the result of their "other" lives in the non-music world. Many of the musicians also worked to create an alter ego more consistent with normative adulthood and enacted this identity from time to time. A majority of the musicians with whom I spoke were employed in other nonmusical work sectors, typically white-collar office jobs or the service sector. Some musicians felt a split in their identities, one that was often met with surprise when coworkers discovered their being musicians in the after-work hours, as in Jen's experience: "In my job that I'm currently in, people always have a funny reaction [when they learn I'm in a band]. Sometimes it comes up in [conversation]. I'll say, 'I'm a musician. I play in a band.' And they'll go, 'Oh, you play in a band? *Really?* I wouldn't have guessed that. How weird. I wouldn't have ever pictured that. You don't seem the [type].'"

While such reactions from coworkers were not necessarily pleasant, they did allow for a more normative backdrop for their adult identities. These contexts were key to their framing themselves as "true" adults.[5] In general, musicians highlighted their "other" (nonmusician) self as consistent with notions of traditional adulthood. They were employed in conventional jobs with traditional nine-to-five work hours. In these ways, they saw themselves as no different from other adults. The only feature that set them apart from traditional adults was that they spent their nonworking hours playing music.

Others persisted in maintaining their musician and adult identities by diminishing particular aspects of traditional adulthood. They avoided such complications of normative adulthood by choosing not to have families and professing little interest in conventional family life. Musicians, women in particular, were aware that starting a family is the normative role associated with adult femininity. By emphasizing the irrelevance of this aspect of adulthood to their lives, they constructed new adulthoods. Although these decisions are not like that of the majority of women who do desire to have children, they are part of a growing segment of the population of young women who also anticipate remaining childless by choice (Gillespie 2003).

Still others suggested their musical experiences helped develop the subjective components of their adult identities, emphasizing in particular their heightened sense of responsibility resulting from their commitment to their bands.[6] They also saw themselves as wiser, more patient, and having a stronger work ethic than many of their nonmusical peers. Some realized "the kind of personal character" they have due to their participation in bands. Heath said his experience in the cultural production of music "helped me learn a certain ethic about myself. If you work hard at something over a long enough period of time, chances are you'll probably get better at it. And I think I'm a lot better at a [range] of music skills than I used to be. So it's a cool reinforcement of the idea of looking past instant gratification and just knowing that if you plug away at something, eventually you'll get somewhere."

They distinguished themselves as having developed and matured in positive ways, even though this development was not always recognized nor appreciated by those outside the musical world. In these ways, their identities as adult musicians were more sophisticated than those of younger, less experienced individuals in the music scene. All of the young adult musicians were independent from the family both residentially and financially, responsible for themselves, and had successfully achieved an identity of their own, all of which are hallmarks of contemporary generations' constructions of adulthood (Arnett 1998, 2000; Kins and Beyers 2010; Nelson and Barry 2005). As such, they demonstrate more qualities of adulthood than do many of their nonmusician peers. Adulthood, as scholars have suggested, goes well beyond simply reaching particular ages, markers, or life events (Arnett 2004; Shanahan et al. 2005). Likewise, contemporary adulthood is more flexible in allowing nonnormative life choices and events to fit within its expanded parameters. Pursuing music, a task deemed adolescent in previous generations, can easily meld with contemporary constructions of adulthood, though these men and women have adult identities that can be and often are still challenged.

Conclusion

As the musicians began their launch into the early stages of adulthood, they contemplated the directions their lives would take. Like most emerging adults in the United States, they used this time period to test out options for the future. Nearly all of the musicians began exploring options by selecting the middle-class "default" life course pathway of attending college. As a consequence, the extension of education also assured that they would have additional time to explore options for their futures. Much to the chagrin of their parents, this testing-out period would come to significantly shift their life directions toward unanticipated career trajectories. Their relocation to a college music town was a critical turning point during the adult years, the consequences of which fundamentally shifted their plans for their futures, due in large part to the culture of the town and the subsequent opportunities that it allowed them.

As they explored college and/or music options, they ventured further into adulthood, discovering themselves and new directions in life. The musicians categorically framed their participation in music as a legitimate expression of adulthood. Consistent with the broader cultural shift in aging today, they emphasized individual criteria of adulthood (responsibility, maturity, independence, self-sufficiency) and saw music as a means to become adult (Arnett 2004; Shanahan et al. 2005). All were grateful to have the opportunities to delve into such life explorations, but they were not without their stresses. The reality of the transition to adulthood is complex. Commitment to music further complicates adulthood, but does not deny musicians its attainment. Instead, what musicians' lives illustrate is the extent to which music can be interwoven with adulthood.

Regardless of age, all musicians spoke of strategies they used to contend with the dilemmas of moving into adulthood. The solutions to those tensions were particularly influenced by their on- or off-time statuses. To be sure, the emerging adults who were on-time had far fewer dilemmas to reconcile, primarily due to their experiencing less pressure to attain an "appropriate" adulthood, while the young adults felt more strenuous and pressing dilemmas. The solutions devised by on-time musicians were much easier to negotiate, while those of the off-time musicians (who constitute a larger portion of my sample) required more effort to successfully alleviate the pressures of adulthood. Some musicians, many of whom were off-time—or felt they soon would be—imagine music to ultimately be a temporary project. Older musicians had similar sentiments, particularly those with no family and no plans to start one in the near future, but they consider themselves a "bit more realistic" in realizing music may not end up as their lifelong career. In general, these musicians are tentative in their expectations of committing to music for the entirety of their lives, but they simultaneously see it as part of the experimental, testing-out phase of early adulthood.

3

I Feel It in My Bones

• •

The Development
of Musician Identities

A hallmark of rock culture is the belief that the best musicians are not necessarily those with the best technical prowess, but instead those with deep passion for their craft. Authentic rock musicians, our culture tells us, have it in their blood; they live and breathe rock and roll. It is not something to be learned, but instead something to be discovered. Iconic musicians frequently tell tales of their developing by chance—often citing watershed moments in which they attended a concert, bought a particular album, or heard lyrics that fundamentally changed the direction of their lives. In this sense, the cultural narrative is that history's best musicians are *accidental* musicians. Fans too are convinced that they can feel the passion of their favorite musicians with every angry strum of their guitars and every guttural scream of their vocals. The passion is something you can't fake, so the story goes.

At the same time, rock culture is founded on the practice of using the literal and figurative stage as a venue on which to intentionally explore identity. The David Bowies and Madonnas of music history have built careers playing with identity, emerging with reconstructed personas that demonstrate a new development in their music and their presentations of self (Goffman 1959). The fluidity and pliability of intentionally creating multiple and shifting selves has an inconsistent reception by the public, however: some musicians with pliable personas are embraced, while others are critiqued as shams with ulterior motives.

Reaction to lounge singer *cum* pop star Lana Del Rey, the self-described "gangster Nancy Sinatra," falls into the latter. Her musical styling and identity is a pastiche of all things Americana. Her presentation of self is read as timeless and glamorous (she was the face of H&M's 2012 advertising campaign), yet contains fragments of contemporary trends in hip-hop and "gangster" culture. Del Rey has been critiqued as co-opting ethnic culture, from her Latina-inspired garb to her cholo teardrop tattoos to her highjacking of hip-hop music production. Some commentators have interpreted her use of multiple racial and ethnic signifiers as the cultural appropriation by a privileged white woman with little understanding of the history and significance of those symbols. Del Rey herself, however, has suggested that her identity is intentional and is as much a fabrication as are the identities of the everyday person in today's culture.

Other artists have more leeway in exploring and playing with identity with less censure. Annie Clark, otherwise known by her stage persona St. Vincent, is one prime example. Regarded as a truly innovative musician, her music is characterized as experimental, nonlinear, and progressive. She appeared on Comedy Central's *The Colbert Report* sporting a new appearance and identity upon the release of her third album in 2014. Host Stephen Colbert, another performer of sorts who has mastered the art of caricature with his satirical crafting of his TV counterpart, nearly fell out of character during his interview with Clark. Discussing the themes in her music on identity in the postmodern world, Colbert asked Clark whether she felt disconnected herself. She responded: "We perform ourselves in a myriad of ways . . . You're wearing that suit and I have this hair, and we're sort of communicating things about ourselves in this analog way. But we now have this other realm, the digital realm, to recreate ourselves [and] make ideal versions of ourselves."

Clark is part of the growing minority of musicians who admit to their intentional crafting of multiplicities of their identities. In years past, there was something of an unspoken agreement to avoid discussing the elephant in room that is musicians' intentional construction of fabricated selves. Today, however, as St. Vincent illustrates, identity construction is part and parcel of one's art. It can be gaudy—think of Elton John's extravagant stage costumes. Alternatively, it can be subtle—consider the everyday slacker look of jeans and black T-shirt (one that is still intentional, despite its seeming negligence), the standardized uniform, if you will, of rock musicians. One's presentation of self always symbolizes something—and for rock musicians, it may be an attempt to convince the audience of their authenticity (Goffman 1959). Furthermore, the shifting significance of identity also suggests a growing awareness of the multiple and fractured selves in today's world, both in and beyond music scenes.

In this chapter, I explore similar issues of identity—the bedrock of which is authentic musicianhood. I begin by tracing the transition to the musician identity. Musicians conceived of their becoming musicians at variable times over the life course. As the musicians discuss turning points in their lives that mark them as musicians, they are also covertly discussing their criteria of musician authenticity. Women and men differ somewhat in their evaluation of what constitutes an authentic musician identity, with the former having more stringent criteria, thus preempting them from soundly identifying as musicians themselves. I then shift attention to the context of Athens and the extent to which it shaped their musicianhood. The women and men highlight the structural components in place in the music scene that seemingly enhance their identities as musicians as well as opening possibilities for their pursuing music more readily. Finally, I compare the working lives of musicians. Their employment sectors, an aspect of their lives they generally felt removed from their lives as musicians, has an impact on their commitment to music and the potential stressors they felt anchored or pulled them away from music.

Transitions to the Musician Identity

In discussing their musical histories, all of the women and men easily recalled the ways their identities as musicians unfolded over time. They spoke of two dimensions of their identity development as musicians: (1) the time period during which they first felt like "real" musicians and (2) the events that instigated their self-recognition as true musicians. Their experiences suggest ways the processes diverge by gender.

Age and Musician Identification

For the musicians with whom I spoke, the development of their identities as musicians occurred during three points in life, each of which varies by gender. The time at which musicians adopt the identity of musician varies, although adolescence was the most frequent time for such an identity to emerge.[1] A few musicians (9 of 48) responded that they have *always* felt like musicians from as far back as they could remember. This population, though small, is dominated by men. For these musicians, there was no turning point per se during which their identities shifted to include musician as a core part of their identity. Rather, it was something they have always felt as a core part of themselves. Beau said: "I always thought I was a musician even before I could play anything. So there wasn't really any grand realization as far as that goes. It was just like life conformed to whatever unconscious idea I had of myself. I found my way to music, like I knew I would [all along]."

Similar to the other musicians with lifelong affiliations with the musician identity, Beau did not believe his musicianhood rested on learning an instrument, writing songs, joining a band, or some other specific marker event. It was a more internal and self-defined realization. These musicians were apt to describe pursuing music as a "calling" in their lives. One musician, for instance, claimed his musicianhood emerged during the kindergarten years, but specified that had he felt like a musician even earlier in life; he simply, at that age, wasn't familiar with the term *musician*. These lifelong musicians also suggested their musicianhood to be intrinsic, almost inherent, in that this life was the one for which they were destined.

The second set of musicians (29 of 48) had specific turning points in their lives during which they began identifying as musicians. This identity shift occurred during childhood for some musicians, while it came about more recently for others. Again, a majority of the musicians with this narrative were men. Some of these musicians cited early childhood as the age during which they first identified as musicians. They had influential musical experiences during the elementary school years, often learning their first instrument or performing in public for the first time, often at a school-sponsored function. Although they had a long road ahead of them to master their instruments and further their musical expertise, they became focused on music early in life. More precisely, they began feeling like a musician, even using the term to describe their identities that early in life.

The more typical trajectory for these musicians was first identifying as musicians during adolescence. These musicians cited their transitions from childhood to adolescence as being accompanied by a corresponding transition to musicianhood. When I asked Aldo when he first "became" a musician, he said: "I've never really thought about that. Once I started playing the drums, after I had been playing about a year or so and felt I had a grasp of what I was doing, I considered myself a musician then, once I knew it wasn't just a passing fad." Damien first began feeling like a musician "when I first started recording on the 4-track with the guitar and stuff. I wasn't looking for someone to say, 'That's good' or anything. This was early [in adolescence and] long before anybody ever appreciated a single thing I ever did. I was like, 'Wow, I'm a musician. I'm recording [music] on a 4-track.'"

Unlike musicians previously discussed, Aldo and Damien do not cite their first experiences with music as the point during which their identities as a musician began to develop. Neither simply picked up an instrument and immediately identified as musicians. It was instead a longer, more prolonged process—one that hinged on developing musicality on their instruments, exploring the music recording process, and the beginnings of musical commitment—that led to the development of that aspect of identity.

To be sure, these musicians do not dismiss their early childhood experiences with music as frivolous. However, it is not until commitment to music and acquiring greater expertise of an instrument occurs that the musician identity can truly develop. And by the teenage years, these musicians felt they had enough of a say in their extracurricular musical activities for their interest in music to not be a simple fad but a permanent aspect of their identity (Guest and Schneider 2003). For example, Shane first identified as a musician early in high school during his audition for a rock band: "I was in the ninth grade. One of my friends was in a band with some other guys and they needed a drummer. I auditioned for them and that was my first time playing with other people in a setting that wasn't just reading music with a band director telling you what to do. So during that time in the ninth grade where we were practicing so we could put it out there [was when I first felt like a musician]."

Shane's independent learning of music without the supervision of band directors or any adults for that matter was crucial to his developing his identity as a musician. Other musicians are similar in citing peer-structured music settings as instigating their developments as musicians (Dagaz 2012). Aldo said: "[Being in a rock band] gave me a bit of an identity in high school. When you're in high school, you've got the cliques. You don't fit in. You're trying to figure out who you are, what you want to be, and *who* you want to be. You have the typical [cliques]: the popular [crowd] and the jocks and everyone else. So being in music gave me an identity, and that was being a musician."

School-structured music programs, though potentially influential in musical development, were not sufficient for a musician identity. Such contexts were deemed too academic, too sterile, and characterized as inhibiting the self-direction that was necessary for a genuine musician identity to develop. As Shane suggests, many musicians clarified that learning and performing music in school-structured settings such as the high school band or choir was not influential in developing their identities as musicians. Some musicians even suggested that structured musical experiences temporarily alienated them from music altogether. Ivan, for instance, said he "just wanted to play by ear. I didn't want it to be work." At the same time, they did sometimes suggest that formally trained music students were far more proficient at their instruments than they were, though again that did not necessarily make those students more adept musicians than they were. Musicianhood also went beyond musical aptitude, often requiring a passion, drive, and creativity that could not be learned. These experiences and sentiments are more common among men, however, since very few women participated in rock bands during the high school years.

Finally, a handful of musicians admitted that their identities as musicians did not develop until fairly recently in early adulthood. When I asked Paul, age thirty, when he first felt like a musician, he responded: "I'm tempted to say this year actually. But that's just because everything came together this year. I started playing more by myself. When I moved here with my friend Dave, we never really got anything off the ground, and we kinda parted ways. So I spent a few years just writing songs and screwing around. The last couple of years I really started to play out more. And when I came to Athens this spring and started playing with [my band,] I hadn't played in a [successful] band in years and years, it was really a very solidifying experience. I'm doing something constructive for a change. It's more real." Paul is one of the few men in my sample to note that taking on a public role with one's music is needed to establish a musician identity. While Paul has played in bands and written songs for many years, it wasn't until he began performing in music venues that his identity as a musician more fully developed.

The remaining ten musicians still have not fully developed their identities as musicians. A larger percentage of women than men fit this category, but it does include some men. These musicians were clearly uncomfortable adopting the identity of a musician as their own. I asked Alicia when she first felt like a musician:

> ALICIA: I don't think I really do feel like a musician, even now.
>
> MR: No? But you're in a [well-known] band.
>
> ALICIA: I mean, when I think of myself, I don't really think, "I am a musician." I guess it's that I know a lot of people who really are musicians, who have gone to school for music, and I consider them to be musicians. I consider what I do to be just for fun.

Alicia suggests that she is missing a core component of what it takes to be a musician. Alicia and others do not consider the musician identity to be a core aspect of their sense of self, despite the fact that they have reached numerous music goals by their midtwenties. For example, midway through our interview, Nate interjected: "The premise of this whole thing, calling me a musician, might be kind of iffy. I never learned how to play other people's songs really well. As soon as I started playing, I started making up my own songs. To this day, I still can't play other people's songs very well."

As his comments suggest, because his repertoire is limited to his original compositions, he restricted his status as a true musician. While others would take this as evidence of heightened musicality—the skill of *creating*, not simply mimicking music written by others—Nate cited this as a limitation of his musical status. One final point vis-à-vis the musician identity is the shaky ground on which it rests. A majority of the musicians, though they ultimately do identify as musicians, do so with a degree of hesitancy. Many felt even embarrassed to use the term *musician* in referencing themselves. By and large, they were uncomfortable with my and others christening them "musicians."

Criteria for True Musicianhood

The lay music fan may regard women and men who perform in bands—as singers, instrumentalists, songwriters, or any other performative capacity—as bona fide musicians. I too entered this world with similar assumptions: the people with whom I spoke, as members of bands who regularly perform, tour, and record music, I imagined would certainly identify as musicians. Early on, however, I realized the adoption of the musician identity was not so straightforward. While the above assumptions were sensible, they were often peripheral—or, at best, only one of many—criteria for musicianhood among those in the music world (Bennett 2009; Drummond 1990).

Identifying as a musician does not simply emerge haphazardly, but instead particular events and musical moments instigate women's and men's adopting the musician identity. As they discussed the emergence of their musician identities—narrating when and how they "became" musicians—they were simultaneously talking about the criteria that constitute an authentic musician, and ultimately their position in the hierarchy of the music world. Authenticity in the music world, as others have noted, is an unremitting challenge in the everyday life of musicians (Vannini and Williams 2009). The "moving target" of authenticity, coupled with its subjectivity, all but assures its precariousness, as will be illustrated next (Peterson 2005: 1094).

Mastering the Instrument

For most of the musicians, acquiring musical proficiency was key to their adopting the identity of musician, a necessary but not sufficient step toward feeling authentic. Gaining knowledge of and learning advanced skills on the instrument helped some musicians to feel as if their interest in music was more than cursory. The formality of learning the instrument mattered, but only to a point. Most musicians agreed that "real" musicians knew more than how to play the instrument; they also know the theory behind it, the "science" of chords and melody, and a broad understanding of music in the theoretical sense. Having a "good ear" for music or being able to figure out the chord progression for a song heard on the radio was indeed indicative of musical familiarity and perhaps even talent, but it was not deemed sufficient for being a true musician. For instance, Roger described what he considers to be his limited mastery of music as barring him from musicianhood: "I don't know guitar technique. I don't know keyboard technique. I do know a lot about music theory. A lot of what I learned, I learned from a friend of mine in high school. But I don't apply it when I play music. I think most people who are professional musicians would think it was a fucking joke that someone like me would say they were a musician."

Musicians whose repertoire included instruments other than the guitar shared similar sentiments.

DEAN: I don't think that there ever was, and I don't think there ever really will be a time [when I'll be a musician]. I don't really consider myself a musician.
MR: You really don't?

DEAN: No, because it seems like drum playing just seems easy to me. And I haven't really gotten a lick better at doing it in years, I don't think. I got to the point where I could hold it down, and I could probably pretty much play with anybody for a little while anyways, and not have too, too much trouble. But playing drums, it's just a dumb thing. You could teach a monkey how to play drums. You could teach a little kid how to play drums. And especially around here, there are so many dudes with guitars and songs that if you own a drum set, and you can count to four, you can pretty much play with anybody. So in that sense I wouldn't consider myself a "musician," because musicians seem to have it together. Musicians practice a lot, and musicians see it as more of a craft. For me, it's more of a glorified hobby, I guess. I spend a lot more time at it than I think most people do with their regular hobbies, but I don't know if I would consider myself a musician. Really because I don't think that I'm good enough to really call myself a musician. I'm good enough to get by I guess.

These and other musicians compare what they consider their simplistic or minimalist music expertise to more "professional" musicians. Their depiction of what constitutes a musician is clearly constructed in relation to non-rock musicians in professional realms.

At the same time, music was more than theory, just as being a musician was more than taking (or suffering through, as some suggested) a minimum

FIGURE 4 Athens, Georgia, supergroup Powers performing at the Secret Squirrel (Photo by Mike White, deadlydesigns.com)

number of years of formal music lessons. Authentic musicians needed the elusive ingredient—be it creativity, imaginative force, in a word, the artistry of music—to claim the label of musician.[2] This crucial element was what many saw as the core of an authentic musician. It was something that could not be learned, but instead was inherent to true artists, said many of the musicians.

Roger's quote above illustrates the importance of genre in acquiring a musician identity. When the rock musicians used the term "professional musicians," they typically were referring to professionally trained musicians in orchestras, symphonies, or sometimes (though far less often) studio musicians. Jazz musicians and to a lesser extent blues musicians were seen as "authentic" too (Grazian 2003). However, they almost never regarded rock musicians—regardless of their talent, proficiency, or creativity in building new musical landscapes—as true musicians. Rock is easy, anyone with a cheap guitar can play it—hence, the genre is outside the confines of true musicianhood. This selective inclusion, of course, pulls them out of the pool of true musicians as well.

Songwriting

Many musicians come into their own—and self-identify as musicians—once they began composing original music. About one-third (15 of 48) of the musicians with whom I spoke cited their initial attempts to compose original music as the key events that led to their adopting the musician identity. Julia remembered: "After I was playing [guitar] for a couple of months, I didn't want to follow any of the rules and layout of how to do it because I started coming up with ideas and started writing full songs and had no idea that I was even capable of doing that. And then once I started doing that, that's all I wanted to do. . . . And [for] the first time in my life I felt like I was unloading who I really was. That's when I really started feeling whole as a person and as a musician." For these musicians, writing music makes their musician identity "seem more real." It also leads to the realization that they not only have drive and talent, but that they more importantly have the prerogative to claim the label of musician.

Being a musician is more than being able to adequately perform songs written by others. The essence of a true musician hinges on the ability to compose original music oneself. Musicians were artists, not simply seasoned performers on their instruments. Penning their first song validates their sense of musical prowess. There is was a lengthy apprentice period in developing songwriting skills. Paul described his songwriting as eventually progressing to the point at which he could "actually come out of the bedroom and play [his songs] for people." This stage in which musicians begin exploring songwriting is informally structured and frequently also self-guided. As such, they do have some sense of control over this aspect of musicianhood. Of course, they could never "force" themselves to mechanically write songs, but once they figured out their songwriting style, many of them felt songs "magically" materialized from them.

In contrast, those who made fewer contributions to the band's music compositions often felt like lesser musicians. Although they learned the original songs and performed them with the band publicly, they were not major contributors to the catalog and hence not "real" musicians. Abby struggled with her limited role: "I feel pretty insecure about it because I really don't write the songs. So I'm probably not a good subject for you to even talk to [about being a musician]. [My bandmates] work on the songs. I'm still trying to get to the point where I can even create enough to put into the [band's songs]."

Recognition by Others

Unlike those discussed above who cite self-identified moments as symbolic of their transition to true musicianhood, other musicians instead suggested the perspective of outsiders as of greater influence. Being "pegged" as musicians by others was often powerful enough to convince them that they are capable musicians who should identify as such (Cooley 1909; Stets and Burke 2000). For instance, Warren recalls first feeling like a musician when he was in high school: "The private school I went to, not a whole lot of people played music. No one really cared about secular rock. So automatically, I kinda got pinned, not [necessarily] as an outsider, not as 'that weird kid,' but just as the kid who does music. And I didn't mind. Technically, that *is* what I did with all of my free time." It amounted to Warren's master identity in high school. This could happen later in life, sometimes after musicians joined bands and developed a following in Athens. Robert said: "When I started getting acceptance from other people, and they were like, 'I like your music. You're a great drummer.' Once people started telling me that, that's when I first considered myself a musician."

Outside validation can act as a status booster or, in this case, an identity booster. It may make the musician label "stickier" for those who receive such accolades. Recognition has long been correlated with a positive sense of self, in the workplace and otherwise (Maslow 1943). Only the men had such experiences, however. In no instance did a woman recall being identified by others as a musician before that identity was firmly established within herself already. Women had lower frequencies of external validation in comparison to men—women, when they were complimented for their musicality, often felt they were being complimented as "a good [musician] for a girl." Perhaps because of such gendered (and diluted) praise, they have a more difficult time using these instances to strengthen their identities as musicians, as the men did. If anything, such backhanded compliments may alternatively make them feel less secure as musicians.

Musical Firsts: The First Band, Performance, and Recording

Other musicians cited their first music-related landmark events as turning points that led them to identify as musicians. Specifically, joining their first band and their first public performances triggered the onset of their musician identities. Instances of being invited to join bands or getting auditions for bands were powerful draws that allowed musicians—especially the men—to internalize the musician identity. They typically described their early bands as "mediocre" or even "embarrassingly bad." However, nearly all of them valued the experience as informal training for future work in bands later in life. The men also credited their early bands as opportunities to explore their musical creativity and discover their sound on their respective instruments, lessons that would undoubtedly benefit their musical development in the coming years.

Daniel's first public performance with an early band in Athens had a lasting effect on his identity. It was during this performance that he began "impressing more than my friends" and therefore thought he "must be doing something right." Lilly's adoption of the musician identity was similar, though earlier in life: "I think the defining moment was when I entered that talent show and played that a cappella song in public. That was just sort of out of character for me, being very quiet—I'm still very quiet—to get up in front of people and just sing. People didn't expect that of me."

Some men had similar sentiments. Dean said: "I'll never forget this: the first time that I ever played at [the landmark music venue] the 40 Watt, I got really excited about the show. I mean, it was a *really* big deal. If there was any time that I actually felt like a musician, it was probably then." Both Lilly and Dean may appear similarly influenced by public performance, but there is an important caveat. Lilly's first public performance in and of itself is the factor launching the development of her musician identity. Dean, on the other hand, focused on the prestige of playing such a momentous club as instigating his musician identity.

While their male bandmates often adopt the musician identity after "joining [their] first 'serious' band," a greater proportion of women musicians suggest they "feel more like a musician when [they] play shows" or "the times that [they are] on stage." Consequently, public performance is a stronger instigating factor for women's development of their identities as musicians. Showcasing one's musical talent in a public—and masculine—setting makes the identity more genuine for women. Other musicians—every one of whom was a man—cited the cultural production of music as key to their musician development. They often cite writing and recording their first collection of songs as solidifying their identities of musicians. For some of these musicians, no one ever heard these early recordings, but merely having them on tape was sufficient to establish a valid identity as a musician, not to mention key to further developing their skills for future musical projects.

Committing to the Band

Others, particularly women, mention specific events with their current band as leading to the realization of their musician identity. For some, it is merely becoming intensely committed to music during adulthood that led to their identification as musicians. Jane refers to her move to Athens, specifically to devote more time and energy on her band, as the turning point during which she began feeling like a musician.

> JANE: It's weird, because I still kind of waffle on [identifying as a musician]. Every once in a while, I'm like, "I'm not a real musician." Around 2000 is when Ivan and I got married and we moved up here, and we had started the [band] by then. And I think by then [I felt like a musician]. I was always real DIY, played in a punk band and things like that. So there's part of me that's like, "Yeah, sure, I'm a musician." I don't know how old I was at that point—twenty-eight maybe. Definitely a late bloomer. But it's probably been in the past five years that it's really become a major part of my identity.
>
> MR: And did that happen when you moved to Athens?
>
> JANE: Yeah. When I moved here is when I made the decision to make it a bigger part of my life.

Others, like Cliff, shared similar sentiments: "It was maybe a few years [into my twenties] when I was living in a shack and [music] was all I was focused on. I had a crappy little job and I was touring and stuff like that. Then I realized, 'All right, now I feel much more like [a musician],' because that was all I was doing. Now I'm definitely a dude that's in a band. [People] look at me and think, 'Music is what he does.' It's not like what I did on the side or anything. It was like, that's what I do."

The musicians suggest that the transition to the musician identity was especially likely to materialize in the emerging adult years once they had completed their education and essentially had to figure out what would come next. Those who chose music over other options, as well as those who intentionally moved to Athens for the music scene, regarded those decisions as committing themselves to music. It was no longer a hobby, nor was it something they did "on the side" while pursuing other traditional pathways, namely, education. Upon graduation, the student identity was shed, making room for the new (and more complete) identity as musician. This shift was largely subjective and privately experienced, but did anchor the commitment to music as an informal career.

Monetary Compensation

A few others who identified as musicians during the early years cited tangible events as marking their transition to becoming musicians. A few musicians, all of whom are men, focus on the economic aspects of music. Adrian, though he had mastered his instruments early in adolescence, did not identify as a musician until he received monetary compensation for his performances. He reasons that he first became a musician in high school: "I guess when people were actually calling me to come play jobs for money. I started doing musical theater, playing bass for orchestras [in high school]. I guess when I started getting a paycheck, I felt like [a real musician]."

Other musicians are similar to Adrian in identifying "getting [their] first paycheck" for musical performance as the moment they became serious musicians. Not only had they developed reasonable performance skills, but they were good enough to demand economic compensation for their performances. This is a turning point at which musicians realize this previously "leisurely" activity could translate into money, and hence be a potential career option (Rothman 1998). Similar to workers in other contexts, they used wages as the axis on which recognition as a real worker rested. It is often challenging for those in positions with no direct or unsteady economic compensation to frame their work as "real" (DeVault 1991). Despite the musicians' nonnormative career contexts, they were able to use the established markers of work—direct economic compensation—as indicative of its legitimacy as "real" work (Rothman 1998). This construction may also allow men to construct for themselves a normative (wage-centered) masculinity that also may allow them to persist in what may otherwise be seen as an unstable, less masculine position. Again, men are the only musicians to highlight the economic aspect as instigating their identifications as musicians, similar to artists in other studies who measure success through objective and economic criteria (Becker 1982). Likewise, this was a key factor that barred other men from identifying as true musicians. Roger, for instance, was unequivocal: "Unless I was making a living playing music, I wouldn't consider myself a musician."

Hesitant Musicians

In general, the musicians did not effortlessly internalize the musician identity. Many of those who did identify as musicians did so hesitantly or with a disclaimer. Roger listed his multiple identities, not all of which were equally central to his sense of self: "I know how to make the instruments do what I want them to do. I feel like I express myself or express something through the music. In some ways that makes me a musician. I have trouble identifying myself as that [though]. I wouldn't identify myself as a writer even though I write [for a regional magazine], and I wouldn't identify myself as a procurement specialist [even though that is my job]. So I guess I *can* identify as a musician since I [do perform] in a band."

Again, part of the tentative musician status may be tied to the informal nature of the rock world: no clear credentials are necessary to participate in the world, nor to claim the musician label. The open-endedness of the world, paradoxically, thwarts musicians' confidence in their position, prompting their insecurity as authentic musicians. Again, these issues of authenticity attend to the positions in which women and men locate themselves in the hierarchy of musicianhood, from impostor to complete musician. They are not simply addressing criteria of musicianhood, but more importantly talking about the extent to which they feel "allowed" to include themselves in this social category.

Gender is another layer that undoubtedly affects the internalization of musicianhood. Women's and men's identities as musicians are generated through interactions with their bands, though in distinct patterns. Women have particular experiences that help motivate them to self-identify as musicians.[3] Many remember first feeling like a "real" musician after their first show in Athens, after which the audience and members of other more established local bands witnessed their performance. It is public performance and recognition from the outside that solidifies the musician identity for these women. Similarly, deciding to commit to the band helped augment women's identities as musicians. Doing so may symbolically validate the band as a serious endeavor, as well as their identities as musicians.

Men's identities are affected by social interactions, but in different ways. External verification, whether by friends, peers, or anonymous audience members, seems key to the process. Outside praise helped bolster men's confidence as musicians. While some of them have felt like musicians for quite some time, comments and praise by outsiders help them firm their identities as musicians. More men than women suggested the role songwriting played in their musical identities. Men seemed to be more prolific (or at least more willing to share their compositions with the band) and hence secured their self-identifications as musicians. Women, in contrast, suggested their lack of songwriting was a key element that barred them from true musicianhood.

In general, the events that instigated their identifying as musicians were cumulative, or perhaps synergistic. Meeting only one of the above criteria was typically not sufficient for feeling secure in the musician identity. Instead, most cited two or more of the above events that solidified their identities as musicians. It was not an easy identity to secure, much less maintain over time. As others have suggested, more than simply cultural, authenticity is also a project of the self (Kotarba 2013; Vannini and Williams 2009). Those who attain markers of authenticity find it easier to self-situate themselves in the music world, while others who do not may feel like impostors. Undoubtedly, moments that bolstered their authenticity as musicians simultaneously helped overcome the challenges of pursuing informal careers in the precarious world of music.

The Influence of Athens

Athens provided opportunities and a unique context for the bands to expand, but was also a critical factor that helped to further the development of musician identities. To begin with, moving to Athens was a godsend for most musicians. They described it, as have rock historians, as a "music mecca." The longer they spent in Athens, the more they appreciated the resources the town had to further secure their commitment to music. Athens is a place unlike any other. It's a curious combination of college town, music town, and art world infused with Southern culture. It had the best and worst of both worlds. Many musicians cited the musical history of Athens—R.E.M. are the most famous residents to spring from the town—as one factor that contributes to the longevity of this musical epicenter. Quite a few musicians, in fact, moved to Athens specifically due to its musical history and reputation.

Musicians felt there was something special about the town that inspired creativity. Athens shaped their bands in profound ways and, more importantly, shaped their identities in that it allowed them the opportunity to explore music and discover their musicianhood (Byrd 2015; Shank 1994). Part of this was due to simply being in a musical space where many bands with many different styles had the room to develop and perform. Living in this "special place" allowed them the freedom to cultivate as musicians. It was like an artist's retreat—a space that magically opened up their creativity in ways they had never experienced. Of course, they could have started bands in other cities, had they moved to places other than Athens (as many of them did earlier in life), but they felt that those alternate locales would be lacking something important to what they experienced, learned, and gained in Athens. Their bands could have existed in other cities of course, but they would be qualitatively different—and subpar.

MR: How different do you think [your band] would be or your music would have been if you had not moved to Athens?

BEN: I probably would have ended up in Atlanta. And I probably would've started a band. I know it would have been different because [my band], the ridiculousness of [my band] could have only happened with Aaron and Marcus. I can't imagine I would've done something as eccentric or weird as [our band] with anyone other than [the two of them]. And I don't think Atlanta would have accepted it. I don't know if Athens has totally accepted it, but we have our places we can play and that we can take our pants off and play. I think if I would've started a band [elsewhere], I'm not sure if it would have done well or not, but it would've been a lot more conservative than [my band], which makes me very happy that I moved to Athens.

Athens was a muse. It inspired art, music, and creativity, and unlocked a realm of decisions and life experiences that would not have been possible elsewhere. It opened up the possibilities of decisions, some life altering and others short term, that shifted life course trajectories in minor and major ways.

Nearly all of the musicians cited the many opportunities available in Athens that are much more limited, if not entirely absent, in other regions. Musicians emphasized the numerous clubs in town that make the regularity of performances possible.

> ANNABEL: There are so many places to play in Athens. I think that alone probably is different than a lot of other places. And it's easy to get shows here. It's not something that's really, really difficult just because there are so many places to play. I think there are so many people that you meet and stuff like that just because it's a compact [scene]. There are so many awesome resources for people who play music in Athens. I think that even the [community] here kind of creates a scene around it that caters to the music scene.

The structure exists for music performance to occur for many bands on a regular basis. Athens yields a sufficient number of venues, culminating in limited, yet healthy, competition in the music scene.

Equally important is the availability of musicians in town that allows one greater chances to start a band. Athens has one of the highest per capita rates of musicians in comparison to other music towns. Vincent lightheartedly said: "If you walk outside and threw a rock, there's a 99 percent chance you're gonna hit a guitar player in this town. I would guess maybe 50 percent of my friends are musicians." In other cities in which musicians previously lived, they cited the difficulty they had in simply meeting other musicians with whom they could start bands. In those contexts, musicians mentioned their low standards for selecting band members. They found themselves simply selecting bandmates based on their availability, while not being able to adequately take into account their ability on the instrument or style, much less their musical chemistry together. In Athens, however, they could be more selective in choosing the musician who was the best fit for the band. The ease with which a hopeful musician could start a band was unusually straightforward. Roman said: "I really love Athens because if you have a group of friends, you can start a band. Or if you don't, you can make them really quickly. If you want to start a country band, you could probably find three guys in a week who probably want to do it with you. And there's a lot of good musicians who just really want to play music. In Atlanta, it's so big and spread out, there's not really a sense of community. It seems like everyone [in Athens], regardless of style, guy or girl, or genre—everybody is pretty helpful [and] willing to lend a hand musically."

Opportunities abound for aspiring musicians in Athens. Every musician was well aware of the resources that were available that allowed for the pursuit of music for those considering music either short term or long term. There was room for everyone, from those with short-term intensions to those with dreams of lifelong musical careers. Musicians did not see gatekeepers to the local music world, but instead assessed a "low barrier to entry into the market," as described by Damien. Paul had attempted the music life in other cities before moving to Athens. He recognized that "it's very easy to be a part of the music scene here if you want to be. It's almost *too* easy." The ease of pursuing music is partly due to the willingness of the music world—especially the clubs—to allow up-and-coming bands to perform at their venues on weeknights.

> JACK: But it really is easy [to be a band here]. . . . I imagine it would have been really hard to figure out how to get a show if we were in Chicago, or Nashville, or some other city. Whereas in Athens, the [chance of that happening] obviously is better. They're especially good about giving some new bands a chance. If you're a local band, you've never played before, if you've got twenty friends, they'll put you first on a three-band bill, like on a Monday night, you know? I mean, you get a chance to play no matter what. The downside is that there's just so many bands in Athens and you have to fight through the noise. There's a lot of good bands in Athens, a very high density of good bands in this town. And they're really good about helping you get those first steps out. But after that, a lot of bands just get stuck. . . . In Athens, it's real easy to get that first show. And it's pretty easy to develop a small following, but just doing that in Athens, no one's gonna care. It's like a bubble around it.

The musicians who had spent a long span of years pursuing music and/or had histories in other music cities were particularly attentive to the advantages available for musicians in Athens.

> ANDREW: It's almost ridiculous how music centered a lot of the community is in this town. It's almost too helpful to a degree where it's like, "Don't get too comfortable just playing in town." Because you can continually have good shows here. People are going to be into it. That's great. That's so awesome. Athens is incredible. [The local newsweekly] *Flagpole* is incredible with helping out all kinds of bands, especially local acts. There's the local music

awards. [The annual music festival] Athfest [is] the fucking South by South-
west of Athens. There's a fucking shit ton of people out for Athfest. Athens
is pretty amazing. We have good venues: Caledonia, 40 Watt, Tasty World,
Georgia Theatre. People don't realize how good we have it.

The multiple resources was not something most musicians took for granted,
having had more difficult and tedious experiences in years past attempting to
start bands, book shows, and otherwise develop musical careers elsewhere.
They fully understood they had access to valuable resources that musicians in
other scenes would never imagine.

Not only was the structure in place to allow for opportunities, but the individuals in the world were mutually supportive of one another, regardless of status or tenure in the music scene. Multiple musicians valued the camaraderie
among bands, between bands and clubs, and between the music world and the
"world outside the music bubble." Part of the camaraderie may be due to its
small population. The town and the musicians are isolated from other bigger
cities and scenes in other parts of the country. Some musicians likened it to a
small town mentality in which everyone looks out for each other.

> ELI: There's just tons of bands. Since Athens is one degree of separation from
> everybody, you eventually know somebody who knows somebody else who
> knows you, and you eventually meet them and you'll end up drinking one
> night together and then say, "Hey, we should do a show together!" You
> meet people through that. People get to know you, and, therefore, this new
> [opportunity] starts out. You have this big community feel. Everybody is
> pretty much in [support of] everybody else.
> ROBERT: It's this camaraderie. We're all these poor musicians trying to do some-
> thing, and I respect you for trying it, and you respect me for trying it. You
> kind of give each other a hand. Not to say it's hunky dory all the time with
> band relationships, but there is a strong sense of that here in Athens. Those
> opportunities aren't there [in other cities]. Here in our small town it's a good
> starting point because there's a lot of options for nobodies.

Generally, musicians cited the solidarity that made the town a true community (Durkheim 1893). Bands were supportive of one another. Some musicians told stories of experiences in other cities in which bands fragmented
into more disparate cliques and splintered groups within the music scene.
They sometimes resorted to sabotaging other bands: removing their promo-
tional flyers for shows, spreading gossip, and speaking ill of them to blackball
them from clubs or disrupt affiliations with other bands. The camaraderie
in Athens went beyond the musicians. Dean, excited to play one of his first
shows, told this story:

DEAN: [My first show] was a big deal. Just seeing this huge crowd, I couldn't believe that they would have a band like us come play there. . . . I was really excited. I called my brother and he was living [in another city] at the time, and he came out to see the show. And we really just blew it. We sucked so bad. And I remember walking around the back [of the club] to the back steps, and I sat down and I started crying. I felt horrible. And I felt like I just let everybody down. And this guy that worked at the 40 Watt—he was probably just a doorman or the dude that took the garbage out or something—came up. I don't know what he was doing walking around behind the place. He came over and said, "Hey, are you okay?" And I told him what was going on. And he's just like, "Man, don't worry about it. You're gonna get tons of chances to play here. Your brother will see you play again." And [he] really just said all the right things. And I couldn't believe it, that this guy I never met before and don't even know if I'd ever run into since, took the time to come over and comfort this poor kid who just played a terrible set. I mean, that was powerful. It meant a whole lot at the time.

These factors culminated into opportunities to extend and secure men's and women's identities as musicians. Doubts they may have had to forgo musical careers were lessened due to the context in place in Athens that allowed for their musical dreams to flourish. Access to resources available within particular music scenes at the individual and macro level influence opportunities to participate in music. In contexts with greater resources and infrastructure, it is "easier" for individuals to discover and participate in music as both fans and musicians alike (O'Connor 2004). While Athens has a reputable place in music history, it has forged a more DIY approach to music due to the fact that it is situated in a locale with fewer resources in comparison to the major music scenes in New York, Austin, and Nashville.

Sustaining the Musician Identity

The musician identity was fluid in multiple respects: it was typically a self-administered identity, criteria were subjective, and, once attained, the status was not necessarily static. Some musicians waxed and waned their internalization as a musician—sometimes feeling more like a musician at certain time than others. They generally felt that the structure of particular lines of employment minimized the toil necessary to be in a band.

BEAU: You can do something like [pursue music] without making your [non-music] job a huge priority because of the low cost of living, whereas if you live in a big city, you have to work sixty hours a week to get by. The more time you have to devote to the band, the more you're able to pay more attention to it. You don't have to worry about other things distracting you [from music] here.

Beau crystallizes the significance of the workplace's influence on musicians' commitment to music. Avoiding excessive overtime in the workplace opened up "free time" to devote to music. They well knew that this scenario would not be as easy to balance in other music cities with higher standards of living.

"Real" Jobs: Degree of Flexibility with the Musician Identity

Despite Athens' low cost of living, musicians of course had to work for pay. And their workplace commitments—which they often referred to as their "real jobs"—had the potential to infringe on their musical careers.[4] In some sense, the musicians personified dual identities: employees by day, musicians by night. Some musicians felt that they had a "split personality" due to their competing professional employments and musical interests. During the day, they were professionals who looked, acted, and behaved like "regular people." In the after-work hours, they transitioned to what they felt were their truer selves: musicians. For many of them, this transition was easily accomplished by simply exiting the workplace at the end of the day. These musicians tended to be workplace segmentors—avoiding overlap in their workplace and social lives or, in this case, their professional and musical worlds (Nippert-Eng 1996). Though they enjoyed their work and got along with their coworkers, they typically did not forge deep friendships with anyone from their office outside of work. They did, in a sense, inhabit two worlds. Such strategies were effortless for some musicians, but other workplace contexts made commitment to the band (and commitment to the musician identity) problematic in that it was challenging to manage both.

Flexibility with Musical Commitments

By and large, the musicians who described a degree of flexibility in their jobs with their musical lives were those in the service sector, music sector, and (to a limited degree) white-collar work. Each work sector had particular aspects that afforded musicians' the flexibility for accommodating their musical pursuits.

To begin, the structure of the service industry and music-centric jobs provided flexibility in scheduled work hours (Golden 2001). These jobs did not require the scheduling of work hours Monday through Friday from 9 to 5, but were instead more variable. Some musicians in these jobs worked four days a week with eight- to ten-hour shifts or five-plus days a week with shorter shifts. Most of the musicians welcomed the flexibility in shifts and sometimes had a say in their weekly work schedules. They may not have had an early morning at work after a late-night show, although some occasionally did. In instances in which their schedules conflicted with their band's schedule, they could attempt to swap hours with coworkers if necessary. The irregularity of their jobs was irritating at times, but they generally appreciated the leeway their jobs provided in being able to devote sufficient time to their bands.

They also appreciated that their jobs, though demanding and exhausting in their own respect, ended when they clocked out at the end of their shifts. Service sector work did not lend itself to employees' having to "take work home," and most of them did not have to think about their work at home, unlike employees in other sectors, particularly the white-collar, professional realm. Service work did not invade their private and musical lives too dramatically, allowing them a degree of work-music balance.

The biggest shortcoming of service sector work, however, was its disparate level of pay. Typically working minimum wage jobs, musicians (as is the case with most workers in the service sector) found it difficult to make ends meet. They did not necessarily frame their economic insecurity as impacting their musical lives per se since it presumably affected *all* facets of their lives. These musicians seemed to voice greater concern over everyday life issues such as paying rent and bills and the struggles of building their savings. Their main strategies to make ends meet included cutting costs by living with multiple roommates, thereby splitting the bills among them all. They often lived with other musicians, artists, or "townies" who were similarly employed in low-wage jobs.

White-collar jobs, in contrast, had little flexibility in work schedules, as all full-time employees worked Monday through Friday typically from 8 to 5. Musicians employed in these settings preferred those hours, suggesting the default, routinized work schedules gave them a structured routine in their musical pursuits. I asked Roger whether his current white-collar job complicated his devotion to his band, in contrast to other seemingly more flexible jobs in the service sector in which he was employed previously. He responded: "It's actually easier, I feel. I bet if more people in bands had a job like mine, they would find it easier to practice because of the [standard] schedule. Every band I've ever been in practiced at night. I work 8 to 5, so I'm free every night. I'm not fighting some ever-changing restaurant schedule. I know what my hours are. I know I can practice any night of the week. I can play a show any night of the week, we can book shows if we want to go out of town, those kinds of things. But not everyone in my band [has a job] like that."

Another valued aspect of white-collar employment was the benefits, especially the opportunities to accumulate leave. Musicians would bank these hours strategically. They would then use their leave to embark on short tours, often up and down the East Coast for a week or two with their band.

MR: Are they flexible with your work schedule and touring?

VINCENT: They are. That's the thing that keeps me there. Over the time that I've worked there, they've developed an understanding about that. I mean, I'm salary so if I have the amount of time saved up, I can use it. If I don't and I wanted to [tour], I guess I'll quit. I haven't had to cross that bridge yet. I've always had the time saved up, the days saved up to do some touring. It's been there when I've needed it.

Lilly's job at an administrative office at the university had similar benefits:

LILLY: I like my job because, working for [the university], you get enough leave time, I can build up leave time to do band stuff.

MR: So if you ever wanted to take a few weeks off to go tour or record or something?

LILLY: Yeah, I can do that. And they're fine with it. They seem to be cool with the idea that you don't have to be a [university] nut all the time to work there. You can have other interests. Where like if you worked at a corporation, a lot of corporations want you to live and breathe that corporation. It's not very realistic. So that's why I like it. I can be a [university] employee and still do other stuff.

Not only do these jobs help musicians generate time off to devote to their bands, but they also do not have an expectation that employees be consumed with their jobs entirely. They do, of course, need to demonstrate commitment and proficiency in their jobs. However, their employers are well aware and accepting of the reality that the musicians "are not [their] jobs" and that employees, musician or otherwise, have other interests outside of their work lives. Their employers knew full well that they were musicians devoted to their bands, and most of them encouraged and were otherwise supportive of their outside commitments to music. They did not necessarily presume nor pressure their employees to devote their lives to lifelong careers at their workplaces (Briscoe and Hall 2006; Sullivan 1999). Musicians in white-collar work who banked their time for touring or recording sessions in other cities did not feel the need to guard that information from their employers. The musicians felt fortunate to not have to "hide" their musician life while at work. Clearly, the structure of the middle-class workplace enabled them to maintain the musician identity with little pressure and no guilt.

These perks were so important to musicians that they sometimes chose to remain in these jobs over accepting offers from other more prestigious, higher-paying jobs elsewhere. Some musicians intentionally declined job offers with higher salaries, more status, and/or more room for promotion because those "better" jobs would more strongly interfere with their music.

> JANE: I'm really lucky because my supervisors are [supportive]. First, [my job] is a nonprofit. And [my boss] has always just been like, "Do what you need to do. Just don't do it in March and April because that's our busy time." But with the [second job I have at the] university, I was [initially] real concerned with getting that job because of that. But they are very understanding about people having passions outside of work. And it's kind of amazing. I don't know how I fell into it, but they are so cool. If I want to, I can take three and a half weeks off. I fear that at some point I'm going to have to choose one or the other. I'm sure that's going to happen at some point. Because you need to start touring more than that to get to the level that we want to be at.

Declining such opportunities was not easy, as many musicians struggled with their decisions. They did not make such decisions hastily, but were fully aware of the implications. Many musicians felt that balancing their work with their music was, for the time being, possible with little complication. Most of them similarly imagined that the sense of balance would not remain forever, and they would have to make major decisions at those points: either devote themselves more fully to their bands and disengage from their normative work, or the other unfortunate option that would require them to step away from music.

Inflexibility with Musical Commitments

Musicians who struggled the most with inflexibilities with their jobs were overwhelmingly those in the white-collar sector. To be clear, they did not necessarily suggest that they experienced the most stress on the job. They did not work a greater number of hours compared to musicians employed in other sectors, nor did they feel their jobs in and of themselves were inherently more grueling than those in other sectors. Instead, latent consequences of their jobs were what made it most difficult to manage their working lives with their musical lives. Like musicians in other work settings, those employed in white-collar work similarly felt like they inhabited multiple identities, of which their work identity and their musician identity were two. However, the consequences of the white-collar world to their bifurcated identities were more severe, exacerbated by their shuffling between the dual worlds in their professional and musical lives (Nippert-Eng 1996).

Some musicians employed in white-collar jobs struggled with the time bind (Maume and Bellas 2001; Schieman, Glavin, and Milkie 2009). They felt overworked and, perhaps coupled with age, no longer had the energy to "run on fumes" like they did earlier in life. They found it difficult to schedule rehearsals, much less studio time, when working forty-hour work weeks.

MR: Then do you find it difficult to balance your work [with your music]?

CLIFF: Yeah, it's extremely difficult. It's difficult enough to where sometimes you wonder why you're doing it. Just because, I mean, you get off work and you're exhausted. It's not even really the money thing. It's more the time [issue]. It's almost like being trapped in a low-energy zone. You work all day. Even if you have a [mindless] job, you work during the day, and get off and don't really have the energy [for anything after that]. I feel like just sitting on my ass and watching TV. But I mean you just have to kick yourself in the ass every once in a while to get [motivated] for the band.

As musicians moved into adulthood, the structure of their lives sometimes dictated less time to devote to regular band rehearsals. While in college, most of them could easily devote themselves to their courses, jobs, and still have the time—and more importantly, energy—to then meet up with their bands for rehearsals or shows. During the college years, some bands practiced every night of the week, whereas upon working 9-to-5 jobs, they had less time and less energy to devote to their band on a daily basis. For most, they learned time management skills in which they devoted less time but were more efficient in their rehearsals and other band endeavors.

Though other musicians in white-collar work appreciated being able to take time off for touring after building enough leave, others saw their working lives as limiting their opportunities to perform and especially to tour.

ALICIA: As far as getting ready for shows, we don't really play shows on weeknights because I have to be at work at 8 in the morning. And Jade and Heath both have jobs where it's hard for them to take a lot of time off and they have to be at work. So whenever we do play a show on a weeknight, it's a hassle for me and especially for them, and [we'll] be really, really tired at work the next day. But otherwise, my job is great because, like I said, it's something where once I'm off at 5, that's it. Or on the weekends, I don't have to think about it at all. So I have a lot of free time whenever I'm not at work to do whatever I want to do, whether it's playing music or whatever. But, it's really hard to be at work all day if you've been out really late playing a show the night before.

Standard work hours in white-collar professions eventually dictate those musicians avoid major band commitments, such as shows, during the week. Instead, they are forced to book shows at the more coveted, more competitive weekend shows. While weekend performances are the favored slots, as there are larger audiences and the potential for increased pay and publicity, it is more difficult to secure shows on Fridays and Saturdays. The foremost consequence is that the band can end up performing much less regularly, as they cannot routinely secure sought-after weekend slots exclusively. This predicament runs the risk of losing momentum, as fewer performances culminate in those bands' falling off local music fans' radar. Popularity is a fickle thing—musicians knew they could only temporarily go on hiatus or perform less frequently before they would be forgotten altogether.

One of the most consistent disadvantages of white-collar work was the limits these jobs placed on the possibilities of touring. While musicians above did describe accumulating leave as a perk of white-collar jobs, this turned into a hindrance when multiple members of the bands were in similar employment positions. It became increasingly difficult for (1) multiple band members to generate sufficient leave to be able to take an extended time off from work and (2) all band members to successfully secure the same time periods off for touring.

> HEATH: We have played in Atlanta twice and Knoxville once and that is the extent of our non-Athens playing. And we've probably played in Athens maybe fifteen times a year times four years, whatever that is.
> MR: Why is that? Is there any reason?
> HEATH: Yeah, I think it's mostly because [nearly all of us have] full-time jobs. We [accumulate] leave, but can't ever take it at the same time.

Heath's band member, Jade, expanded on the complications that arose from multiple members employment in white-collar work: "I don't know if we would even be able to go [on tour] because Alicia has a job, Heath has a job, and I have a job. Beau has his recording studio. Dean's probably the most flexible, but for [the three of us employed in office jobs], it's our vacation time." Jade highlights the ultimate consequence of devoting the entirety of one's leave to the band: the musicians never have time off for themselves. Most consider it a privilege to be able to take leave for short regional tours with their band ("Who else gets the chance to do this?" some of them gratefully acknowledge), but it comes at a cost. Many of them eventually feel exhausted and get to a breaking point. Some admitted to being burnt out and having considered stepping away from the band to have a "normal life" and take "normal vacations," like Lauren: "I find it exhausting a lot of times because I don't get a vacation. My vacation time gets used to go play shows or things like that or to record an album. Yeah, it can be tiresome. . . . We've been really busy lately because we have a new album out. But it's not always crazy. It's basically just never really having a break. That can be exhausting." By allocating their leave for tour and studio time, musicians, as a result, are not able to take time off for holidays, personal time, or leisurely travel.

Between working full time to devoting to remainder of their free time to the band, their schedules are grueling. The musicians fully realize these decisions are theirs, and any frustration they have at not having "any real time off" is entirely their own. They, however, sacrifice their vacation time because they see it as the only way to pursue their musical dreams.

The workplace is a greedy institution (Coser 1974). Scholars have examined ways in which workplace commitments infringe on other spheres of life, from family commitments to leisure to sleep (Hochschild 1989; Maume et al. 2009). However, the workplace also steals from musicians' true passions, their subjective careers—their music (Stalp 2006; Stebbins 1970). Maintaining the musician identity is more problematic in particular workplaces due to the tension between shuffling between multiple worlds that require distinctive and contradictory identities. While some employment contexts, such as the service sector, can prolong musicians' commitment to music, white-collar employment is yet another force than can begin to cast doubt on musicians' commitments to musical careers as they move more fully into adulthood.

Conclusion

Pursuing careers in music was a commitment interlaced with numerous challenges and demands, and equally tenuous was securing a firm grip on one's self-identification as a musician. The transition to the musician identity varied, with some identifying early in life as musicians, others more recently, and still others who were still early in the process of internalizing the identity. They also had strongly developed ideas regarding the criteria for inclusion as a true musician. Many musicians focused on technical aspects, such as proficiency at instruments, music theory, and improving songwriting skills. Others suggested musicianhood rested on monetary and business-centric responsibilities with the band. In general, a majority of the musicians felt that they were, at best, "partial" musicians or, at worst, frauds and impostors. Attaining the musician status, much like acquiring other achieved statuses, is more of a development, a gradual process. They implied seeing musicianhood as a continuum, not a clear dimorphic typology in which one is a "complete" musician or not one at all. Paradoxically, the *informality* of entering and pursuing informal careers in rock music imposes self-administered and symbolic barriers that impede musicians' feeling authentic. Those men and women who felt more comfortable with claiming the musician identity were often those who had accomplished business components of the music industry.

Structural components were also critical to the development of the musician identity. Athens was described as a space for music consumers to explore music, and correspondingly for musicians to continue to explore the possibilities of their identities. The history and culture of the town inspired such exploration. The structure of the town, particularly its having venues and cultural space in which music and the arts were valued, lent itself to identity development as musicians. The musicians sustained their identities by virtue of finding their niche in a larger musical world that is Athens.

Finally, the musicians' work lives outside the music world influenced the depths of their musicianhood. The sectors in which they were employed exerted strong influences on their ability to embrace identities as musicians. By and large, service work was more aligned with the musician identity. Musicians could maintain their musical identities while in these work sites. Those employed in professional or white-collar work, however, often faced more interference with their musician identities.

In sum, the musicians experienced some measure of freedom in constructing their musician identities. However, many musicians self-imposed strict limits on authentic musicianhood that resulted in their being less "qualified" to claim those identities themselves. Overall, the interplay of structure and culture worked in tandem to influence the emergence of the musician identity, although the process was unusually erratic. Only the rare musician's life course featured key factors that worked to ease the transition to and internalization of the musician identity. For most, however, it was a challenge.

4
Men and Masculinities in a Musical World

• •

Listening to the Beastie Boys' debut album *Licensed To Ill*, released in 1986, you would have never guessed that the three members, Mike D, MCA, and Ad-Rock, would grow into the men they would later become. As is often the case for musicians with lengthy careers and cultural longevity, listening to the discography of the Beastie Boys is like watching them grow into adulthood. Their debut album, though popular and influential, was not exactly a bastion of progressive masculinity. Songs like "Girls," "She's Crafty," and "Brass Monkey" did not present women—or men for that matter—in particularly positive lights. Their lyrics were often draped in misogyny, painting women in tired tropes used time and time again throughout popular culture. The Beastie Boys also personified elements of homophobia, as, to take one example, *Licensed To Ill* had the working title *Don't Be A Faggot*. Suffice to say, numerous identity groups—women, men to a degree, as well as the LGBTQ community—were systematically ridiculed in their early work.

Fast forward a decade later to the release of their seminal album, *Ill Communication*, and we see their principles on life, culture, and (especially) women to have progressively evolved. On this album, the Beastie Boys are far removed from depicting women as sex objects and gold diggers, and instead seemingly respond to their twenty-something younger selves in their most heartfelt rap in the third stanza of "Sure Shot." Fans have taken this verse as the three members more or less apologizing for disrespecting women in their earlier work. The album is a marker of their growth as men. During this time period, the world also witnessed their exploration into religion and their resulting spiritual growth, not to mention their social activism. In later years, Ad-Rock[1] went even further, issuing an apology via *Time Out New York* for their past lyrics: "I would like to . . . formally apologize to the entire gay and lesbian community for the shitty and ignorant things we said on our first record, 1986's "Licensed to Ill." . . . There are no excuses. But time has healed our stupidity. . . . We hope that you'll accept this long overdue apology."

The Beastie Boys do not need to be singled out—many men musicians have used (and unfortunately continue to use) misogynistic and homophobic lyrics in their music since the birth of rock, rap, and every genre in between. Nor should the music world necessarily paint them as martyrs to be worshipped for their growth—they are simply demonstrating simple civility by treating women and the LGBTQ community with the decency any human deserves. Instead, the trio is a sound illustration of the historical mainstays of masculinity in music culture. Popular music—especially in rock and rap—has long been dominated by men who reify normative, harmful masculinities. The Beastie Boys (fortunately) are not the only musicians to grow into profeminist identities. Their music, their activism, and their politics have impacted music culture—thus influencing masculinities to evolve into a more open and progressive direction that incorporates a broader spectrum of perspectives on gender, among other issues. If a couple of off-the-wall rap kids have the ability and drive to grow into more inclusive masculinities, it gives the rest of us men some hope too.

In chapters 1 and 2, I traced the life course trajectories of musicians, examining the events that individually and collectively influenced their possibilities of pursuing musical careers in adulthood. In this chapter, I focus explicitly on men musicians, identifying particular aspects of their life courses and growing up male that enabled them to pursue music. By so doing, I am able to forge the ways in which the life course is structured to advantage men over women in the music scene, one factor that explains the historical domination of men in this aspect of culture.

The Head Start

As discussed in Chapter 1, most musicians had an introduction to music early in life. Both men and women began developing an interest in music and subsequently picked up their first instruments often in the early childhood years. The first major difference to emerge in the sequencing of the life courses of women and men was centered on their learning rock instruments. Boys learned those instruments far earlier in life than did girls. The reasons were twofold. First, boys asked "permission" well before girls did. The idea of considering learning a rock instrument entered the minds of boys far earlier than it did girls. Boys remember the moments at which the initial idea to pick up a rock instrument entered their mind. It was typically in the middle school years, though for some it occurred even earlier. Of course, the earlier ages which children begin learning instruments will advantage, though of course not guarantee, their musical prowess by the time they reach adulthood.

Most boys, as was the case with girls, learned classical instruments before having the opportunity to learn rock instruments. However, boys were able to more successfully negotiate the obtaining of rock instruments well before girls did. For some of the boys, it may have been due to the masculine culture of rock and roll coupled with their parents' perceptions of normative boyhood (Ashley 2011; McHale et al. 2003). Parents seemed to be less than surprised when their sons eventually pushed and prodded for a guitar or drum set, especially after witnessing their sons becoming devoted fans of rock bands early in life. Parents expected these requests, and though they often delayed making those purchases, most surrendered to their sons' requests early in childhood. Furthermore, many of the musicians recognized the advantages with which learning multiple instruments endowed them. The faster transition from classical instruments such as the piano to rock instruments such as the electric guitar benefitted boys, as Roger speculates:

> Music theory from [piano lessons] was one of the things that helped me play guitar. I got to the level of my [more experienced] friends pretty quickly just because of the piano music theory base. I didn't have to learn what key was, or why a C chord sounds like this. Some of that stuff already made sense to me. And most of the time, when I'm thinking about music, the few times I do in a theoretical sense, I see it on a keyboard. That's how I feel about it. Because [although] I still play it, I'm not a keyboardist. I'm not even *really* a guitarist. What I mean is I really don't play an instrument. I mean, I *play* them. I think I play them pretty well. I think I do what I do pretty well. I can jam. I can jam with a bunch of guys. I can get on it and blow it out.

Roger is clearly advantaged on the guitar due to his experience with the piano. Boys in general were able to transfer the music theory knowledge base they gained from learning other instruments to their learning rock. This was a less viable knowledge base transition for girls due to the longer number of years between instruments, and hence the fading of music theory from their minds by the time they picked up rock instruments later in life.

Though the family influenced musical interests early in life, it did not seem as if fathers (or mothers, for that matter) singled out their sons as the only children who should develop interests in music consumption or music performance. Perhaps due to their identifying with the musicians whose music they heard as children, the boys felt like playing an instrument was a viable option for them. Siblings had an influence as well, especially older brothers. Most men who had older brothers singled them out for the influence they had on their musical interests generally.[2] They not only became fans of their older brothers' favorite bands, but also viewed them as musical role models who inspired them to pick up rock instruments themselves. Jacob remembered the influence of his older brother:

> And then my first cassette I bought—well, *he* bought—was *Led Zeppelin IV*.
> I heard Led Zeppelin and I thought, "Wow, I'm gonna do that." And I still remember it—all I had was a little cassette [player], and I remember getting the tape and going in my room, no one else is around, and then listening to *Led Zeppelin I* from the beginning. And then of course he fed me music off and on, but what happened was he got into problems with drugs and was sent to rehab a couple of times. So it was like he came in and out of my life, but I ended up with a bunch of his tapes he would leave around. So yeah, he definitely influenced my early listening a whole lot. I think when you have a three-year-older brother, you usually think he's pretty cool.

Many men singled out the influence of their older brothers in guiding their musical tastes in the early years. Other family members had significant influences too, though in distinct ways. Mothers, for instance, seemed to specifically nurture creativity in their sons. Many men described their mothers as former artists or creative in nature, though few of them had careers in the arts. For some mothers, their pushing of the arts to their sons may have been due to their dreams deferred. Unable to take up the arts themselves, they may have subconsciously encouraged their sons to do so.

Second, boys had a tendency for more limited extracurricular pursuits compared to girls (Eccles and Barber 1999), a factor that oddly increased their likelihood of discovering music. Their participating in limited extracurriculars is in contrast to the normative experience of boys, as there have historically been more diverse options available to them: athletics, music, art, drama, and academic clubs, to name a few. Despite the increased selection of activities from which boys could presumably choose, many of them did not actively explore many options (Bielby 2004). As a consequence, time that would have otherwise been spent exploring various athletic or academic endeavors was instead devoted to not only listening to recorded music but also learning instruments, sometimes more than one. Participation in music outside the formal context of the academic environment also amounted to a recovery of and, in some instances, a boost in the social status of boys removed from athletics. In the high school context, adolescent boys find "few alternative paths to peer status outside of organized sports" (Bielby 2004: 8). Music, however, is one of them.

Some boys did demonstrate curiosity in a wide range of activities, including athletics. Though they suggested having interests in many extracurricular activities, most found it exceptionally difficult to align participation in sports with any other additional pursuits, due in large part to their incompatibility. For one, the time structure of extracurricular activities essentially forces boys to choose one and only one activity in which to immerse themselves. Selecting certain activities require an uncompromising commitment of time, energy, and focus, particularly in athletics. Likewise, the constructions of masculinity that boys "should" embody within each often conflict with one another, rendering them incompatible pursuits. Sport masculinities prioritize competition, physical strength, and the flushing of all femininity (Hauge and Haavind 2011; Swain 2006), while other pursuits allow for more inclusive masculinities that incorporate less hostile, volatile, and aggressive elements. Ironically, however, the impetus for boys pursuing sports mirrored that of boys selecting other "softer" activities—the motivation to connect to others and gain status (Messner 1992; Swain 2003).

Third, their social networks early in life provided boys opportunities to learn instruments during adolescence (DiMaggio and Useem 1978; Marsden et al. 1982; Stebbins 1976). Boys more often than not had friendships circles composed primarily of other boys (Thorne 1993). Boys had a greater likelihood of owning and playing instruments and thus provided opportunities for boys to informally learn from their peers. In fact, it was only the boys who had friends who taught them how to play instruments as they were coming of age, typically in middle and high school. Girls almost never discussed such experiences while growing up.

> JACK: I did take some lessons for about a month, but I took them about eight months after I started playing. When I first got the guitar, a couple of my friends had already been taking lessons on guitar. So they had already learned a few things. They would show me certain things. My friend made me this chart of all these chords that I needed to know, and he showed me how to play a few songs. The summer after seventh grade, I didn't have a car yet and none of my friends were my neighbors. So I literally didn't see my friends the whole summer. I sat in my room and played guitar, like eight hours a day. Getting past that breaking point of switching between chords and it not hurting to push the strings down. For three months, I just did that.

The three months of practicing his guitar using the foundation of his friends' informal lessons paid off. Jack soon hit his stride with the guitar and began further developing his musical prowess on the instrument. Jack's experience was typical of many men with whom I spoke. Their friendship circles clearly illustrate the extent to which boys had larger and more accessible musical networks early in life in comparison to girls. Consistent with Bielby's (2004) work on the social organization of rock culture, access to this social network allowed boys more ample opportunities to not only discover but also to learn and contemplate pursuing music.

Music Icons Organized by Masculinity

Men developing interests in rock earlier in life than women is due also to the culture and history of rock music. Rock, as a genre and cultural history, is organized by masculinity (Bennett 2001; Walser 1993). Cultural critics of music primarily celebrate men as the biggest influences in rock music. Rock was born of the King (not Queen) of Rock, Elvis Presley.[3] Classic rock icons from the 1960s and 1970s were primarily men: Led Zeppelin, Jimi Hendrix, and The Who were typically cited as provoking boys' interest in music. Even less normatively masculine artists such as Elton John influenced boys' growing passion for music. In the years since, men have continued to dominate rock, with bands such as The Clash and Nirvana, among a host of others. The rock world is a man's world. Boys are the heirs.[4]

During boyhood, the musicians could easily see themselves transplanted on stage alongside their iconic rock stars (Bennett 2001; Bielby 2004). It was by no means a stretch of their imagination to see themselves with the same instruments, performing as their heroes did. They highlighted the role of rock music history in structuring the gendered trajectories of contemporary musicians. Namely, the men musicians sometimes recognized how their shared gender with rock icons may have influenced their interests. From an early age, some were attentive to the trend of rock bands being composed of a collective of men and men only. Even those men who did not explicitly identify the connection still told stories in which they remembered particular male artists inspiring the men themselves to follow suit and pick up a guitar.

At the same time, masculinity goes deeper than the gender of the music icons on record. The culture of rock is one steeped in masculinity (Eastman 2012; Haenfler 2006). Musicians, men and women alike, often referenced the atmosphere of music culture as aligned with masculinity. The loud, blaring music, the screaming of the vocals, the pounding of the drums: nearly every sound that emanates from the rock records that influenced the direction of their lives was categorically masculine. It was easy for men to identify with Jimi Hendrix, Led Zeppelin, the Ramones, or Nirvana at early ages. Daniel said: "I think a lot of it is contextual. There are certain bands where there is a sense of masculinity. You're never going to get past that with bands like the Rolling Stones obviously. Even in more current bands, [there's] still that air of masculine sexuality."

Similarly, Paul said: "I think a lot of it goes back to there haven't always been many [women in music]. There are female role models in music obviously, but it's just been very male centered. It's just always been male oriented and I think that just perpetuates itself. I certainly think the macho aspects of it definitely appeal to men."

Ironically, the masculine-imbued world of rock was also a safe space for nonnormative boys to seek refuge. Boys who did not particularly feel comfortable in the bastions of childhood masculinity that is athletics instead saw the music of gender-benders like David Bowie and Lou Reed as comforting to and accepting of them. The very act of becoming a Bowie fan was an act of rebellion against normative adolescent masculinity at play on the sports field. Regardless of their alignment or misalignment with heteronormative masculinity, most boys could find a musical space in rock that let them be who they felt they were (or perhaps wanted to be).

Mentor Selection and Recruitment

Professional life in virtually any career trajectory is far easier to navigate with the assistance of mentors, whether formal or informal (Dobrow and Higgins 2005; Johnson and Hager 2008). Mentor relationships are one of the key markers of future success in one's professional life, regardless of occupation. Mentors are critical to not only learning the ropes of one's trade, but also to avoid making the same mistakes others have made before. They provide a key aspect of on-the-job training for young and less-experienced workers who are new to the workplace. Though mentorship is typically associated with professional and formal lines of work, the musicians spoke candidly of mentor figures who benefitted their lives, professionally and otherwise.[5] Gender was at play in mentoring relationships in numerous respects. At its most general level, men's lives were structured in ways that enabled greater opportunities for mentorship early in their starting days as musicians.

First, mentors were more easily accessible to men via their social networks. Friendship circles in which they had long been involved since the teenage years, as well as more recent friendship networks they entered in early adulthood, provided opportunities for mentoring, though informal. They often had a good number of friends and acquaintances in the music industry in some capacity, either as experienced musicians themselves or as producers or recording engineers. By virtue of their shared relationship status as friends, the musicians were able to learn the trade of the music world. Sometimes this occurred directly by firsthand observation and/or training, while other times it was more indirect in terms of the musicians simply observing from the fringes of the world. A few of the musicians did not even realize until some time later that their friendships with insiders in the music world had inadvertently provided them with insight to be used in their music careers later.

Other times, men were tactful in clandestinely learning from their friends (McDonald et al. 2007; Philip and Hendry 1996). These instances were "covert" mentor relationships. In one telling instance, Nate discussed who he considered to be a key mentor in his musical life, one of his bandmates:

NATE: [My mentor is] probably our drummer, because he had already played in another band and they had been on tour already and released an album, so he kinda knew how to be in a band. All the stuff I wouldn't have known were it not for [him], just little things. He already had a home studio and a practice space. None of us [in the band] would've known what to do . . . If you talk to him and you tell him he was my mentor, that's gonna cause a lot of trouble between us. Oh my God, I would never hear the end of that.

MR: So it was an unofficial? He would have no idea that you consider him that?

NATE: Probably not. He knows that we wouldn't know what the hell we were doing if it weren't for him. But I don't think he'd ever think that I would say he was my mentor.

In some instances among men, such as with Nate, mentors were secretive. Not only was Nate's mentor unaware of his influence on him, but Nate also felt there would be consequences were his drummer to find out how he perceived him. There is apparently an undercurrent of masculine norms guiding covert mentorships. Men have questions and need training and other forms of assistance, but may feel inclined to avoid asking directly for assistance through formal mentorships. The safer alternative to secure their independent masculinities is to secretly be trained at a distance, through relationships never disclosed.[6]

Second, men discussed their being mentored symbolically from afar by their musical heroes. Men often cited the careers and lives of icons such as David Bowie, Marc Bolan, and others as acting as their symbolic mentors over the course of their lives. The men often seemed to be the expert biographers of their favorite musicians, having spent years upon years not only listening to their music, but also reading their biographies and learning details about their lives. They used this information to gauge their decisions in music as well. When I asked Seth about mentors in his life, he initially was stumped.

SETH: That's a difficult question. There are indirect mentors: David Bowie, Bob Dylan, David Byrne.

MR: What about them would you say sets the criteria for them being a mentor to you?

SETH: Bowie and Dylan, they're to the extreme of what I talked about earlier with how people became more like actors in a stage performance where they became—a lot of people hated them. They pissed off a lot of people because they had this goal, both of them. They were like, "I want to be a rock star. I want to change this fucking planet by being a rock star. I'm going to do whatever it takes to get there. I'm not concerned with people's feelings." I've always been really concerned about how people perceive me and not pissing people off—I want everybody to like me. I want to be friendly and make people feel like they're accepted. You can't please everyone. That was what Bowie and Dylan did to an extreme example. "I'm not interested in doing what you want me to do and pleasing you. I'm not going to let you put me in a box. I'm going to keep going. If you resent the fact that I've left you behind, so be it. I've got a fucking goal and mission. I have this passion that drives me to the extent that I don't care what you think about me." I really respect that in a lot of ways because it's the exact opposite of me. Not as much anymore as it used to be. I'm more like that now. That's what fascinates me about them.

Men suggested that they not only learned tactics to survive and succeed in the music world, but also that they began to learn a musical masculinity via their musical icons.

Third, men were the only musicians who were resistant to the idea that anyone—mentors or otherwise—assisted them in their careers. Men were more likely than women to suggest having had no mentors, much less no one from whom they sought any advice. Their entrance to the music world was framed as entirely independent and self-directed. They were lone wolves who blindly and independently ventured into the world. They admitted to some stumbles, but reveled in their ultimate success that was due fully to their navigation entirely on their own. They aligned themselves with an independent masculinity in that they forged their own roads into the music world, figuring out the intricacies of the world on their own.

MR: When you were first starting out, is there someone that showed you the ropes?

BRANDON: No. That first band that I was in that started playing out, that guy was in a band in Montréal and he was in that band for several years. He was ten years my senior, so he had done all that already. I just let him kind of take it. As far as recording, when we were in the studio, I would just listen. But the truth is, with any of it, with anything you do, if you just sit down and do it, if you know what you want and you are willing to be patient to get it to sound like you want it to sound, that's all there is to it. I know what I like and I can get it. As far as live shows and all that, I still haven't learned that networking aspect. Back to your former question, no one showed me the ropes, I just watched. And bartending helps. You meet doctors, lawyers, people that are in clubs. You hang out with them enough and they are like, "Yeah, we'll let your band play one night. Sure." So my route was different than everybody else's. Everyone else, you've got to send a demo.

These musicians of course did have informal mentors, often bandmates, friends, or others they came into contact with via their networks, who advised them similarly to other musicians. However, in stark contrast to other musicians, they refused to see these relationships as bearing even an informal mentoring dimension. Mentoring involves a status differential: mentors have more experience and wisdom imparted upon the younger, inexperienced mentees. This seemingly put the mentee's masculinities at risk, as they sometimes felt secretive or embarrassed having a mentor show them the way. They showed some hesitance sharing these stories. In other more formal contexts, mentor relationships are badges of status. Organizational newcomers, for instance, who are taken until the wing of experienced and powerful mentors often are satisfied with and proud of those relationships (Chao 2007). In the rock music world, it seems as if the independent masculinity that is part and parcel of musicianhood is threatened by having any semblance of outside assistance. The musicians whose independence remains fully intact are those who suggest they entered and succeeded in the music world on their own.

Musicianhood, Masculinity, and the Adult Status

As discussed in the previous chapter, the musician identity is coded as masculine, similarly to the ambiguous model worker in the formal work sector (Acker 1990). It is easier for men to fit the generic model for the musician identity than it typically is for women. The musician identity is more imbued with tropes of hegemonic masculinity, the construction of manhood held most dominant and most valued in a given cultural milieu (Connell 1987, 1995). Not only is it a male figure, but it is a carefree, independent, assertive, and wild prototype, one easily aligned with masculinity. As such, being a musician has the potential for boosting men's masculinities. Men become more masculine as they move into the world and identify as musicians. Their cultural status is boosted as well. Their access to fame and women—key indicators of a valued cultural masculinity—is heightened. In general, the social consequences of shifting one's identity to that of a musician is a status enhancer.

Despite these and other advantages men experience over the life course that ease their contemplation of and eventual pursuit of musical careers in adulthood, they nonetheless experience obstacles that work to push them away from their musical trajectories and onto normative pathways. Here I examine the ways in which musical commitment poses challenges to normative masculinities. In particular, parents, families, and peers regard musicianhood as lacking the attainment of full adulthood, as well as a lesser achievement of normative masculinity. The primary injury men may receive by virtue of internalizing the musician social identity is the potential impairment of their attaining a normative adult identity. However, much like men in other lines of nonnormative work, musicians strategically counteract accusations that threaten their masculinities.

Challenges to Musical Masculinities in Early Adulthood

As the men reached early adulthood, they contemplated the directions to take in terms of education, career, and music. While they did exhibit some diversity in their backgrounds, all of the men with whom I spoke were similar in their considering possibilities of pursuing musical careers in adulthood. As they deliberated their decisions, they were also confronted with the ways in which their musical career choices would potentially pose challenges to their attaining hegemonic masculinities.

One of the primary influences in reaching musical decisions bore on others' expectations of the men (Ramirez 2012). Parents and other adults shaped the musicians' ideas of what constituted an appropriate adult career. Such influences from individuals central to the musicians' lives became more frequent and imposing as they aged. Some men highlighted the tension between their chosen careers in music and their parents' expectations of them. Owen discussed at length the impact of adult family members on his decision to pursue music as a career. He cited his mother's former profession in music:

> I think it's important to remember that my mom gave up a career in the opera to raise two kids. So the behavior that I saw modeled for me was that music was an impracticality and that you should not dwell on it too much because it will distract you from the really important business of making a living. . . . It's a constant struggle. A foot in two worlds. Impractical for all society's messages you get from parents, teachers, vocational counselors, grandparents: the music is a luxury. There's no way to make a living, so you tend to second guess the impulse as a musician. And also you don't allow yourself the luxury of enjoying some of it. I see that behavior in my band members when we travel. They forget to have fun because they've been told that what they're doing is stealing away from their responsibilities by deciding to be creative. "This is irresponsible. It's indulgent." The thing is, I made a fairly decent living, not a great living, but a decent living in [my previous band], so I've seen that it's possible to make a living as a musician. . . . It's hard to help people see [that it's possible] when they've got twenty-plus years of their parents telling them, "Music is not a career. Art is not a career."

In contrast to other studies that illustrate how women's career histories can provide a supportive network for sons to try out nonstandard occupations (LaRocco 2007), Owen's history illustrates a counterargument. His mother's experiences seemed to trigger his contemplating a more normative avenue himself. Although he had been able to make a "decent" living off music in the past, Owen's anxiety carries on to this day. Parental warnings coupled with norms of adulthood exacerbate musicians' doubts as to whether music was an appropriate path to adulthood. The musicians' stories also illustrate how these tensions are coupled with social class. On one hand, their middle-class socialization encouraged them to appreciate and participate in artistic activities. On the other, as they grew older, they were expected to shed these interests and instead focus on more lucrative careers. They experienced a mounting pressure that maintaining a solidly middle-class status is paramount to all else. A few musicians, such as Brandon, had family members prepping them for the family business at an early age. While he realized it would secure his status in the upper middle class, he knew that music "would be one of the sacrifices that [he] would have to make." To risk losing status and security at the expense of an artistic career is—or should be—too big of a risk for the men. And for some, it is, as exemplified by their surrendering their musical interests.

For other musicians, parental tensions arose in other ways. During the early college years, a majority of the musicians' parents not only accepted their sons' pursuits of music, but took pride in them as well. As the musicians neared graduation, parents fearful of their sons' continued pursuit of music attempted to steer them back to conventional paths of normative adulthood (Ramirez 2012). For a number of musicians, the parental advice was direct. Those who decided to quit school to devote themselves to music were typically warned to not ask parents "for a damn thing." Roger's predicament was similar. Upon finishing college, "my dad was like, 'Get a job. Get a job now. You're a college graduate. Get a job.'" Even musicians who were several years into their postcollege life still wrestled with their parents' expectations. Adrian admitted that he contemplates abandoning music "every day. I phone my dad about twice a week. And in some way, it always comes up in every conversation. Maybe not directly, maybe in just tone or something. Just the ever-looming call of reality. It's definitely there. There's always the feeling of impending doom and you've got to regroup and do something practical." In reaction to these situations, musicians attempted to simultaneously accede to their parents' wishes while continuing their devotion to music. Roger took his father's advice and got a "regular" (i.e., white-collar) job, although one for which he was far overqualified as a college graduate. These attempts by parents to veer musicians to conventional pathways were simultaneously attempts to shift men back to normative wage-earning traditions of masculinity (Williams 2000).

Men also described situations of parents being supportive of and, in some cases, even encouraging music careers early on, only to later witness it wane over time. The musicians' devotion to music was once a thing to be admired and proud of, only to be an annoyance as time pressed on. Many of the musicians suggested their mothers were more consistently supportive, while their fathers' support plummeted or altogether vanished over time. I asked Aaron about both of his parents' levels of support for his music career.

MR: One other thing you mentioned, I think you said that your mom has generally been more supportive of the music than your dad, even though your dad was more into music?

AARON: No, he's very supportive, but is [apprehensive] about showing it. The weird thing is, is there was this split probably when I turned eighteen, that he kind of just turned off general interest in what was going on because he was like, "You're an adult. You're in this other realm now." Still a super great person. He's never come and seen a show whereas my mom has seen [my band perform live]. It's a little much, but she listens to it. And that's the great thing. It's so crazy, the shit we try to get away with, and she loves it. . . . But yeah, my dad started it, got me really interested in music [initially]. But mom's just been the one behind me the whole time [consistently].

It is more than parental support waning as the men moved more fully into adulthood. More precisely, fathers attempt to instigate a more forceful, demanding push out of music than do mothers. The gendered behaviors of parents are partly responsible for this discrepancy. Mothers generally were more supportive of their children's decisions, music or otherwise. They also are more likely to allow a more exploratory experience for their children as they move into adulthood. Fathers, in contrast, consistent with normative masculinity, prescribe plans for their sons. Both mothers and fathers have their children's best interests in mind, although those interests emerge in vastly different parenting styles. Mothers see their children's maturation as arising through exploration and perhaps even a few false starts in life. Fathers want their children to learn from their mistakes, their experiences, and use their family wisdom as a template to avoid pitfalls for themselves as they move into adulthood.

The breadwinner status has historically been a defining marker of hegemonic masculinity (Kimmel 2011). And true to form, the wage-centered masculinity was internalized in many of the men's lives. Furthermore, the tension between pursuing music over other more stable jobs was a daily stressor for most musicians. When the men disclosed their hesitations to fully pursue music, they typically framed their hesitations in economic terms. They questioned whether the self-fulfillment they gained from music outweighed the minimal economic compensation they could expect to receive. The economic limitations of music seemed to threaten men's identities, as masculinity has historically been "measured by a paycheck" (Gould 1974). Men musicians were concerned with the disadvantage their pursuing music may have not only on their economic futures, but also on their masculine gender identities.

Last, the potential economic consequences of musical careers were even more apparent for men who were married and/or had children, as well as for those who believed they may want to have children at some point in the future. Owen discussed his views on a future-oriented fatherhood: "I think I want to have kids, but I don't want to do it right now. And [my family] see[s] music as an impediment to that because of the lack of financial security in being a musician. So yeah, the pressure exists." The pressure is even stronger for Owen's bandmate who, in contrast to Owen, does have parental responsibilities. Owen says of his bandmate: "And Michael, he fights a daily battle of poverty. He's a father. He's got a nine-year-old son. He has never really beaten those voices out of his head that say, 'This is no way to make a living. You're stealing from your son's future.' It's constant."

Their status as a culturally masculine musician is at odds with the masculinity required of the outdated, though still powerful, father-provider role. Men in comparable situations struggled to come to terms with which path they should take. Notions of the archetypal family man prompted men to consider abandoning music for the sake of the family or, more specifically (since more men imagined the possibility of children than currently had children), for a *potential* family in the future. All in all, while men musicians felt unique in many ways from the average man, they nonetheless felt compelled to maintain the traditional role of the breadwinner. As other studies have illustrated, employment and fatherhood are "mutually reinforcing, for having children provides a motivation for dedication to employment, and supporting a family is crucial to successful fatherhood" (Townsend 2002: 78). Contemporary fathers, musicians included, realize that being a "good father" means going beyond the role of economic provider, yet they continue to value contributions as the provider more than anything else (Ramirez 2012).

In general, normative masculinities influenced men's decisions as to whether to persist in music. The men highlighted various aspects of hegemonic masculinity as they made sense of their career decisions. On the whole, conceptions of a normative adulthood shaped men's career decisions and subsequent reactions in constructions of their masculinities. The economic implications of musical decisions weighed on men as well, as the potential for a less lucrative and less stable payoff may result. Finally, worries of starting and/or supporting a family inhibited men. These factors—all of which are bound to career and working life—are ultimately woven with constructions of masculinities. Other studies have characterized young men's entrance to adulthood as an extended adolescence in which they avoid serious careers and relationships (Kimmel 2008). The men musicians were similar in that they did frame emerging adulthood as a time to focus on themselves; however, they did not have unrealistic expectations of career success being easy and immediately attainable. In this sense, musicians were more closely aligned with "traditional" notions of adulthood than contemporary men studied in other contexts (Kimmel 2008).

Masculinities in a Musical World

In describing their coming of age within musical contexts, nearly all of the men musicians with whom I spoke shared the impression that musical participation shaped their gender identities as men. As I illustrate next, their identities as musicians were often critical components in their constructions of masculinities. I also highlight the extent to which musicians strategically framed music as appropriately masculine in response to challenges of masculinities they experienced by others.

Nearly every man with whom I spoke regarded his musician status to be a core part of his social identity. They were many things: students, college graduates, professional workers, artists, fathers, social activists, to name a few, but the central, most critical persona they saw in themselves was that of musician. Music, they discovered over time, was critical to their understanding of themselves (MacDonald et al. 2002). It provided a self-awareness that no other part of their life could shed light on. It was also one aspect of their identity that they imagined would remain consistent for the rest of their lives. Some musicians compared their devotion to music to other men's lifelong interests in sports, motorcycles, or carpentry. Cliff said: "Why do people jump out of planes and things like that? Why are people into [motorcycles]? My dad's big into Harley [Davidson motorcycles]. He's been a bike rider for forty-five years. Why does he do it? He's sixty, but he still [does it]. He goes riding on some highway, and it's like he feels complete. When you're on stage, you kind of feel the same way. You feel complete. Like everything makes sense." Similar to many other men, Cliff saw his commitment to music as a core part of his identity, and one that he anticipated would remain for the entirety of his life. Like other men who spend their time playing pick-up basketball, doing carpentry in their garages, or tending their gardens on weekends, music was something enjoyable, therapeutic, and a defining part of his sense of self.

The men consistently suggested that their musical identity (though not necessarily their *musician* identity) would be a part of what defined them evermore. Sentiments such as, "It will always be a part of who I am" and "It's the most important thing to me" were recurring thoughts among the many men with whom I spoke. Other men went further by suggesting, as did Owen:

I don't think you could know me without seeing me play drums. You couldn't know who Owen was without experiencing [my band] or some

FIGURE 5 Bryant Williamson of Cinemechanica (Photo by Mike White, deadlydesigns.com)

other band that I was in in the past. My wife never saw me play drums at all until we moved to Chicago. That was the first time she ever saw me play music. And I thought it was really strange that anyone would find me interesting at all without having seen me play drums. . . . Now, I'm a pretty broad guy: I work on my own car, I grow my own vegetables, I work on my own house, fix computers, and I play music. There's a lot of stuff that I do. But music is [central].

Music was one of many interests and passions in which the men participated. However, they did feel it was the core of their identity, something that anchored who they were to the world in which they lived. Without music, they felt like a key part of them would be missing. As I will examine next, musicianhood was also the pivot on which constructions of masculinity often hinged.

Musician Masculinities as Traditional, Innovative, or Something in Between?

The Traditionalists

Just over 20 percent of the men (7 of 33) believed men musicians' gender identities to be consistent with normative constructions of masculinities. Personally, they regarded their participation in music as having no influence on their gendered lives and were consistent in believing men musicians adhered to characteristics of hegemonic masculinity. They certainly recognized the way they spent their nonworking, nonschool lives as unique—often feeling that they "eat, breathe, and live" music—but did not see it as consequential to their lives or identities as men per se. Some men were of course familiar with the trope of men musicians being more sensitive, emotional, or in touch with their feminine side, but they essentially believed this to be a fiction or, at best, only a partial truth that only pertained to some musicians. Eli believed all men, whether musically inclined or not, to be "all basically the same. People up there rocking with their cock out are no different than frat boys screaming at football games. . . . Some people are passionate about SGA [Student Government Association], make T-shirts for SGA. We just make T-shirts for our band. Just a different type of personality, but the same way of thinking." Eli simply assumed music, though an interest in his life, to be detached from his gendered sense of self. Of course, these men did value their role and social statuses as musicians, and they did feel like they were part of a "special club." However, it did not lend itself to their developing a particular masculinity. These conceptions of music's minimal influence on masculinities, however, were rare.

Musician Masculinities as Nontraditional

Most men (26 of 33) instead believed music had soundly shaped their identities, both their "everyday" social identities and specifically their gender identities as men. These musicians expressed two variations of this theme: (1) the "innovators" believed musicians to be categorically distinct in comparison to nonmusician men, and (2) the "dualists" recognized musicians' masculine gender identities as innovative in some respects, but conventional in others.

The Innovators

One-third of the musicians with whom I spoke (11 of 33) were consistent in their beliefs that men musicians have masculine gender identities wholly unique from other men in contemporary society. These "innovators" believed musicians were worlds away from nonmusician men. Many musicians could easily speak of men musicians' nontraditional masculinities in generalities. Ivan, for instance, said: "I would say whether they like it or not, yeah, at some basic level [men musicians] are a little bit different. I think *how* much different they are varies a lot, because you can be in a band in high school and never do it again. But if it is something that you persevere at, even if you are a jock in every other way, there is something weird about you. . . . I don't know what it is that sets them apart, but I think there is something special about musicians."

Some musicians, similar to Ivan, found it difficult to speak precisely about how men in music were different from their nomusical peers. Part of the difficulty in enunciating these differences lay in the multidimensionality of musicians' lives and gender identities (Butler 1990). When pressed to pinpoint exactly what it was, Isaac believed it encompassed men musicians' entire lives— their identities, their goals, their perseverance, and their relationships. Others, such as Cliff, believed men musicians' alternate constructions of masculinities "probably [have] something to do with creating art, similar to someone being a writer or an artist." He more pointedly suggested creative professions lend themselves to flexible ideas of gender. Indeed, a number of the men were critical of hegemonic conceptions of masculinity. Adrian said: "I really hate it when men come across in a very masculine way. At least in the mainstream culture, you get so much of that where things have to be so masculine. Anyone who flirts with the notion of femininity is laughed at in our culture." Music provided a safer context for these men to express their alternate (and subordinated) masculinities and to otherwise play with gender (Ramirez 2012).

The men suggested that men musicians are more likely to exhibit two particular elements of nonnormative masculinities in their identities: a heightened emotionality and the incorporation of elements of femininity into their identities. First, numerous men described musicians as being more attuned to their emotions (Bannister 2006). The musicians who were songwriters themselves saw the act of composing music as more than simply a talent. Instead, it was aligned not only with the ability to be in touch with one's emotions but essentially as the only suitable outlet to discover their complicated emotions. Furthermore, they often framed emotionality in music as a necessity for men's survival in their worlds. Israel, a songwriter himself, said:

> The people who write [music] for bands are complex people in the sense that a lot of times they are confused. They are in touch with their emotions, but they also feel the need to express this masculinity. And I do think the history of rock has tended to lead towards that obviously, with the amount of male bands as opposed to females. I don't know why that is. I think it started off as a real male thing, a tough guy, rebellious James Dean kind of thing, what with Elvis and all. But you always see even the toughest guys writing in these bands. You have

to be in touch with your emotions, but I don't think you have to understand [them]. There's always been that confused sort of thing, with Nirvana and others. A lot of people who have a mental imbalance, they can't deny their emotions, they tend to be run by them. If you're run by your emotions, you can't turn it off. So if you have any musical talent, you put that together. . . . You're in touch with your emotions, but what people don't realize is that you're in touch with the whole spectrum.

Stewart spoke about men musicians' emotional lives as well:

The people who are really into [music], yeah, I'd say are pretty in touch with their emotions. I mean I think everybody is in touch with their emotions, but [musicians] have got that outlet. And it's *public*, which is different. Because a football player dude is not necessarily less emotional about things than a rocker dude. It's just that where you see him when he's in his [element,] the football player's hurting people on the field. And with [musicians], there's this guy singing about his girlfriend on stage. [They both] may be the same person offstage and [off] the field. But that's what he's showing people while on stage.

Both Israel and Stewart saw musicians are more emotional, implying their masculinities to be more aligned with normative conceptions of femininity. At the same time they suggest that emotionality also has a masculine dimension. They in some ways were critiquing our cultural markers of emotion and love as being culturally tied to women (Cancian 1986). Musicianhood by default requires a more public performance of the innovative masculinity (Cohen 1997). They may in actuality not be too different from, nor necessarily more emotional than the "average" man, but their role as a musician requires that aspect to be demonstrated in public via their songs and musical performances. Men with similar emotive masculinities may have the protective barrier of a private professional life that does not necessitate their "disclosing" their emotions publicly with others, as is the case with musicians. In this sense, the structure of the musician role itself may require men to be more disclosing of their emotions, which in turn may alter their self-perceived masculine gender identity.

The second element that musicians recurrently saw as an ingredient of musicians' masculinities was their being prone to claim elements of normative femininity in their identities (Ramirez 2012). Many musicians, such as Isaac, discussed the ways in which the masculine world of rock requires a significant deal of femininity in its performance:

As maybe a consequence of having musicians like Alice Cooper or David Bowie who blend femininity with masculinity, is that somehow dressing like a woman is about the most masculine thing that could ever happen. I think a lot of "dude" dudes are just such dudes that they'd probably be afraid to put themselves out there to have their masculinity dissected. So yeah, I think that there're a lot of guys in bands who are probably more inclined to [do things] like cross their legs like a girl and even look like a girl and not think twice about it. Whereas, dudes like your typical [college] football fan would never do that because it might make them perceived as girly or [gay]. In that sense, guys that play in bands are probably more comfortable with themselves.

Musicians may have more security in their masculinities, thus warding off any negative reactions of their identities by outsiders. What is a negative repercussion to most men in US culture (having one's masculinity critiqued or marked as deficient) is a badge of honor for musicians. Seth was one musician who has particularly reveled in blurring the gender lines:

SETH: I'm very outgoing and very flashy. I've got some makeup right here. I wear makeup and put on these crazy clothes and go out.
MR: Not just when you're playing [onstage with your band]?
SETH: Not just when I'm playing. I probably get more ridicule than anyone else I know in Athens. I get accosted on the street if I'm walking from one bar to the next by myself. People yell, "Fucking faggot!" All this crazy shit. I love it though. Before I would be like, "Oh God. I'm scared to death. These people think I'm weird."
MR: Who's saying that stuff to you?
SETH: Anybody. We have rednecks rolling down their windows driving past me yelling that shit. One of the more interesting ones was—this was when I was so camped out that it was ridiculous. I'm wearing these platform boots that have a three-inch heel on them. I'm wearing bright red pants, this fur jacket, I've got makeup on. These guys are walking towards me, and I'm walking by myself from the Go Bar to probably the 40 Watt. These guys coming towards me, and I'm like, "Oh, shit. I'm gonna get heckled." These guys were some of the most homophobic people ever. As soon as they get up to me, I'm literally about from me to you [about two feet away]. The guy looks up and he notices me. He's like, "What the fuck? Is it a man or a woman?" He yells it in my face as they're walking past me. They're all yelling at me. The other guy is like, "I don't know, but it looks good enough to fuck." I was like, "I love that shit."

Seth does not limit his gender bending exclusively to the stage. Instead, he often ventures out in makeup, heels, and other markers of femininity. In this sense, his gender bending is not limited only to his stage performance with his band, but is part of his day-to-day public identity. His appearance has consequences not only to his masculinity, but also potentially to his safety. He anticipates negative reactions—even harassment and the threat of assault—in public settings, particularly those outside of musically centered contexts, but ultimately redefines those interactions as positive.

The Dualists

Upon closer inspection of men's lengthy and complex discussions of masculinities in the music world, the story that emerges is more convoluted. Almost half of the men (15 of 33) felt that they and other men in music scenes enacted a range of masculinities that incorporated both traditional and nontraditional qualities of masculinities (Connell 1995). Rather than seeing musical masculinities as wholly innovative, they instead emphasized a duality in their masculinities (Ramirez 2012). Many men with whom I spoke believed not only that men musicians exhibited a range of gender performances, but also that most enacted both hypermasculine *and* hyperfeminine attributes.

What distinguishes these characterizations from those described above by the "innovators" is their seeing musician masculinities as comprising the entire spectrum of both masculinity and femininity, often simultaneously. They spoke of men musicians as comprising sets of dualities that, at first glance, do not seem reconcilable. The men described themselves, their bandmates, and other musicians generally, as enacting normative and transgressive gender performances simultaneously. They characterized men who performed music as being "meatheads" but having meaningful lives, as being narcissistic but having intense empathy for others, as being selfish but antimaterialistic, and as adhering to normative masculine expectations while adopting feminine personas on stage. For many men, of whom Owen is one, they believed these contradictory dualities at play were typical of men who create art:

> I think that is the essential duality of being a rock-and-roll musician. That's what makes the best rock-and-roll musicians great. It's that combination of toughness and vulnerability. Think about the way that you perceive David Bowie, especially in the 70s: the rock-and-roll animal, [during the] *Diamond Dogs* [era], but also in drag. That duality intrigues people and draws them in because they are experiencing that on their own. And then when you're a teenager, you're overflowing with emotions and you feel both like your balls weigh five pounds each, but also that you just want to be loved by someone. That's rock and roll in a nutshell. I think that [my band] is the most overpowering, heaviest band out here [today]. It's very masculine. We're all pretty much guy guys. We work on our own cars. Everybody but me has a physically laborious job. But we also feel things really intensely. Every one of us has wrestled with depression and every one of us has wrestled with anxiety and every one of us wants more than anything to be with someone who loves us and to be safe in the world. But part of being in [my band] is understanding that you're never really safe. Life is a constant struggle

against irrelevance, against superficiality, against being co-opted and sucked into a life that doesn't allow you to completely be who you are. So I think that both of those stereotypes, they are both completely wrong and absolutely right. I think the central conflict of being in rock and roll, being a rock-and-roll musician is that kind-hearted killer mystique. And all the great rock-and-roll artists personify that.

Owen's analysis of the contradictions in musicians' gender identities mirrors dueling expectations faced by men in contemporary society. Particularly among musicians, accepting one's vulnerability is increasingly more acceptable for men today. In many ways, divulging one's vulnerability as a man (and doing so through music) may be a therapeutic solution for dealing with the unattainable demands of hegemonic masculinity. Masculinity, in this music scene in particular, seems to be constructed in opposition to hegemonic ideals of appropriate manhood (Connell 1987).

The men felt positioned in dual worlds—the musical world and what some jokingly referred to as the "real" world—with competing prescriptions of appropriate masculinities in each. Musicians deviated from normative masculinities in some ways but still clung to elements of them in other ways. While men who play music may very well be distinct from nonmusical men, they believed the idea of a stereotypical gender-inclusive musician to be a myth. Aldo said: "That's the thing. Everybody has this picture of the stereotypical musician, but I don't think there is one. There are probably some that are real sensitive and poetic guys. There are also the macho, metalhead guys who like sports and drinking beer and that other side. It's a wide spectrum of people. You can't just put musicians in a [single] category."

The dual worlds they lived in complicated their ideas of masculinities. The more fluid opportunities they felt they had to construct innovative masculinities in the music world did not necessarily erase the normative prescriptions to which they had been socialized to value and instill in themselves in larger culture. In other words, though possibilities for new masculinities existed due to their participation in music, it continued to be a challenge to fully cast aside the adherence to normative masculinities. Some musicians even recognized such contradictory constructions in the larger history of rock. Paul believed contemporary musicians to perhaps be more innovative in their constructions of masculinities, but suggested they still stem from a particular masculine prototype in rock culture: "Especially if you're a songwriter, writing songs and performing them might separate you emotionally from the average man. But there's also a very rock-and-roll, macho image to playing guitar. And no one is immune to that. No matter how sensitive you are, you're connected to a certain history, there's a certain phallic-ness to the whole process that is inescapable. So there's a couple of different things going on." These musicians were attentive to the nuances of musicians' masculinities. They were not necessarily entirely traditional nor unequivocally revolutionary. Like most identities in transition, they borrowed elements from multiple tropes, often in ways that mirrored and complicated existing images of men and masculinity. These gender identities among men were complicated, exhibiting a "both/and" quality.

The musicians with whom I spoke suggested the music world to be a site in which *purposely* playing with gender is standard (Schippers 2002). Men musicians "do" masculinity in nonnormative ways. Some performed in makeup, in feminine clothing, and adopted androgynous personas on stage in other ways. Charlie liked the ways his band challenged gender: "I don't think the dudes in [my band] intentionally say, 'We're going to present ourselves this way and write songs like this [in a nonnormative way].' But at the same time, what I think is cool about [my band] is there is sort of that sexy, androgynous thing that maybe fosters some comments or at least gets people talking about it, or even thinking about it." Some musicians who wittingly enacted subordinate masculinities purposely did so in reaction to stereotypical images of men in rock, as discussed previously. Marcus recognized male heterosexist sexuality as a historic core component of rock musicians. He believed it still to be the case today, although bands are increasingly playing with notions of gender and sexuality. For instance, he cited a local band in which the lead singer intentionally complicated ideas of masculine sexuality. He attended a show in which "the singer would come into the audience and sort of just feel up on guys. Not to say that he was gay, but [he would do it] just because the guys were uncomfortable with that. And that's entertaining. That's what he's trying to do. He's trying to make people upset." This singer was trying to "make people upset" by disturbing heteronormative expectations of male sexuality in rock culture. In other interviews, a number of men critiqued musicians who were in bands to increase their access to sex with women. While Marcus's example does parallel traditional enactments of sexuality on stage, it does so in a way that threatens ideas of hegemonic (heterosexual) masculinity. The singer, according to Marcus, was not intending to flirt with men in the audience, but rather to tease the boundaries of acceptable masculinity. The stage is literally a platform on which to engage in "gender maneuvering" and reshape the gendered order (Schippers 2002).

Playing with masculinity in new ways was not limited to the stage only, though. For a few men, their participation in the music world led them to rethink and reevaluate larger identity issues such as sexuality. Nearly all of the musicians identified as heterosexual, either directly or implicitly. A handful of men, however, had more complex sexual identities. They wavered between identifying their sexuality through their practices versus defining them by their attraction (or possibilities of sexual attraction).[7] Their making sense of their sexualities was tied to heternormative practices of sexuality. Seth's take on his sexuality illustrates the nuanced understanding he has of male sexuality:

Women are the pinnacle of [beauty]. What about another man? The knee jerk reaction in our [culture] is no! Can a man be attractive? Can I admit that? I'm not attracted to men at all, but I'm attracted to anything living. I can find a man just as beautiful as a woman because I allow myself and free myself of that stigma that men can't find other men attractive. Once I allowed myself to do that, that brought up a lot of difficult decisions. A lot of it informed my concept of sexuality. That's what got me interested in reading things about human sexuality. It's interesting to see how different cultures view sexuality.... There's no right or wrong to it. I came to the conclusion and I was like, "Well, I'm going to open myself up for anything goes. I guess I'm going to experiment." Which is funny because a lot of the bands that I like all have the sexual ambiguity. There's this British band from the '90s called Suede . . . [whose lead singer] said, "I'm a bisexual man who has never had a homosexual experience." When I found out that he said that, I thought that's kind of how I feel. I think the possibility of me being attracted to a man is possible, but it's never happened. I've toyed with the idea and wondered how that would work out, but at the same time, it has never felt right.

Seth's sexuality was fluid, complex, and still in process. He was comfortable enough to acknowledge his seeing men as potentially attractive, though he had never felt compelled to initiate a romantic or physical relationship with a man. He did, however, ultimately identify as bisexual. In US culture, sexual identity is defined by practice (Fausto-Sterling 2003). Seth and a few other musicians were more nuanced in their examination of sexual identities and practices. Participation in music opened them up to new ideas and considerations beyond the normative practices they had internalized up this point in their lives.

Many musicians performed masculinity in contradictory ways. A number of men maintained a masculine front externally, but simultaneously highlighted their emotional vulnerability through music, two seemingly contradictory notions of their musical and gendered performance. Ben, whose band had a reputation of not taking themselves too seriously, consistently straddled the line between normative and novel masculinities. He emphasized the contradictory nature of his band: "A lot of [my band] is very much the masculine, power riff end of the spectrum, [but] it's very tongue-in-cheek. . . . It's all done with a sense of humor. . . . I've never genuinely been like, 'Let's write a "dude song."' And, you know, that would be funny if we wrote a 'dude song.' We would do it intentionally—because it's funny—not because we're tough." Ben's performance in his band (both in terms of music, as well as gender) complicated ideas of masculinity. While his band has a solidly masculine sound—loud guitars and aggressive rhythms—they also were critical of hege-monic masculinity. Likewise, their masculine performances were intended to be satirical critiques of hegemonic masculinity. While some men in female-dominated lines of work are "ironically feminine," musicians at times seem to be *ironically masculine* (Robinson et al. 2011: 42). In a site in which hyper-masculinity has been the norm for generations, these musicians mimicked hegemonic masculinity in an attempt to reveal its fabrication (Ramirez 2012). Though men revised constructions of masculinity within music culture—with clear sanctions in some instances—their nonnormative masculinities remain fairly safe and quite privileged. While men did complicate gender at the indi-vidual and performative level, perhaps even at the cultural level in their music, their revolts in masculinity were not entirely disruptive to the system of gen-der as a whole.

The Pastiche Masculinity

The men with whom I spoke, though they shared some overlap in their backgrounds, interests, and career trajectories, expressed a varied approach both to the extent to which they saw the relevance of masculinity in music and especially in the ways in which they constructed their personal mascu-line identities. This is not entirely surprising as gender is easily manipulated and reconstructed regularly in culture. The musicians, like a number of other people today, have significant agency in piecing together their gender identi-ties. The musicians used a pastiche or "pick-and-choose" approach in recon-ciling their individual masculine gender identities. The world in which they lived may have eased those possibilities, as they were aware of and observant of other musicians who played with gender in creative ways.

There may be a payoff for such identity constructions. Other research has illustrated how gender conformity has different consequences for men and women on the job. In some contexts, men who enact cultural expectations of femininity may be regarded more positively than women who do so (Meltzer and McNulty 2011). Such may similarly be the case for musicians. Their work requires a softer masculinity in which they "wear their hearts on their sleeve" through the emotional and artistic vulnerability inherent in their work. Men who perform music were, by and large, rewarded for nonconformist displays of masculinity.

Musicians' constructions of their masculinities prompt a final important question: Which influenced which? Did their participation in music prompt men in their innovative masculinities, or did their atypical masculinities in place beforehand play a role in their moving onto musical pathways? A few thoughtful musicians voiced this "chicken or the egg" question during our interviews, a question I had not considered up to that point. The musicians who addressed this issue were attentive to the complexities in their development over their life courses. Nate was one musician who had spent time considering the relationship between his masculinity and his life outcome as a musician: "I have always been not-so-masculine because I have always been small. I think that being a musician has something to do with it, but I think that always being a small guy has always made me not very 'uggg-uggg!' I definitely don't think that I'm as cavemanish as a lot of other people. It's not necessarily because of the music. I think [understanding] who I was as a guy came first. Maybe that's *why* I got into music in the first place." He sees his physicality as a factor potentially having influenced his masculinity, which in turn may have triggered his venture into music and the arts. Musicians, Nate included, did not imagine the relationship to work in a simple, unilateral direction, but instead imagined both their interests in music and their subversive masculinities to have mutually influenced one another. In other words, they presumed that their masculinities were somewhat distinct from their peers early in life, and music may have prompted them to relish those differences and accept their nonnormative gender identities.

Conclusion

In conclusion, two general factors come to light in men's experiences in the music world. First, the pathways to musical participation are structurally and culturally quite direct for men. Men begin their discovery of music early in life, often in the context of the family, but not entirely. Many cite their social networks as key to their delving into learning instruments. This is not an isolated activity, as many of the boys develop their musicality alongside their peers, nearly all of whom are of the same gender. While their exploration in music is outside the structure of school and other adult-controlled settings, they nonetheless mimic the confines of formal organizations in the extent to which boys have more access to and an easier "fit" into the music world than do girls. The informal organization of music leisure activities is one still coded with masculinity, albeit one in contrast to the hegemonic form most valued in adolescence worlds. Though men stay off the beaten path to pursue music as they venture into adulthood, they ultimately remain on a highly regimented path of masculinity. The sociohistorical and cultural legacy of rock is one founded on masculinity. The experiences of the rock musician are generally organized by masculinity. It requires skill, risk taking, independence, and persistence, among other traits. In a word, musicianhood requires masculinity.

Second, musicians used musical milieus as a foundation on which to construct a range of masculinities. Most men used music to build new, innovative masculinities that challenged customary conceptions of appropriate manhood. Other men, in contrast, used their statuses as musicians to maintain normative masculinities, thus reinforcing the construction of masculinity as independent and generally opposed to femininity. While the music world is a site in which men may feel freedom to play with gender, they have been historically constrained by normative masculinities and expected to perform them in particular manners. Their masculinities intertwined aspects of both hegemonic conceptions with their subordinated innovations. As a result, they simultaneously reaffirm and challenge normative constructions of masculinity.

5

Women and the
Challenges of Musical
Life Course Trajectories
• •

In the early 2010s, electro-pop witnessed a resurgence in the independent rock world. Two notable acts, Grimes and Chvrches, each released impressive albums (*Visions* and *The Bones of What You Believe*, respectively), generating lavish praise in both underground and mainstream music outlets. Grimes's Claire Boucher and Chvrches' Lauren Mayberry made the press rounds, and attention quickly and predictably (unfortunate as it may be) detoured to the objectification of both women. Both Boucher and Mayberry were reduced to young, attractive, thin women who men (and sometimes women) both sexualized and infantilized. Commentary, particularly from anonymous "fans" on their respective social media outlets, was unfettered. Some offered unsolicited counsel: "It's just one of those things you'll need to learn to deal with. If you're easily offended, then maybe the music industry isn't for you." Online responses to Mayberry's retorts turned vile: "This isn't rape culture. You'll know rape culture when I'm raping you, bitch."

Both artists found themselves in a precarious position. Mayberry admitted the toll such commentary had on her mental health, writing in a piece for *Guardian*, "I am embarrassed to admit that I have had more than one prolonged toilet cry and a 'Come on, get a hold of yourself, you got this' conversation with myself in a bathroom mirror when particularly exasperated and tired out. But then, after all the sniffling had ceased, I asked myself: why should I cry about this? Why should I feel violated, uncomfortable and

131

demeaned? Why should we all keep quiet?" Boucher posted an open letter on her Tumblr, a veritable inventory of issues she refuses to accept any longer: "i dont want to be molested at shows or on the street by people who perceive me as an object that exists for their personal satisfaction. . . . I'm tired of men who aren't professional or even accomplished musicians continually offering to 'help me out' (without being asked), as if i did this by accident and i'm gonna flounder without them. or as if the fact that I'm a woman makes me incapable of using technology. I have never seen this kind of thing happen to any of my male peers. . . . I'm sad that my desire to be treated as an equal and as a human being is interpreted as hatred of men, rather than a request to be included and respected" [sic]. Episodes such as these underscore the recurring issues that women have come to expect in the male bastion that is the music world. While pop artist after pop artist has regularly voiced the "I'm not a feminist, but . . ." disclaimer (often with little to no understanding of feminism's basic tenets), Boucher and Mayberry have tenaciously voiced their frustrations, as women, as artists, and as women artists.

In Chapter 4, I examined men's life course experiences to magnify the experiences, opportunities, and limited constraints they faced as they came of age in musical contexts. In this chapter, I focus my analytical lens on the gendered life course experiences women musicians face as they forge into musical careers, paying particular attention to the ways in which coming of age as a girl and moving into adulthood as a woman influences the arcs of women's life course pathways into music. Throughout this chapter, I examine women's opportunities and constraints that structure their experiences in the music world, though women face far greater of the latter in contrast to men. I highlight women's dominant inroads to the music world in adulthood, as well as the role interpersonal relationships play in this process. Finally, I examine musicians' awareness of and speculations on the gender imbalance in the music scene.

As Boucher and Mayberry's cases suggest, women musicians are prone to experiences in the music world that can be sexist, misogynist, complicated, and threatening. Their involvement in music can also liberating, allowing women to create not only musical art, but also a vivid life experience that is personally satisfying. As I will show, women's participation in male-centric musical landscapes is about gender, but it is also about other dimensions of their positionality.

Women's Delayed Starting Points

Musical trajectories that enable pursuing musical careers in adulthood do not simply crop up overnight. Like any other occupational trajectory, they unfold over time. As the men's stories in Chapter 4 demonstrate, starting points were often situated in preadolescence. Women, however, had a somewhat different experience. In the middle school years—the first opportunity for many of them to begin sampling a range of extracurricular activities—most of the women participated in a number of school-affiliated activities, typically drama and theater, athletics, cheerleading, and academic clubs. Two-thirds of the women were involved in school-structured music programs earlier in life. In contrast to men, however, women were less inclined to join the school band and learn instruments, though a few of them did. Instead, they were more likely to participate in activities that concentrated on the vocal aspect: chorus, show choir, and/or musicals.

> JADE: Well, as early as I could, I was in the school chorus. And then I also lived in North Carolina and [there] I was in a show choir—
> MR: What's that?
> JADE: It's like singing and dancing with partners. It's very lame. [laughs] But I got to [explore] singing.

Though Jade jokingly remembers the school chorus as "very lame," it was important and influential to her eventual development in rock music, though she would not take note of these links until well later in life. Her interest in chorus also illustrates a more general theme among women: as early as adolescence, women were less likely to specialize in learning an instrument in contrast to the boys. Historically, music culture has mirrored this trend (Groce and Cooper 1990): likely not accidentally, but illustrative of the extent to which early exposure to music influences—or in the case of women, may limit—their participation in bands later in life.

Women's musical interests outside of school settings were fairly similar to men's early in life. At roughly the same time periods in childhood, girls began developing interests in music. Similar to boys, this was often the result of early familial experiences in the home. Their parents' love of music had a rub-off effect on the girls. Like boys, the church played a role in their general developing interest in music, particularly singing. At this point in life, girls were on virtually the same life course musical pathways as boys.

However, a crucial difference in women's life courses that offset their entrance to the music world occurred during adolescence. While the boys often were devoted to music—some described themselves as "obsessed"—the girls often had a wider range of interests and activities in which they participated (Eccles et al. 2003). Of course, the girls' explorations down multiple avenues was beneficial, as they began discovering many potential interests for the adolescent and early adult years.[1] This, however, was at the expense of music. While music was on their radar in the childhood and adolescent years, it typically was not the single or "obsessive" focus as it often was for boys.[2] Typical of many women musicians, Julia talked about her many interests during adolescence, only one of which was music:

JULIA: My stepfather, he really kind of pushed me into sports. He was a very commanding figure in my life at the time, so I pursued it wholly. There was a while where I was very passionate and obsessed with basketball—

MR: Was this in high school or middle school?

JULIA: From like [age] 10 to 17, something like that. I practiced all the time. I guess I started getting serious about it when I was about 12 maybe. . . . I just slept it, ate it, breathed it. At the time, I was like, "I'm going to play college basketball." That's what I wanted to do so. I practiced every day and every night. I wish I would have put that energy into what were my obvious leanings [when I was] very young, like I said I was writing poetry and I liked to draw and I loved music.

While she did enjoy the sport at the time, she now wishes she had stood her own ground and put her adolescent energy toward her true passion—the arts and music. A number of other women were similar in regretting not putting their commitment toward music earlier in life.

Relatively early in life, both girls and boys began learning their first instruments. Again, there are general patterns among these experiences. Many children, regardless of gender, began learning their first instruments in the elementary school years. For nearly all of them, the instrument was a classical one, more often than not, the piano. Women began learning their first instrument in the early elementary school years, typically at age seven. This is, on the average, two years later than the men began. Some of the women even had a much later start. For example, Jane is a self-described "late bloomer" who didn't learn her first instrument until much later after graduating from high school. Other women voiced similar sentiments.

The typical entry to musical pathways for women contrasted sharply with men's experiences in one most consequential way: the starting point at which they began to actively learn rock instruments. While all of the men and most of the women had learned their first instrument by the end of middle school, many girls did not pick up their first "rock instrument" that soon. Girls transitioned to rock instruments much later than did boys, during high school at the earliest, though even that was rare. Parents often prodded their children—both girls and boys—away from rock instruments early on, only to later acquiesce to their increasing and recurring requests. For example, Annabel said: "I guess I first started being interested in playing music probably when I was about 10 or 11 and I wanted to take guitar lessons. And I told my mom that. And she, for whatever reason, didn't want me to take guitar lessons. She wanted me to take piano lessons. So I ended up taking about four years of piano lessons and then ended up getting tired of it. I mean, I really liked it, but it just wasn't what I wanted to do. After that, it was okay for me to take guitar lessons, so I started taking guitar lessons when I was about fifteen."

While parents were the obstacle impeding some girls to switch to rock instruments, similar to Annabel's situation, a greater number of girls' delayed adoption of rock instruments was more self-induced. They were less likely than boys to have rock instruments on their radar early in life. As a result, it was not even a possibility that most girls considered during the middle school and teenage years. While the women musicians with whom I spoke could not say precisely why, some of them suggested it was at least partially due to the masculine culture of rock music. While they did not necessarily think they had no place in bands, the rock world was categorically regarded as a boys' club (Cohen 1997; Frith 1981; Frith and McRobbie 1990).

Most women eventually developed an interest in pursuing a rock instrument, albeit much later in life. The main consequence was that their transition to learning those new instruments was delayed in comparison to men. For most women, it was not until well later in life, typically the college years, that they took agency to pursue their rock instrument of choice. Like many women, Jane had been involved in music throughout a majority of her life, but did not learn her first instrument until the emerging adulthood years.

JANE: [My first instrument was] actually the bass.
MR: Oh, the bass? So how old were you?
JANE: Twenty-one, twenty-two. I was a late bloomer. I was in chorus all
    throughout elementary, junior high, [and] part of high school. But I was
    actually a visual artist, focused more on that. I was [also] in marching
    band, on the flag team. . . . I wanted to play in a band for a long time. I
    [eventually] met this guy who was a friend of a friend. He played gui-
    tar and he had a bass that he said he could sell me for twenty dollars. I
    [bought] it, and I just started.

Women learned the basics of their rock instruments in two main ways. First, some were self-taught. A few may have been in enrolled in lessons, but they were often a "joke" and they decided they would make more headway by learning on their own. Lilly said:

In high school, that's when I got a guitar and started playing. I started out on the acoustic because some of those hair metal bands at the time had their ballad songs, and I wanted to learn how to play those. I learned it on my own. They had a deal at the music store where my parents bought the guitar, that if you bought a guitar at Christmas time, you would get a year of free lessons, but the lessons were a complete joke. Half the time they didn't have a teacher. And when they did have a teacher, it was just some twenty-year-old dude who didn't really care. . . . I didn't learn anything about theory. Not anything. I finally just stopped going because it was pointless. I figured it out [on my own] over time.

Others, however, learned with the assistance of others—often the men they were dating or other musicians they knew. Paige, for instance, said: "His band broke up. And it was just me and him hanging out. We had been dating at that point for [some time]. We always knew, 'Oh, that might be such a bad idea if we were in a band together.' But we liked the same exact music in such a ridiculous way. Our tastes are pretty much identical. So it was just like, 'Fine. Your band broke up. I have [an instrument], so why don't you just start teaching me how to play?'"

The above discrepancies are notable in assessing gender disparities in rock. These experiences may explain women's lesser numbers in the population of musicians. They may also explain women's limited variability in instrumentation in rock bands later in life (Fournet 2010). Finally, women's inexperience may lend itself to their relying on men for musical introductions.

The First Rock Band

A critical turning point in pursuing musical careers involves joining one's first rock band. Women became involved in their first bands later than men did. The typical trajectory for boys, as discussed in the previous chapter, was to join their first band during the middle school years. By high school, 18 of the 22 men had played in at least one band. Women, however, joined their first bands at much later ages. In stark contrast to men, not one woman started her first band in middle school. Again, in contrast to men, only four women participated in rock bands in high school. Their experience typically included playing a handful of parties or talent shows. Lauren gained experienced during adolescence, with her band achieving significant exposure: "In middle school, I wasn't really involved in any extracurricular activities related to school. I just did my own thing and took guitar lessons on the weekends. In high school, I was in an all-girl band. . . . where our gigs took up most of our time [away] from school. It was cool though. All the teachers thought it was awesome. And everyone thought we were going to be famous because we had gigs every weekend and were [promoted] on the radio."

While four women had performed in rock bands by the time they graduated high school, the norm for women was to not join a band until their post–high school years. The remaining eleven women started their first band well into the college years. It was almost necessary for women to be ensconced in the college world to secure opportunities to join a band. It was exceedingly difficult for women to do so outside of the intersections of the college and music worlds. These worlds overlap, and women's experiences deemed it necessary to be involved in both environments to make their entrance to music more direct. Such was not the case for men, as they typically did not need to use their access to the college world to enter the music world. (The men were more likely than women to have never attended college, yet still pilot their entrance into the music world with relative ease.) In this sense, entering the music world required navigating two arenas—the college world and the music scene—for women. Only one woman, Jane, started her band after high school removed from the college context. She started a band with acquaintances with whom she was connected in the music scene—and she was the single exception to the gendered trend of women's requisite music scene access via college networks.

Furthermore, while men had extensive experience in a few, if not several, bands in their pasts, women had much more limited experiences in bands. My conversation with singer-keyboardist Jade took me by surprise:

MR: And is this the first serious band that you've been in?
JADE: Yeah, it's the *only* band I've never been actually.
MR: Oh, it's the *only* band you've ever been in? Wow!
JADE: Yeah, I know! [It's] kinda crazy.

Three other women had the same one-and-only-one-band history, but not one single man had this type of experience. Clearly, women have shorter tenures in bands and fewer total bands of which they have been members. Similar to Jane's experience described above, Emma *learned* her first instrument as she joined her first band: "Actually the summer before I came to Athens, I bought my first bass. It was a cheap one. I never picked it up [though]. I just didn't have time to think about it. It was cool that I had this instrument, but there was nothing really motivating me to learn it. And to learn an instrument, you have to really be motivated by yourself or through others. You've really gotta want to learn how to play it yourself. So, yeah, [when I joined] the band actually was when I first started learning how to play."

Though this type of experience was not typical of all women with whom I spoke, it was *only* women who voiced such histories. Men, in contrast, never learned an instrument at the time during which they joined their first band. Since women were about the same age as the men were when they first became interested in music and about the same age when most learned their first instrument, it was surprising that they joined their first bands at considerably later ages than did most men. Several factors seem to contribute to this difference. First, many women didn't learn their first rock instrument until well after men did. While men typically picked up their first rock instrument in middle school, some women did not learn theirs until much later, and for women musicians such as Emma and others, until they actually joined their first band. Second, peer networks may affect the age at which each gender typically joined their first band. As discussed in the previous chapter, men typically learned their instrument with the help of male peers and music was a centerpoint of same-sex peer activities for the young men. Only one woman, in contrast, discussed playing and learning the guitar with the assistance of a peer in high school. The majority of women develop their playing on their own, sometimes through private lessons, but more often through trial and error. Adolescent girls are less likely to play rock instruments (especially the guitar) and are less likely to have friends who play rock instruments (again, especially the guitar). As a result, women do not typically learn how to play rock instruments until much later—often when they develop mixed-gender friendships after high school. Their delayed entrance to the music world is due the lack of opportunity to do so. There are virtually no avenues for women to explore music until they exit high school for the college context that has fewer obstacles blocking their entry.

Women's Inroads to Music

The degree of visibility and prestige among the various roles in the rock band is directly tied to status and gender. Clawson's (1999) analysis of women in the Chicago rock music scene illustrates the clustering of women in particular roles in music to be tied to their lesser status and compromised access to the music world. Furthermore, women's lesser prestige in rock is tied specifically to their instrument specialization: the bass guitar. These trends are mirrored among the musicians with whom I spoke as well. Women never took lead on the masculinity-imbued instruments of lead guitarists or drummers. Those spaces were reserved exclusively for men. Alternatively, women were more likely to enter bands by concentrating on two particular aspects of specialization: keyboards and/or vocals. Exactly one-third (5 of 15) of the women play the keyboard and/or synthesizer in their bands. This is in stark contrast to the men, only one of whom plays the keyboard and synthesizer in his band today.

To be clear, it was not that women were not interested in the guitar. A good many of them owned and played guitar on their own. They, however, were not able to find inroads to bands via those instruments. The reasons were twofold. First, the market was saturated with guitar players. Most of them were men, and they often "hoarded" those positions in bands for themselves. Second, and perhaps more informative, the women often—as a result of their delayed introduction to the guitar—were not nearly as well versed in guitar as were their male counterparts, who often had an additional five to ten years of experience

FIGURE 6   Nico Cashin of Psychic Hearts performing at the Caledonia
Lounge (Photo by Mike White, deadlydesigns.com)

on the instrument. By simply having more time to experiment with the guitar, men were advantaged in securing those roles in bands.

The bass guitar, in contrast, was deemed easier to learn. Furthermore, it is not considered "all that fun to play," as some musicians who had experience on the instrument suggested. In this sense, despite it being a historically requisite instrument in a rock band, it is less prestigious. (In recent years, some rock bands even forgo a bass player altogether, the White Stripes being among the most famous. It is partly shtick, but also highlights the extent to which particular instruments, the bass in particular, are disposable.) Many women, such as Lauren, stumbled into opportunities that prompted them to switch to the bass: "I actually never learned the bass. I started out as a guitarist and played [guitar] in my previous bands. I was always interested in rhythm and when I was asked to play bass [in a previous band], I was pretty excited and stuck with it ever since." Among a number of the women with whom I spoke, the bass was initially not their instrument of choice, but instead developed through either limited opportunities as guitarists in bands and/or other musicians' pushing them to switch to the bass.

Also deemed feminine is the keyboard, another prime avenue for entrance to the rock world for women. In a majority of bands with a keyboard (all bands except for one), women were responsible for those instruments. The women similarly frame their instrumentalization as supplemental, but not crucial, to the band and their songs. Most keyboard players spoke of their contribution as adding touches that often made the songs unique. Similar to women bass players, their instruments—and hence the women's contributions in general—are not regarded as the center point of the band. Women have a growing presence in rock bands, but they are in downgraded roles. These instruments, however, are critical to women's entrance to the rock world. Their odds of landing positions in bands mount when they take on instruments in which fewer musicians specialize. Women, in some ways, are simply playing the odds in their favor—learning instruments that have the smallest pool from which bands recruit to fill those necessary, though undervalued, positions. Knowledge of and experience with piano-based instruments may allow women the greatest opportunities for entry into bands, but, at the same time, women's specialization in keyboards and synthesizers may limit their options in rock bands, since keyboards are not considered essential.

Vocals provide a similar illustration, yet one that is more highly regarded in the bands. As described earlier, women's musical training early in life often included a vocal component. About half (7 of 15) of the women specialized in vocals in school-structured music activities early in life. This trend continued and perhaps facilitated the beginnings of their musical aspirations in the rock world, as 60 percent (9 of 15) sing in their bands. Singing is an entry point for women into musical activities, both in high school and later as performers in rock bands. Women singers are in more secure, more valued, and more highly visible positions when they are lead vocalists.

Mentoring Relationships

A mainstay of musicians' life courses included the vital mentoring relationships that provided informal training to enter and succeed in music (Kay et al. 2009; McDonald et al. 2007; Philip and Hendry 2000). Women, like the men, had mentors who had helped them along their pathways of musical careers. Generally, women's mentors were drawn from the same pool as were men's.[3]

Women typically cited other local musicians from the music community as taking on informal roles as mentors, providing them with strategies as to how to book shows, organize tours, record albums, as well as other tips to further their musical careers. However, women's mentors were likely to be drawn from within membership of their bands. They often discussed how their unofficial mentors were their more-experienced bandmates.

> NIKKI: And I owe it all to this guy who was the first drummer in the band. He really got it going because I tried to for a while before and I didn't really know what to do. I was working really hard, writing songs all the time, diligent work ethic, playing and practicing, and even tried a couple of different cities out and never really got it moving. And then I moved here and met him and it was much better than [before].
>
> MR: What specifically did he set in motion?
>
> NIKKI: Just about everything—because he had done it so much before. He set up the first shows and just basic things that I didn't even think about. [He] got it moving, just made it happen, whereas I would probably just be in the practice room, writing a million songs, you know what I mean? He just got everything started.

Some women mentioned that more experienced musicians in their bands helped them personally learn about the music scene and how to deal with the business aspects of music. It appears as if women's limited experience and/or late start to the music scene made their bandmates, who were often men, more likely to take on mentoring roles. Alicia remembers:

> When I was [in my] first band in college, neither [my bandmate] Wendy or I had a lot of experience with playing shows out, but Beau did. And Beau also at that time was recording a lot of local bands, so he had a lot of contacts as far as knowing people in bands and stuff like that. So, of the few shows that we did play, I think he set up a few of them. And then the drummer in our band, who's now in lots of other bands in town, also had a lot of contacts as far as people who played music and stuff. So whatever other shows we played, he set up a lot of them too. . . . There wasn't really one person who showed me the ropes, but I think it was just more like making friends and knowing people and just learning as you went along.

Only one woman with whom I spoke identified having another woman musician as a mentor. Lilly's mentor was a musician in another town with whom she often played. In Lilly's case, her mentor counseled from a distance and was an effective mentor and advocate. With rare exception, women did not suggest having a preference for a particular gender in forging mentoring relationships. However, this was essentially a moot point as there were so few women in the music scene to potentially act as mentors for other women, even if they did have those preferences. Rather, they were likely to select mentors from within their existing peer networks who had experience in bands, a vast majority of whom were men. Hence, women de facto choose men as their mentors.

By far the most unique aspect of women's experiences with their mentors concerns the consistency with which men to whom they are romantically linked take on this role. Just over half of the women (8 of 15) cited their then boyfriends as their central mentor when they were first starting out in the music scene. The boyfriends usually were usually similarly aged as the women, but much more experienced in performing in bands. Beth, who was dating a member of another well-known Athens band some time before joining her current band, was quick to assess how their relationship benefited her music career. When I asked whether she had a mentor figure, she responded: "Yes, unfortunately so. My ex-boyfriend, when I first moved here . . . He books shows [at a local venue] and plays in a band . . . that does a lot of touring all across the US and Japan and Europe. I would be around when he was booking a lot. And I would sometimes go with him to the [music club] when he was booking and talking to other bands and seeing which bands [were suitable] and checking out the press packs in question. Just seeing which ones he and the owner of the club liked and what they didn't like helped. . . . I learned a lot from that."

These mentoring relationships were by no means quid pro quo situations, but they were indeed precarious in that women's status in bands were tied to their relationship status with their bandmates. Dating within the band was fraught with potential drama. In some instances in which the romantic relationship did not work out, potential lineup changes were options the band considered to rectify the tension. In only one instance did a band "fire" a woman after she and a male band member ended their relationship. The man's position appeared entirely secure in the band, as his departure did not seem to be an option considered. In most cases, however, bands acted with maturity in these situations and discussed the future of both members of the band (and sometimes the possibility that the entire group would disband). At the same time, romantic relationships had the potential to complicate and even end one's tenure in bands in those instances in which the couple split up. Because women's positions often seemed more precarious than the men's—women often had less prestigious roles, were not founding members, and were less likely to contribute to songwriting—women were the ones who were at greatest risk to find their tenure in the band come to an end in these predicaments.

The "Push" by Men

In addition to the mentors who provided occupational socialization to the musicians, the women noted that other men in their lives had encouraged their pursuit of music as well. Many of the women discussed how particular men in their lives nudged—and in some cases pushed—them to pursue music. Julia noted that her uncle had strongly encouraged her to invest herself in music. She said: "Once I had an interest in it, but wasn't doing so well in teaching myself, he offered me to come live with him in Jacksonville, Florida. He had a bunch of [musical] equipment there already. He was like, 'If you have any questions, ask me and I'll tell you what I know.' He was really like my mentor for learning how to play. For six months he really kind of pushed me in a sense. Just being around him and watching him helped give me that extra drive to keep doing it really, since I started so late. It was really cool. I pretty much really owe it all to him, seriously getting into music."

Similar to Julia, Kayla was frank in discussing the role her then boyfriend played in nudging her to perform music as well. Kayla remembered never truly considering forming a band herself, even though she plays instruments and considers herself to be creative. However, she grew to be enthusiastic about performing in a band once her then boyfriend suggested it, inviting her to join his already-existing band. Lilly's experience is slightly different in that her then boyfriend (and current husband) urged her to start a band of her own before eventually starting a band together: "Well, Jason taught me a lot. He was always there when I was contemplating even starting a band of my own. When I was starting [my previous band], he really encouraged me to do it. . . . He said, 'Hey, go for it!' Because I was unhappy just being in college and writing papers. I felt kind of bored and I needed to be doing something else too. He said, 'Well, play music.' And I looked around and was like, 'I'm not very happy. Maybe I *will* play music again.' [And he said,] 'Go for it!' That helped."

This prodding to pursue music was remarkably unique to women, as not one man who I spoke with ever cited a woman in his life as urging him to pursue music. This does not mean that a man's encouragement to "take the plunge" is required for women to pursue music, but the women did cite men's prodding as a factor that helped them to initially do so. In some cases, women specifically said that were it not for their boyfriends, they may have likely never joined a band. For other women, their musical trajectories were less definitively tied to men's insistence. These women instead speculated they "probably" would have pursued music on their own accord eventually, but they did specify the assistance men's encouragement was to their entering the world earlier than they imagined they otherwise would have on their own.

Greater Parental Sanctions

Eighty percent (12 of 15) of the women reported that their parents had fairly clear aspirations for their daughters' careers when they were young, and musical careers typically were not among them. While parents' ideas of their daughters' future careers did range from careers in archaeology, business, engineering, journalism, and law, among others, they were all similar in their hopes for their daughters to enter a profession of some sort. Beth's parents had clear preferences for her to pursue a career in teaching, an aspiration that apparently persists. Beth shared with me: "I still get calls from my mother saying, 'You would just make such a *good* junior high math teacher.' I mean, completely pestering me. All of her friends think that's what I'm studying. Whenever I go back to visit, they are like, 'So how is it going, studying math?' Sorry, that's just my mom's dream of what she wants me to aspire to be. No thanks."

Consistent with men, women's parents hoped that their daughters would attain a high level of education and to pursue stable, high-status careers. Women appear also to have faced more parental restrictions than did men. For example, Emma's parents assumed she would pursue a lucrative job in the business world (particularly after earning a degree in business), and they disapproved of her pursuing music as a career. When I asked how her parents reacted to her committing herself to her band, Emma admitted, "They are pissed. They hate it. They hate it so much." While some men have parents who hoped their children's music pursuits were temporary, none had experiences with their parents who expressed such strong disapproval of their musical involvement. Paige said: "I'm the oldest of four [siblings], which made it even harder telling my parents. They want me to be a good example [to my younger siblings], and here I am in [this band]. They think I'm just playing around. They know I work hard, but it's not the path they would have chosen for me. . . . When I go home, they just don't talk to me about the band. And when they do, it's kind of awkward. So they just want to pretend that nothing is going on."

Furthermore, some women had brothers invested in other artistic aspirations who witnessed a differential level of support from parents:

ABBY: I think that my family feels like I'm just kind of trying to discover myself or something. Now they don't really take it that seriously at all.

MR: Do they see it as a phase or something?

ABBY: Yes. They relate to [my brother's career choice] more. He says they have been more involved [in his pursuing a career in art]. They are more involved in the arts. They have a better appreciation for it. But not so much for [music].

Truncated Timelines for Success

The occupational trajectories for musicians are typically a sequence of steps that—with a little bit of talent and whole lot of luck, as many musicians would say—can amount to a bona fide career. Unlike normatively structured career trajectories, that of the musician is one that is widely variable.[4] Some musicians experience a lightning bolt of musical genius early in life that ignites a career in the emerging adulthood years, while others toil for decades on end with only a modicum of success. Frustration and anxiety were the normal responses, often coupled with self-doubt and serious considerations of abandoning music for another "safer" career. Musicians were notorious for making agreements—sometimes with themselves, sometimes with their families—that they would set time limits for success in the music world. Women musicians, like Emma, set self-imposed timelines for a successful musical career: "Do I think this is a phase? You know, maybe when I'm like thirty-two I'll be tired of it, but right now I'm enjoying it. I don't want kids until I'm in my thirties. I don't want to get married until I'm in my thirties. Right now I'm just on my own." Like other musicians her age, Emma realizes that emerging adulthood is the ideal (and perhaps only) time she will have to give music a chance (Ravert 2009). Delaying marriage and parenthood allows her the flexibility required to pursue a career in music. Other women were similar to Emma, imposing age-graded deadlines upon which they would exit music if they were not to reach substantive goals by then. Sometimes the goals included getting signed to a national or reputable record label, regularly touring, generating national exposure, and most often, securing steady incomes to cover their living expenses.

Age was often a central marker in deciding when success should be attained. Women, more so than men, felt apprehensive to continue to devote their time, energy, identities, and essentially the entirety of their lives to music in the absence of tangible and recognizable compensation. Though women spoke about their time limits in the music world using language of adulthood and responsibility, there seemed to be an undercurrent—voiced directly by some—of the social consequences of aging being a detriment that pushes them out of the music world. Women seem apprehensive of growing older as musicians. One half-jokingly asked, "How sexy would it be to be a forty-year-old woman to be on stage?" Other women in their early twenties suggested that if they were not successful by age thirty, they would likely quit music. Women distinguish adult femininity as incompatible with musical performance. Women's apprehension to maintaining a musician identity while growing older illustrates how an aging femininity results in a lessening of options and truncated life chances, all of which impact women earlier in life than men (Calasanti and Slevin 2001).

The Impostor Status, Self-Doubt, and the Culture of Rock

Throughout women's stories of their musical history and devotion to musical careers, there were moments of self-doubt. They were unquestionably embedded in one of the most male-dominated industries in US culture. Women musicians align with Collins' (1986) concept of the "outsider-within"—those individuals who live in border spaces in our social world, inhabiting two worlds that seldom overlap. A significant consequence of their precarious status is that they feel like impostors. Women musicians grow to suspect that they do not belong in music, as if they have duped their way inside the world, and as if they are essentially not worthy of being there. The reality in the music world is that many musicians—both women and men alike—often drown in self-doubt and anxiety that they lack what it takes to be a "real" musician. Women, however, have fiercer doubts than do their male counterparts. This may be due to their relative inexperience in contrast to men. Their token status as "the girl" in the band may also motivate their wavering status (Kanter 1977).

All musicians learn via occupational socialization to "fake it 'til you make it," but it is a more tedious process for women. Many have difficulty shaking the feeling that they are faking it—in a word, that they are inauthentic. Some women consistently felt that their comfortability, familiarity, and skill with their instruments were always deficient in comparison to their (male) bandmates. Nikki had a long history in a few bands, yet pointed out, "pretty much everybody I've ever played [in a band] with has been a better musician than me. I'm always asking, 'How do you do that?'" While she does use these contacts as opportunities to advance her guitar playing, she nonetheless remains in her mind as less proficient on the instrument. For others, their lesser contributions to songwriting exacerbated their worry. Beth said: "I think it's always been something that I enjoyed, but I'm not competent enough in songwriting by myself, the way that Brandon is with his [prolific] songwriting, I don't think I could do that. I maybe could eventually write my own [songs], but it would take me a long time to get [to that point]."

Ironically, when women were the focal point of the band—as the lead singers—they sometimes felt a heightened sense of the impostor status, characterized by the musicians as a fear of being found out as "frauds."[5] This was more likely the case for women singers who were not the primary songwriters in their bands. They often felt guilty for being center stage while they were not central to the composition of songs. They imagined that their fans may incorrectly presume that they, as the lead singers, were the primary songwriters. This assumption—one the women had no role in initiating—was the impetus for their guilt. For some women, the consequences of doubt acutely emerge when on stage. April, who was a regular contributor to songwriting in her band and a skilled guitarist, said it was "normal" for her to get nervous at the beginning of every show: "Sometimes I think, 'What am I doing? Why am I doing this?' I'm nauseous and I can't figure out why. I'm like, 'Am I crazy? Why do I do this?' But then when I get up there, I end up finding it to be really enjoyable and I like it. I always get nervous. I usually get a little a nauseous. But then once I'm up there, I'm okay." Women feel they are outsiders who have somehow managed to "infiltrate" the music world, unbeknownst to the true insiders who truly belong there. They worry that they will be exposed and banished from their bands, the music scene, and all future opportunities in music. Some women, due to this fear coupled with their doubt and other gendered obstacles, ultimately exit on their own.

Gender Imbalance in the Music Scene

Every musician with whom I spoke—regardless of gender, age, or tenure in the music industry—was well cognizant of women's lesser presence in the music world. For most of them, the gender imbalance was something of which they had long been aware and had experienced firsthand. All the women recognized that they, as women in rock, were rarities. These experiences stemmed far beyond the women's personal experiences, as many of them had women friends who were musically skilled but not in bands, nor were they even seriously considering starting one.

Women's Speculation

Women had given considerable thought as to their gender's lesser presence in the music scene. When asked why women participate less frequently in music than do men, every single woman had clear ideas on factors that contributed to women's lower likelihoods of participating in music. They all recognized the scene as a boys' club. None of the women had this realization dawn on her upon her joining her first band. More typically, women realized the male-heavy composition and uber-masculine culture of rock early in life—usually in the time span during which they became major consumers of rock music and fans of rock bands. As such, gender inequality in the music world was on their radar well before entering the music world as musicians.

The women easily constructed hypotheses to explain women's lesser participation in rock bands. Their responses gave the impression that they had spent time considering reasons for the gender imbalance both in the local scene and in rock music historically. Women often had multiple explanations for their absence in rock and framed their many speculations as working synergistically to impede women's entrance to music. All in all, women had four dominant speculations for explaining women's lesser participation in rock music, each of which I discuss in turn.

Socialization. By far, the most recurring explanation women considered was socialization. Eleven of the fifteen women, nearly 75 percent in total, cited differential gender socialization as the root of women's lesser participation in music in adolescence and adulthood. They were well aware of ways in which they and other women had far different experiences in the family, school, and peer culture that inevitably taught them different lessons than boys. Julia characterized the gender imbalance as "fairly frustrating. I think it's getting better, but I think it just kind of mirrors life [outside of] music: how we were all sort of similarly raised in this culture. I don't like to think of [women in music in terms of] as what's accepted and what's not accepted in society. But it's definitely not in balance."

They typically contrasted either their experience or that of another woman with whom they were acquainted with what they imagined the typical man's venture in music to be like. Paige explained:

> I think males come off as stronger and seem like they have more ability, even if that may not necessarily be the case. That's just how it is in society in general. Women, I feel, aren't as encouraged to try as hard to be better at what they do. I mean, I'm sure it's getting better, but it wasn't like that even in [the recent past]. Even in the Seventies, women were never encouraged to be businesswomen. They were encouraged to stay at home. They were never encouraged to be awesome at something, to work at something. You probably find more girls learning how to knit than playing music now even which is messed up, but that's just a matter of fact. It's just going to take several years before there's an equalization as far as actually getting out there and doing it. It's true, you see a lot of women at shows, but not in the band.

Paige emphasizes the similarities between women's historical exclusion from the business world with her observations of the music world. Women are pushed into traditionally feminine leisure activities that deter them from music careers in the future. Other women have sentiments similar to Jen, emphasizing gendered socialization and the extent to which "girls aren't really encouraged" to learn an instrument and/or pursue music. In contrast, men's typical socialization experiences may facilitate them in the daunting pursuit of music. To be sure, many of the women cited experiences, either due to their atypical (read: masculine) personalities, egalitarian parents, or sheer luck that provided them with what they saw as a more gender-neutral or even feminist upbringing. They were quick to regard these experiences as influencing their unique place in adulthood—in bands pursuing musical careers in a male-dominated industry.

Gendered Personalities. Second, women discussed supposed differences in each gender's personalities as contributing to differential outcomes in music. In particular, they suggested the development of women's gendered personalities as constraining their pursuit of music. Most women agreed that becoming a musician requires traditionally masculine characteristics. In particular, they emphasized the critical importance of confidence. They cited men as "typically more confident" and more likely to "come off as stronger and seem like they have more ability, even if that may not necessarily be the case." A masculine personality was key, including the provision that the successful musician be skilled at "faking" confidence even when it was lacking. Women believed men were more successful at living the adage "fake it 'til you make it." Men echoed such ideas, stating that music is more a "game of confidence" than one of skill or superior songwriting talents. Jade noted another potential gender difference that may be of consequence as well: "I do think you have to be brave to perform, no matter what you're doing. And maybe that has something to do with it. Maybe it's just more women are shy."

Jane had similar sentiments: "People still don't expect a lot of times to see female musicians. More of the musicians that I know that are out there performing, they do have to make some different decisions about having kids. . . . It seems I haven't met nearly as many women musicians, but they do seem to have a different kind of courage. I know lots of female musicians who don't play out and a lot of times [it's] because they are afraid to or because they have other [responsibilities]. I think there are a lot of really creative women out there who just aren't feeling okay for whatever reason to be in a band. It's seen as irresponsible. And it's a little more acceptable for men." Jane's comments are quite telling in theorizing women's lesser outcomes in the music scene. She highlights consequences to women who may want to pursue careers in music, particularly in terms of work-family conflict. Similar consequences may come to light in men's lives, but the choices women make have a presumably stronger impact on the question of children than do the choices of men.[6] Jane also sees pursuing music as more appropriate for men since women may be expected to a greater extent to be "responsible" more so than men their age. Because "boys will be boys," parents and other adults may be more willing to acquiesce to their pursuits of music (at least during the emerging adulthood years).

April, in contrast, characterizes women musicians who are likely to be most successful: "It's a strange field for a woman to get into. There is so much testosterone in it that you have to be tough. I think that a lot of women who play music are a lot tougher, even if you can't see it on the outside. You've got to be because you have got to stick up for yourself. You can get taken advantage of. You've got to look after yourself." Abby too emphasized the possibilities that women's hampered confidence may influence their likelihood to pursue music: "I just think that guys are typically more confident. It's easier for a guy to get himself out there. Because I think that in general girls worry more about what people think about them. So it's easier for a guy to be confident enough to perform for people."

On the other side of the coin, some women suggest that women's traditionally feminine personalities inhibit their entry to the musician life. Women's supposed tendencies to be shyer, less confident, and less aggressive makes their entrance to the music world more problematic. Embodying stereotypical feminine characteristics is at odds with music culture, as femininity is generally not aligned with the traits necessary for a "good" musician. Iconic musicians are brash, outspoken, and forceful—in a word, they embody a "masculine" presence and personality.

Gender Discrimination. Third, some women were attentive to ways in which discrimination emerged in the music scene and structured their lesser participation. Discrimination took a few forms, according to women. Some felt that women musicians were held to a different and higher standard than were men. Part of what makes rock music profane is the fact that authentic rock is centered on passion. Rock bands, punk bands, and grunge bands, among others, have measured the worth of a band by their passion, not their acquisition of skill, intricacy of chord progressions, or vocals pleasing to the ear. Many iconic bands revel in the fact that they are not skilled musicians and know little formal music theory. However, women in rock at times must contend with the possibilities of critics, fans, or other outsiders questioning their skill levels and credentials. Beth describes it like this: "A lot of times if a girl is in a band, it's just like [trends in] television and other [media industries]. It tends to be a lot more about looks and personality than it is about music. So I think that for a girl to be a musician and for it to work out, they have to be pretty confident and have worked really hard at it because you have to be perfect if people are going to give them the chance initially. And you really do you have to probably be better than guy musicians because people are not necessarily expecting as much out of you."

As studies of other occupations have suggested, the bar is often higher for women than it is for men (Foschi 1996; Roth 2011). Although music is an informal vocation in which credentials are less quantifiable than in traditional careers, women encounter a different set of expectations in securing positions in the music world. Julia's experience reflects these trends: "It's definitely not in balance, but it's never kept me from doing anything. It's pushed me to try to be that much more of a dominant player. And I certainly never felt impaired or intimidated at all, but I think a lot of people do. I think maybe there's an intimidation factor for a lot of [women]." As a result, women sometimes must reach a higher level of musical proficiency to be considered as potential recruits for bands. The subtext in these decisions is that unless a woman reaches a particular threshold of skill with her instrument, she is not worthy of being a musician.

Only a few women experienced overt gender discrimination. It was rare for anyone to forthrightly tell a woman she could not join a band, play in a club, or pursue music ipso facto because of her gender. Instead, women had experiences of more subtle forms of discrimination in which other musicians assumed they would not be adequate at their instrument or implied they were incapable of handling the demands of music life. Some women, like Jen, had friends who gave up on music as a result of such persistent discrimination: "I have a friend. She's a great guitarist, has a great voice, but she's terrified to get out and play again. She's just like, 'I just can't hold up to the guys.' And I too have had lots of guys who have done crappy things to me like cheat me out of [opportunities]."

The differential treatment and stolen opportunities take a toll on women, prompting some of them to contemplate leaving the world behind. Others, however, such as Julia in her quote above, suggest that facing discrimination increased her personal motivation to commit to and succeed in music. Regardless of the insistence that many women musicians have to persevere despite challenges they face due to their gender, they still must contend with such challenges that are not a part of men's typical experiences in music.

Gendered Possibilities. Finally, a number of women suggested that women have in mind a different set of prospects for the future when considering leisure and occupational pursuits. Women could of course easily develop their identities as fans and connoisseurs of rock music, and, likewise, some developed interests in learning instruments. However, the step to envisioning music as an occupational possibility was a leap far too great that many women did not fathom. They believed careers in music were so far removed from their conception of possibility that the thought rarely entered women's minds. Those women who did fantasize of futures centered on music often kept their dreams at bay, as the aspiration was too otherworldly.

Most of the women musicians had women friends and acquaintances who loved music and played instruments. Some even had a stockpile of songs they had composed themselves. However, a number of these women were not looking to join bands. They participated in music to a degree, albeit privately. The women musicians strongly suggested that impeding thoughts of doubt either sabotaged women's plans to join bands or pushed them off the table of possibilities entirely. Emma discussed her friends' limited experiences in music: "Many of my girlfriends have always wanted to be in a band but have never taken the time to learn the instruments or put the effort into actually *being* in a band. Almost every one of my boyfriends who have had the musician bug has taken the time to learn an instrument and experienced a little with being in a band. It's really sad because I sometimes wonder if the reason behind my girlfriends not taking the time to learn an instrument or joining a band is because [society] has always expected women to put their hopes and dreams on the back burner."

Emma's friends did not seriously consider pursuing music as a result of gender norms coupled with gendered possibilities. While most men who play instruments may at least consider the possibility of making a career of music, women may be less likely to consider those prospects and are consequently less represented in the musician population. Jade links her own experience in her limited, though successful, career in her band to this idea as well. She had this to say about women and their participation in music: "As far as music goes, there are a lot less female musicians than male musicians and maybe it's just that girls don't even *think* about it. Just like me, I wasn't ever like, 'Oh, I'm going to start a band!' . . . If I hadn't had met Heath [her then boyfriend who invited her to join his band], then I probably would not have *ever* been in a band. . . . Maybe it's just that [women] don't even think about it."

Expectations, of course, are partially reflective of social realities. Women, in a word, lack opportunities that allow for informal socialization into the occupation. While men have multiple pathways for entering musical careers, women seem to enter music in a much less predictable manner, and often only with male sponsorship or encouragement. Were it not for their ties with men in bands—romantic or otherwise—many women doubt they would have ever attempted to join a band on their own. The culmination of these explanations leads to the lesser likelihood of women contemplating careers in music.

Men's Speculation

Men musicians too were keyed in to women's general absence in rock music. They recognized men's all-embracing presence in rock at both the national and local level, both in the past and today. Most men, similar to women, saw the gender ratio in the contemporary landscape of rock to be improving, though not necessarily nearing equity. Men's ideas regarding women's absence were generally thoughtful, perceptive, and insightful, but, in contrast to women's multiple and intersecting explanations, they often had a single rationale for the gender imbalance. Many of their speculations echoed those provided by women, citing the impact of both socialization and gender discrimination. Their other speculations were unique, however, and stemmed from their vantage point as men.

In particular, a majority of the men (19 of 33) discuss the impact of culture on the gender ratio in rock bands. During childhood, many men became fascinated with rock music. Often a particular band or musician planted the seed for adolescent boys' desire to learn a rock instrument and subsequently petition a parent to allow them to do so. This was in contrast to most women who simply adored the bands and became fans from afar, not necessarily considering emulating them by becoming musicians themselves at this point in life. In my conversations with men, nearly all clearly remember their favorite bands while growing up being composed entirely of men. As such, they identified with them quite easily: either in terms of the musician's perceived identity or the content of their music. In any case, they could easily imagine themselves in the roles of these men since they shared the same gender. Even "far-out, bizarre" bands such as KISS with extreme, sometimes cartoonish identities, makeup, and costumes were not a world away in how the boys could imagine reconfiguring their identities. After all, behind all the props, the boys were not too fundamentally different from the men hiding underneath the makeup and attire. As such, many men, such as Warren, imagined it difficult for adolescent girls to similarly identify with the same musicians the men did: "When girls my age were growing up, I don't know how many girls there really were to look up to be a musician. Like I said, growing up, every band that was on the radio when I was in the fifth grade was a male rock band."

Andrew has similar thoughts on historically gendered rock culture: "I really think it has a lot to do with the whole beginning of rock music and what we see rock music as. Rock music has been four dudes in a band since the fucking Beatles, [even] prior to that really, since forever. Over time, you start having more girls playing. In rock music now there's probably more women than there were ever before. It was never like that before, and I really think it's because of the beginning path of rock music really." Men seem more attuned to the masculine trajectory of rock culture, perhaps because a number of them identified with the musicians' music they grew up listening to (Ashley 2011). For many of them, connecting to a band was the most powerful inspiration early in life to learn an instrument. The men considered the extent to which teenage girls would be likely to gain inspiration from a group collectively composed of men and anticipated it would be more difficult for them.

What's more, the men also contrasted gendered outcomes in rock music to those in academic settings. Men, like women, often had experience in school-structured music programs and spent several years performing in marching and concert bands affiliated with their schools. The men were attentive to the extent to which gender and music was differentially structured in these settings. Andrew contrasts differences in rock and school-structured music cultures: "Think about being in a marching band and high school band, orchestra, symphony orchestra. There's not an outstanding number of men versus women in that. Women can do it just the same as a man. It's been that way for a long time, right? So in rock music, I really think [the gender imbalance] is from past tradition." During the high school years (and beyond), girls and women participate in other music cultures to the same extent as do boys and men. While women seem equally interested and capable of learning instruments and performing in school-structured bands, their representation severely declines in rock music culture (Bielby 2004). The primary explanation Andrew and other men have for women's "drop off" in musical participation outside of academic settings is the extent to which rock culture is structured by masculine norms, which operate as an impediment to women's entry.

In contrast, school-sponsored music activities are generally characterized by comparable numbers of girls and boys. Neither gender seems to relish a majority of the higher positions or generate a disproportionate share of status in these settings. There are, of course, significant gender differences in instrument specialization even in this context. Boys are more likely to play the bigger, heavier, sometimes lower-tonal instruments such as the tuba and trombone, as well as "aggressive" instruments such as percussion. Girls tend to dominate the smaller, higher-pitched instruments such as the flute and clarinet.[7] Despite this clear gendered organization of music, both girls and boys are visible in these music settings. Charlie worked at a rock music camp for kids and had insight on the transitions from school-structured music programs to rock. In discussing women's waning participation in rock, he said:

> I think it has something specifically to do with [becoming] a rock musician. Rock and roll is loud and girls aren't supposed to be loud. So there's a push during a girl's adolescence away from that. I don't think it's as socially acceptable as it should be, specifically on the drums. In the camp that I do, you see the numbers of kids that come in, and you see that they all have an interest to play the drums or the guitar. . . . I see kids *really* interested in the drums. Everybody wants to sit down and play them when they come into the practice room. So I guess, citing that push away from loud [instruments] with kids of both sexes, I would apply that to girls and say that parents don't want their [daughters] to do loud stuff. . . . If a male kid is more interested in playing the drums, there's a better chance that he's gonna do it than his sister who has that same [interest].

Early in their entrance to rock culture, boys and girls experience differential access to rock instruments, particularly those deemed as loud and masculine. Rock is anything but an open playing field for women. With few exceptions, the culture of rock prescribes men to easily secure nearly all positions in rock bands, as well as the lion's share of the visibility and status in the rock world.

A few others suggested that barring women's access to the interior of the music world was essentially an impression management strategy that protects men on the inside, specifically those musicians who exploit the perks of musicianhood. These men believe that women's presence would complicate the sexual exploits musicians take advantage of by virtue of being in a band. Not having women present to bear witness to what happens after the show is a simple tactic to hide the masculine norms and behaviors of musicianhood (e.g., sexual promiscuity). Women's absence works as information control—they are less privy to see the goings on in the world if they are not allowed in. Seth recounted this story:

> I've met a lot of guys who say, "I won't play in a band with a girl." It has less to do with the fact that they don't respect women as musicians. Other guys say, "Hey man, I don't want to be in a band with a girl because I'll feel like I have to be on my best behavior all the time. I can't just loosen up and be a dude. I don't want that pressure. . . ." They'll be straight up honest with me. "Man, I play music because it helps me get laid. I feel like a shithead when I'm in a band with a girl, and she sees me night after night running after girls all night. She's not going to respect me." They're afraid of being judged because they're guilty. They don't want some girl to tell their friends what a dog they are. They want to keep that under wraps. I can go into town and be as mischievous as I want, but if there's a girl watching this night after night, I'm going to feel guilty.

Part of men's controlling and limiting women's access to their bands may have to do less with women themselves and more with men's desires to hide their exploits from them.

The Marketability of Female Sexuality

Femininity takes on a special meaning in the music scene as it inevitably intersects with women's sexuality. Most women must negotiate issues of sexuality in the music scene and consider its implications on their careers and statuses as musicians. Some women suggested they were recruited to their bands at least partially due to their identities as women. They did not experience pressure to sexualize their identity on stage per se, but their recruitment was a bit of a marketing ploy. April said: "Well, having a girl in the band makes it more easily marketable. I mean, that's the truth. And that's probably why they wanted me to be in the band."

Beth had a similar experience:

BETH: I don't know how much [the singer] told you about how he asked me to join the band. I work at [a bar in town]. He used to work there too, so he is always hanging out there while I was on [shift]. He had just always been looking for a girl to play in the band with him and [eventually] asked if I was interested.

MR: For the voice? Like to harmonize?

BETH: Yeah, and kind of for a pretty face too. He'll admit it and so will I. I said, "I play the piano. I sing." He had played with a bunch of different girls, but nothing had ever worked out. I went over to his house and recorded a few songs. We just kind of clicked. He and I have a good chemistry, a friends dynamic, we get along, we don't irritate each other all that much, as much as bandmates can. And that was about a year ago March that we started playing together.

While April and Beth did not necessary feel pressure to engage in a sexualized identity on stage, they seemed to be invited to their bands due to their pleasing femininity and normatively attractive appearances. Other studies find women musicians endure frequent pressure from both the audience as well as other band members to enact and display a sexualized identity on stage (Groce and Cooper 1990). By and large, the women with whom I spoke did not cite the sexualized component of their femininity in their experience. It was not a pressing problem for most women, as only a few experience difficulties with this. A few women musicians, Emma in particular, did reflect on their early days in theirs bands during which they gained reputations as the "hot girl in the band." Most saw it neither as a boon nor a restraint to their identities as a woman musician in their respective bands. Nor was it something they exploited or honed to generate status, interest, or attention. At times, however, such attention was unwarranted. Lauren played a show in which "a guy in the audience threw money at me because I was a hot chick on the bass. It sometimes sucks, [but it] comes with the territory." While she refuses to speculate on all women musicians' experiences in the music scene based on her single instance, she did not recollect any instance in which men musicians (in her band or others) were ever "tipped" because of their appearance.

Other musicians, such as Lilly, cited the recent "schtick of the token female" in rock bands quickly becoming a tired trope in the music scene: "It used to be [a trend] in the past. I think it's getting away from it, but it used to be if you're a girl in the band, then you had a gimmick. You had dress really sexy, or be like Courtney Love, not wear any underwear and curse a lot. You had to have some kind of shtick. I've seen more and more bands now where it's just there's a girl in there and it's not really a big deal. She just happens to be a girl. More and more I see that. You don't have to have some gimmick—be it a short skirt or the tough girl [persona] or the baby doll dress, or the cursing, abrasive person—to be in a band."

Most women felt similarly; women's relegation to the periphery of the band as eye candy was not a suitable avenue for entering the music world or building one's fan base. For this reason, many women tried their best to contain or minimize their sexual identity in the band, although, truth be told, the male gaze of the music world was difficult for women to counteract.[8] Beth, however, was one woman who strategically enacted an element of her sexuality on her own. Her stage persona incorporates a hint of her sexual identity with a particular intention in mind: "I think that when I'm on stage, it's just another side of my personality. I'm kind of a flirt I guess. I dress cute. I know what makes guys want to come see your band play, which is kind of shallow, but the truth sometimes. And it's what brings people initially to see us. But then, unlike [other bands with a token female], we actually have the music to back it up. If it's a good performance and if the music backs it up, then they will appreciate it and come back again." While on stage, she uses her sexuality as an incentive to get men to attend shows with the intention to increase her band's fan base. Her strategy is relatively tame, but does profit from her feminine wiles to enhance her band's position in the scene. She and other musicians of course believed any musician—woman or man—has the prerogative to use any tactic in their arsenal to further their band's career. A few likened using the image of their attractive band members as no different than creating eye-catching posters and flyers advertising their band's upcoming shows. The intent is generally the same: capture their attention with something pleasing to the eye and then use the opportunity to hook them with the music, even when it was at the cost of women's femininities.

Conclusion

In this chapter, I have examined elements in women's lives that influenced their musical trajectories. In some ways, their lives were no different than men. However, most points of their musical life courses were marked by gender. During the early years, the girls experimented with and became invested in a wide range of extracurricular activities. Music was on their radar early in life, but it was not the focus of their attention. As such, it took longer for them to focus more directly on musical pursuits, not to mention develop skills in musical performance and songwriting. Their wide-ranging interests, though they helped them to become well rounded, in some ways hindered their start to focusing on music.

Although they became fans of rock culture at similar points in life as do men, women typically developed their interests in participating as musicians far later in life. It is a more difficult deal to strike, with parents in particular, to learn rock instruments. Their foray into their first bands begins early in adulthood, acting as a disadvantage in that they are "late bloomers." Upon becoming musicians, they must then confront and subvert the consequences of their being women in rock. By far the biggest distinction between women and men musicians is the role of romantic partners in their musical careers. The norm among women was having a man in her life who provided her the "push" to pursue music. Women were the only musicians to ever cite their romantic partners as mentors or role models. Women seem to be less inclined to pursue music without the guidance or support of an outside (and male) figure.

All women were aware of and frustrated by the gender imbalance in the music scene. They readily discuss potential factors that may contribute to the imbalance, perhaps because they have considered such ideas previously. They believe that, especially today, it is possible for women to overcome these obstacles. Perhaps because these women came of age after the Second Wave, they are well aware of the gender imbalance in various lines of work and education systems, as well as aware of the historical (but limited) improvement in these inequalities. The factors that impede women's pursuing music are multiple and synergistic. Women of course do find their place in the world of rock, but it is a challenge. It also comes at a price.

6

The Great Beyond

• •

Commitment to Music and
Looking toward the Future

Art, music, creativity: these are the things that make us human. What would this world be without music? Hip hop artist Princess Superstar contemplates such possible worlds in the opening track of her 2005 album *Last of the Great Twentieth Century Composers*, as a pair of astronauts years into the future explore the remnants of life on earth. Their archeological dig leads them to a long-abandoned apartment, presumably Princess Superstar's, in which they stumble upon music in the form of thousands of "spherical discs made from a primitive synthetic plastic" (better known to those in our time as albums). They wonder what ever happened to music. It's long since disappeared from the world. And with its absence, their world as they've known it has always been muted.

What would this world be without music? A lot quieter, for one. Daily life is peppered with music in various forms from morning to night. Music, for good or bad, is ubiquitous. Ours is a culture of media saturation, one component of which is the ever-presence of music: it surrounds us not only in our cars and on our smart phones, but in commercials, in grocery stores, in gyms, and on phone lines when put on hold. In those moments when we do not have a choice in listening to the music, it may not necessarily be enjoyable. But in the moments we actively and purposefully choose music we want to hear, it can bring us comfort and enjoyment. Music influences emotions and states of being in the listener. Music consumers seek solace in music: melancholy songs to accompany our heartbreak; upbeat, peppy songs to complement our celebrations.

A world without music is a muted world, both figuratively and symbolically. It would be an empty world were there no music. And for many of us, a deeper layer of ourselves would go unrecognized were it not for music in our lives. The musicians, as I will illustrate in this chapter, shared similar sentiments, though theirs were often more fervent. Music gave them understandings of themselves and their place in the world. Without music, they imagined, they would be adrift. It was the conduit that allowed for their development, for their connection to an otherwise empty and bland world.

In this chapter, I focus on two distinct yet interrelated issues: musicians' levels of commitment to music and their plans for the future. I begin by exploring musicians' perspectives on their self-defined levels of commitment to musical careers. The most highly committed musicians foresee a lifetime centered on music, though one that will not be without struggle, while a larger portion of the musicians instead see their commitment to music as temporary. Many have alternate ideas for their future and are in the process of planning their exit from the music world. I next focus on the consequences of their lengthy participation in the music world. Musicians regard their time in music as shaping their lives in countless and significant ways. Many of them believe music was a tool that enabled a better understanding of themselves throughout life, as well as their place in the world. I conclude by exploring musicians' speculations on paths not taken. They speak in great detail about what they imagine their lives would have been without music, illustrating what they consider to be the ultimate function of music.

Degrees of Musical Commitment

The musicians not only discussed the trajectories their life courses took from early childhood up to the present time period but also carefully considered the directions in which they imagined their lives to go in the future. They were attentive to the ways in which their past had shaped their present positions in life and recognized their present-day choices would similarly influence what was yet to come (Elder 1985; Holstein and Gubrium 2003). As such, all of them spoke freely and in depth about the future. With little hesitation, they speculated on the role they anticipate music to take in their upcoming years. Like all other human beings, they of course did not know with absolute certainty whether their premonitions would pan out, but most of them had strong signals as to where they were headed next in life. Of course, their ideas about the future often hinged on the role music currently played in their lives, specifically the extent to which they were committed to music as a lifelong endeavor. As such, I examine the musicians' levels of musical commitment as the backdrop for their anticipated futures.

Music as a Career: The Lifers

Just over half (25 of 48) of the musicians were devoted to pursuing musical careers for the rest of their lives. They posed their commitment to music entirely—with no hesitation, no disclaimers, and no uncertainty. Music was their lifeblood, what they lived for, and they saw no possibility of anything diverting them from their passion. These musicians unequivocally framed their musical commitments as permanent, like Nikki: "I want to do it until the day I die. So the more I can play, the better. I want to play music as much as possible. I'd be much more content if we were playing shows every [week], maybe had a cool [record] label hook us up. But yeah, I definitely want to make a lifelong career out of it. For sure." In no uncertain terms, they foresaw themselves bound to music for the rest of their adult lives. They could not imagine any possible outside influence diverting them from music, describing themselves in some ways as powerless to its hold on them. Adrian put it this way: "Yeah, I think at this point I'm a lifer as far as music goes. It has to be there in my life from here on out. If I'm not writing [songs] or I'm not playing, I would just roll over." The lifers characterized music as a "compulsion"— something that was uncontrollable. Despite their efforts to ward it off, they could not convince themselves to do something more "rational" with their lives (Hamilton 2006). It was their calling, their destiny. Even in instances in which they attempted to move away from music, a new project or request to record or invitation to tour emerged, prompting them to further delay (and avoid altogether) their abandoning music.

The self-defined lifelong musicians by no means imagined they would one day be on the cover of *Rolling Stone* or play to sold-out arenas. Rather, their hope was to develop a modest, though national, following, perhaps get signed to a small record label, tour regularly, and generate enough income to survive, living a simple, unassuming life. Even this dream, though much more attainable than ideas of becoming the next Beatles, is a long shot. Warren is initially torn as to whether he considers music to be his career or hobby: "It [making a career in music] seems impossible. The numbers are just that you're probably not going to make it. But so are the odds of opening up a restaurant or starting a magazine. Whatever you do, there is a high percentage that it just won't work out the way you hoped it would. So I don't really have any other options. What, am I going to *not* do it?" He rationalizes his decision by stressing that no career choice is a sure thing. He also seems so invested at this point that giving up his dream is not even an option. He and other lifers felt symbolically so far along the musical pathway that they were beyond the "point of no return" with no way to alter their course now. At the same time, Warren and others understand the chances of making it big are not in their favor.

However, success does sneak up on bands from time to time, often for musicians who are not necessarily striving for nor expecting it. For instance, Dean's previous band released an album that generated praise, attention, and a surprisingly high number of sales, all of which was unanticipated: "That really just kinda came out of nowhere. Nobody would have expected that. So that idea [of reaching success] was prevalent for a while until I realized that it's kinda the same sort of thing as the lottery. You can buy a lottery ticket, and you can expect that you really have a legitimate chance of winning millions of dollars buying a lottery ticket, but is that gonna happen? Probably not, probably not." Similarly, Seth said: "[My dad] was talking to me about the future. I was like, 'Dad, let me break it down for you like this. Me playing music is about the same as me going down to the convenience store every week and buying lottery tickets. I have about as much chance as making a career in music as I do buying ten lottery tickets a week and hitting the lottery.'" The lottery analogy was recurring in musicians' contrasting the dreams and realities of success in the music business. The adage "You have to play to win" is pertinent to both the lottery as well as musical careers. The odds are consistently stacked against the musicians breaking out at the national level, but they have witnessed it among their local peers. For those wishing for success, it keeps their hope alive.

Music as a Job: "It's Just Like Any Other Job". Career-oriented musicians were also similar in conceptualizing music as a job that was not necessarily pleasurable (Schieman and Young 2010). Granted, they did gain personal satisfaction from performing and typically had fun while on stage, but as a whole their day-to-day life as a musician was not what they generally described as fun.

> SETH: I got into a huge debate with my bass player because I was being really intense in practice. I said, "You know, I want to apologize for being a little too intense in practice [recently]." He said, "Yeah, man. It does make it awkward sometimes. Music should be fun. If you don't have any fun, there's no point in being in the band." I said, "I disagree. My definition of fun and yours don't coincide." For me, having fun with music is when I get up on stage, I feel like I'm performing to the best of my ability, and I'm presenting something to people that is exceptional and something that should be remembered. In order to do that means putting in a lot of hard work. By reaping the benefits of hard work, that's fun for me. Getting to practice, cutting up, playing sloppily, and goofing off isn't fun. Shit, let's just go to the bar and drink and talk about girls. That's fun. In the context of a band, that's not fun for me. I don't want to sit here and waste time. When I get into practice,

      I'm like, "Let's do it. Let's go." You can tell us the funny story of what hap-
      pened at work later. We're going to do this now.

MR: You treat it like a job.

SETH: It is a job for me. It's a job that pays very poorly.

For Seth and other committed musicians, music was not a leisure at all, but instead the undertaking of an informal career, one characterized as indistinguishable from work in the professional world. A long-term commitment to a musical career changes the practice of and meaning of music.[1] First, serious musicians personified seriousness at rehearsals. Gone were the days of lollygagging during band rehearsals. Rehearsals were not for enjoyment, but to hone the band for future performances. Band practice was regarded as clocking in hours at work. While "on the clock," many musicians did not act in jest, drink, or otherwise treat it as a time for social recreation. It was, in fact, work. This was a given for some musicians, as they likened avoiding recreation at office jobs as professional and as the identical bar for expectations in the band. Furthermore, such expectations allowed for more efficient and productive rehearsals, something particularly important when they rented practice space by the hour.

    Second, the social-psychological function of music changed after committing to music. Early in life, music was therapeutic for musicians. Consistent with research recognizing the therapeutic functions that listening to music and playing instruments has on individuals, doodling on the guitar and writing preliminary drafts of songs had a calming effect on the musicians (Christenson

FIGURE 7   Pegasuses-XL performs at Athens Popfest (Photo by Mike White, deadlydesigns.com)

and Roberts 1998; DeNora 2000). The other side of the coin, however, is that once the stakes are higher—once music is a calling in one's life—the therapeutic functions vanished. Music instead became work, and hence metamorphosed into a mode of stress for musicians. A few musicians acknowledged having to adopt new hobbies in their private lives after committing to music, as it was now centered in the realm of their work life. Some of them took up other artistic endeavors such as painting or creative writing, while others used "zoning out" with TV, video games, and other media (something many of them had avoided previously) as a means to relax during their down time. Playing their instruments "off the clock" became something to be avoided, much like professional workers strive to distance themselves from checking e-mail or completing any work tasks on weekends or holidays. In sharp contrast, the less committed musicians who likened their bands to a hobby (to be discussed below) were far more likely to describe their musical life primarily as fun. "Once it's not fun, I'll know it's a sign for me to quit" was a sentiment the hobbyists often expressed regarding the relationship between pleasure and music.

Some career-oriented musicians were concerned with what a "career" in music would look like. They were consistent in avoiding national fame and platinum record sales as the criteria for a bona fide music career. But what precisely a "true" career in music did entail was far from clear. Most musicians suggested that being able to make music, generate some income (however modest), and occasionally tour constituted the type of musical career they hoped to achieve. Ideally, some hoped their music careers would "mean that I'm not having to go to my cubicle" and would make sufficient income for some sense of stability. Others, however, felt that instances in which they simultaneously juggled multiple jobs, often in the service industry, while maintaining their musical life constituted a musical career. Both musicians below were attuned to the consequences pursuing their musical dreams would have on their economic futures.[2]

> PAUL: I definitely would like to be doing it at a level where I was making enough money to be comfortable and not necessarily have to work regular jobs. But I'm resigned to the fact that that might not happen, and that's fine with me. I have no problem doing both: working and playing to make it work. It's worth it to me.
>
> ADRIAN: You have to love it. You've got to be a little bit insane to accept the fact that for the most part of your life, it's gonna be in poverty. So you've got to be a little bit crazy to agree to that, but you've definitely got to love it enough and have the drive and motivation.

Commitment breeds further commitment. Musicians' love of music is an impetus for holding steadfast to their musical pursuits, despite the consequences.

Equally important, however, is their suspicion that their blinding devotion to their passion has curtailed other alternatives. Without question, some of them have declined other ventures at the expense of music. They have devoted so much of their adult life to music that they feel there is no turning back. All of the most highly committed musicians, no doubt, said they would hold fast to their musical pathways even if possibilities arose in other work worlds. They fully recognized the benefits and satisfactions far outweighed the limitations in persisting with music. It was a choice in which they felt confident.

Music as Tentative: The Provisionals

A number of other musicians framed their thoughts on their musical futures in uncertain terms. Even when I would probe, asking what conditions were necessarily for them to commit to a life of music, they pushed back with increasing hesitation. There was no formula, nor a specific milestone they needed to achieve to fasten their commitment to music. Instead, they simply could not say for certain what would happen next, as they were "on the fence" about their role music would play in their futures. These "provisional" musicians were, for the most part, early on the path to musical commitment, but not far enough along the path to not consider other avenues.

Their uncertainty (and, as some would phrase it, reluctance) to committing to music took two forms. One subgroup of the musicians framed their commitment to music as important, though likely temporary. Nearly all of them were age twenty-five or younger, clearly in the emerging adulthood years. The second subgroup speculated and often was in the midst of planning alternate careers away from music performance, though they were still embedded in the music world. Each group had specific experiences and suspicions for the future, each of which will be discussed in turn.

Temporality of Musical Commitment. First, some musicians regarded their pursuit of musical careers as one to which they were committed, but perhaps only temporarily. Many of their provisional devotions to music took the form of their having the privilege of not having to commit entirely (Arnett 2006; Swartz et al. 2011). Theirs was a conditional commitment in which they felt they would soon have to make a decision, but not quite yet. Abby expressed it this way: "Ideally I'd like for it to be something that I could make enough money off of to make a living. That's really a difficult thing to do. Really difficult. So realistically, I'm not counting on it. But I guess I don't really think that far ahead for now. I'm just enjoying myself."

Abby implies a temporality to her commitment; music is something she will ultimately decide on later. Abby's tone, especially her focus on the here and now, was typical of other provisional musicians. They enjoyed and received immense satisfaction from music, and they currently devoted themselves entirely to their musical endeavors. At the same time, they did assess other options for the future, as is the case for many emerging and young adults, some of whom were even planting the seeds for future shifts. Their designing alternate plans was an indication that they were contemplating leaving music behind. Until they knew for certain they were ready to exit music, many musicians refused to conceive too precisely of a substitute plan.

Other provisional musicians voiced a devotion to music, but one in which there were limits to their commitment. Some reasoned that the economic toll could only be tolerated for so long. Others maintained that their blind commitment stemmed from a deep-seated passion for music, but one they were aware had the potential to hurt their private lives, relationships, and families. And in those cases, they would step away from music.

> ISRAEL: I've been trying to make it a career for the past fifteen years. I don't know if I can call it a career. It's more of a vocation than a career. I haven't made a lot of money doing it at all, but I've done it on a semiprofessional level for the last ten or twelve years. I would love to have it as a career. It would be a lot tougher now at my stage in life, having a kid and settled down, but I would like to see if there was some way to work it out. . . . It would be nice, but I don't think I'd make the sacrifices that I make at some point. There'd have to be some lines drawn. I don't want to ruin my relationship [with my family]. It's kind of a sad thing when you look at people who have full-on careers in music [at the expense of their families]. I wouldn't want to sacrifice my marriage or my relationship with my kid. I think it can be done. It might be better at this point since we're older and a little wiser, as far as how to balance things. If I could support my family, that would be awesome.

Older musicians, particularly those with increased responsibilities of mortgages, marriages, and family lives, such as Israel, were more attentive to the challenges committing to music had on day-to-day life. Older musicians—those in their early thirties and beyond—often compared their present situations to earlier times in life in which they recognized more fluidity in the decisions they made. Good or bad, and often a mixture of both, the provisional musicians learned during their tenure in bands that musical commitments took consequences of greater significance after the emerging adult years.

The emerging adult years are marked as a time of exploration (Shanahan et al. 2005). For musicians, a middle-class status allows more time to explore—and hence more time to test out music as a career option well into their midtwenties. Those musicians who felt the exploratory period of emerging adulthood was coming to a close—or that they were stagnating in this period for far too long—and hence felt more pressure, often self-conceived, to contemplate other options.

Musicianhood as a Springboard for Alternate Careers. The second grouping of the provisional musicians is resigned to the fact that their musical commitment is wavering. They love their bands, but do not see their musical performance careers panning out. Instead, they suggested their time invested in bands would instead be used as a springboard for entirely new career trajectories in other fields, though typically still embedded in the music world.[3]

Often times, their time spent devoted to bands inadvertently gave them insight and/or provided training for a nonperformative career in music. These musicians' experiences in bands shifted their interests away from performance and toward other dimensions of music, similar to other studies of musicians' arcs in music as they age (Giffort 2011; Schilt and Zobl 2008). Lilly, like other provisional musicians, imagined for the longest time that her commitment to her band would be lifelong, only to recently have a change of heart.

> LILLY: Well, what I'd really like to happen is to one day make some connection from this band to where I could have a job that's music related, whether it be as a publicist or writing jingles for commercials or something like that. But I just don't see it for us making it big on [the national level]. That rarely happens. I honestly don't see that happening. And even if it did happen, I don't know if I would like it. I'm a pretty quiet person. I don't really know if I want to be in the spotlight. I would just like to get to a point where I can have a job that's somewhat music related and have gotten that connection through being in a band. . . . I think that's the most realistic thing that might eventually happen.

Her considering other options outside of music performance took her by surprise, as she had invested a significant span of her emerging adulthood years to her band.[4] Lilly, however, also recognized during that time that the most "successful" people with whom she was acquainted in the music world were able to develop careers in other, nonperformative segments of the music industry (Arthur 1994; Schilt and Zobl 2008; Wagner 2015). Modeling her potential career track off of what she witnessed firsthand, she was now taking the initial steps to begin sowing the seeds for a new career in the music world.

While Lilly was taking the music business route, other musicians were gaining experience that was placing them on pathways leading to careers in the music production. After some time in the recording industry, these musicians weighed the pros and cons of switching more fully to the recording and production side of music. Economics spurred these thoughts for some musicians. Those who were contemplating such transitions, like Jason, recognized that, were they to desist from musical careers, they would have to stop the performative aspect entirely.

JASON: Right now, the return that we're getting for the effort and the money that we're putting in, it's just not paying us back anymore. And at some point, the mortgage has got to outweigh being in a band. I imagine that if I stopped doing it, I would stop cold turkey. I wouldn't be able to do it as just a hobby. . . . But even if I stopped having my own band, recording [other bands in my studio] is what I do. That's how I make my money. And I do make quite a bit money off of that. Even though that's much less person- ally satisfying, it's paying the bills a little more. I will always make music, I imagine. I've only been [recording] professionally for a handful of years, and I've got tons of credits at this point. I'm competing with people who've been doing it for twenty years longer than me.

As Jason illustrates, many of the provisional musicians are inching away from music as a result of unanticipated options opening up in what was initially an unintended career choice. This trend is consistent with the experience of men and women outside the music industry, as most "stumble" into their ulti- mate careers (Heinz 2003). Furthermore, these musicians stressed that their years spent in musical performance was a requisite part of their pathway that allowed them the opportunity to stumble into or discover their ultimate career choice outside of music. They surmised that they would have not discovered those interests, nor developed the necessary skills for them, had they not been involved in musical participation in bands. Perhaps most importantly, some of them realized they would have never made the contacts and expanded their social networks that allowed them to enter the production world were it not for the people they met and befriended while they were in their bands.

Music as Leisure: The Hobbyists

One-third (15 of 48) of the musicians consider music to be their hobby, having no intentions of pursuing it as a lifelong career.[5] The hobby-oriented musicians had a broad age range—the youngest being twenty-two and the oldest thirty- seven—and were a mix of both women and men. Like the career-oriented musicians above, most of these men and women liken making a career in music to a "roll of the dice," but, unlike the careerists, seem less willing to play those odds. They do not give the impression they are burnt out or bitter at the music scene. They do, however, state that music, though central to their lives, is only one of many interests they have, and only one aspect of their identities in which they are invested. Most of them imagine stepping away from music in the relatively near future, though nearly all suspect music will always be a part of their lives in some way.

Many of the hobbyists framed their temporal status as their being "more realistic" about forging successful, long-term careers in music (Hodkinson and Sparkes 1997). For example, Jade said: "If it happens, great! It's certainly more fun than sitting behind a desk at a computer all day long, but I've never seri-ously thought that it would happen. Sure, I'd love it, but I don't really think that will happen." The hobbyists insinuated they would not walk away from the promise of a music deal, but also were not expecting it, nor were they nec-essarily devoting themselves wholeheartedly into the band to increase the like-lihood of musical career flourishing. Their musical aspirations had an escape hatch—though one they considered only when all options had been pursued. These musicians were often deeply invested in music, but over time felt they should slowly move away so as to not be too disappointed were their musi-cal plans not to pan out. By voicing their allegiance to music, the musicians hinted that it would hurt that much more were their dreams to be deterred. Being "more realistic" about the possibilities of musical careers was often coupled with two trends. First, the musicians tended to be older—beyond emerging adulthood and firmly into the young adult years. Second, they were more prone to have significant responsibilities in life—family (they were typi-cally married, though not necessarily parents), mortgages, and other standard markers of adulthood.

The hobbyists also consistently framed their musical participation as ful-filling, something they enjoyed with every moment they devoted to their band, yet also as something that they were not "cut out for" in the career sense. They had no complaints about the time commitment or even the expenses that went into making their participation in bands possible. It was a casual leisure, sometimes a costly hobby, but something they participated in "just" for fun (Stebbins 1997). They understood the satisfaction in life that sprang from their musical leisure. But they did not have serious intentions of turning their hobby—even when they had a significant local following—into a full-blown career.

> JADE: I definitely enjoy it and it's really fun and I really like everyone in the band, they're my friends. It's fun—the performing and everything. So I don't know, maybe it was [my career goal] when we first started, I guess. But it's kind of hard to say, because I'm not someone who's consumed by music all the time. I mean, I love music, I love to listen to it, but it isn't my life. It's definitely my most important hobby, but I feel like I'm too practical, you know? If we got this awesome record deal and they wanted to pay us and we could travel through Europe, sure, I would make it my priority in a heart-beat. But I just don't ever see that happening. And maybe that's why it won't ever happen. I definitely love it, but it's not my everything.

This trend may have to do with the intersection of age, gender, and experi-ence. For many of the younger women, their current band is their first serious band, and the novelty of the activity may support their heavy investment of time and energy. The women beyond their midtwenties have played music for a significantly longer period of time. They have put in difficult years holding down dual jobs and attempting to balance music and work. Many realize that making it big is a long shot. Second, they are fatigued from the economic hardship of the musician lifestyle. Finally, the excitement of being in a band and performing in front of audiences may have dimmed. These women are more likely to describe aspects of their participation in bands as "work" and, hence, less enjoyable. Their aspirations, as a result, are fading.

The musicians were quick to catalog the endless array of tasks that accompanied the "fun" job of being a musician. A good many of them regarded those aspects of musicianhood as the least satisfying moments in their bands. For some musicians, touring was not intrinsically satisfying. Nate said: "I don't really like the whole playing shows thing that much. I like recording. As far as playing shows goes, I like the hour that you're actually playing, but all the other stuff—booking a show, promoting it, setting up, soundcheck, waiting around, and nobody showing up—is a drag. Going on tour is the worst thing in the world. I wouldn't recommend it to anyone. It's weird because you'll drive all day in a van with no air conditioning. [You] get there and wait around and it's just a miserable day. But that fifty minutes that you're actually playing, it's like you forget about all of it. *That's* really fun." Touring is a hallmark of building a band's reputation. It was grueling for some musicians, though. Musicians estimated that between traveling and setting up for each venue for each performance on tour (along with the countless other tasks described by Nate above), they clocked in a minimum of fourteen hours of work for each hour-long public performance.

Their commitment to the bands took additional tolls on their lives as well. The musicians with a lengthier tenure in bands recognized the toll the bands had on multiple aspects of their health. Some felt that they were "run ragged" because their bands had taken a toll on their physical health, leading them to adopt less healthy lifestyles. Jacob said: "I had this conversation with an old friend of mine the other day. She said, 'You look like shit.' I said, 'I'm exhausted.' 'What happened?' 'We played last night. Got home at 3:00 [in the morning], was in bed by 4:00, up at 6:30 to go to work.' She's like, 'Is it still bringing joy to play like that? This band? This music?' I said, 'Yeah, of course it does. It's not always fun, but it's important [to me].'"

Sometimes this was coupled with sheer mental exhaustion. The band was in some cases negatively impacting musicians' mental health. This was exacerbated in the lives of musicians who felt the constant anxiety of making music a career, alongside the pressures to exit. The juggling act of balancing their musical and personal lives, compounded with relentless travel schedules and deprived sleep routines, took a toll on musicians. As described in

Chapter 2, those musicians who were in college and/or in their early twenties did not find it challenging to go to work or class with a scant few hours of rest. Older musicians (in their thirties and beyond), however, struggled with maintaining a disrupted schedule long term. Health and mental well-being were valued over their musical dreams, and they were increasingly attentive to the diminishing returns that stemmed from such stressful routines. Some of the hobbyists voiced frustration with the workload and effort required for their bands. Many of these musicians started off with ideas of building careers in music, but only recently began doubting those plans, due in part to the toil.

The musicians who founded or were more heavily invested in their bands voiced the greatest frustration. Despite nearly all musicians portraying the band in communal terms (never was it framed as "belonging" to a sole band member), some of those with greater investments did feel they had a larger stake in the musical project. Its success rested on their shoulders, so they felt. And the obligatory work sometimes became their sole burden, as with Andrew: "It was supposedly an entire group effort. And then it turned out that I'm actually doing everything. When I try to get people to do anything to help me, or when it's not done well enough, or they don't get it done, and are just unreliable, it's draining. I end up having to do everything. And people are constantly like, 'Oh, we want to help.' But then I feel kind of like to a point where I ask people to do it, and it takes me more time reminding, 'Hey, do you have that done?' So I'll just do it myself. And honestly, that gets really draining. For me, right now, I'm taking a break from the business side." A few musicians likened the sole burden as being a single parent—not surprising, considering these musicians sometimes described their band as their "baby." Research on parenting negotiations has shown that would-be parents who anticipate bearing a majority of the domestic responsibility (often women) often do not foresee those arrangements as fair or satisfying (Gerson 1985). Musicians had similar responses, citing those circumstances in which they had sole responsibility as too burdensome, stressful, and unsatisfying. Given the choice between maintaining the band with the unbalanced responsibilities or stepping away from music, many of them contemplate or begin executing their departure.

As some of the hobbyists ventured more into their discussions of their musical futures, some of them came to realize (and verbalize) their true motivation for music: pleasure, not career. The hobby-oriented musicians create music for music's sake (Stebbins 1997). They have no interest in attempting to build a career in music, in part because they recognize they would be somewhat at the mercy of not only the record label, but critics and fans as well. Damien, in discussing his intentions to not pursue music as a career, said:

A lot of the arts are very subjective, whether you become successful as recognized by the greater world. You could be a great artist and nobody would know it until you're dead. Or *never* know it. And maybe what you'd have to do to get acceptance while you're alive is that you'd have to change what you're doing a bit to please others. And even then, if you try really hard doing that, it's really just up to a few critics or people to decide whether you're going to be successful in the sense of getting signed to a big record deal or making an amount of money to do it as your living. Whereas if you keep it as a hobby and you never really want it to be more, you just do what makes you happy and you don't ever really have to worry about any of that. You like doing it. My real job is fine with me. I don't have some huge desire to escape the life that I'm in.

The arts are subjective. While the music world offers a degree of open-endedness to enter informal careers in music, waiting for the business side of the music world to "recognize" musicians' art becomes too taxing over time. There are no gatekeepers per se that allow musicians to enter, but the key figures in the music industry (record labels, higher-end clubs, etc.) come to function as gatekeepers. Without their "approval," persisting becomes more difficult. As such, part of stepping away from music is the stepping *into* more a private practice of the arts.

> ROGER: Yeah, I definitely think I'll do music [in some capacity in the future]. I don't think I'll do it for [my entire] life, but at this point, it's in my soul. I can't explain it. I told that to a couple of other people. They might have thought it was cheesy. It's just, I have to have [music]. And another thing is, a lot of musicians describe themselves as artists . . . and one thing about real artists [is that] they feel compelled to do what they do. It's *in* them. It's definitely in me. Music is *in* me. Not any other type of artistic expression [does it] for me. The music is constantly in my brain. It's an integral part of life. I really believe that at this point. It took me a long time to really think that way, but I now know it to be true.

Relinquishing musical careers is often the musicians moving out of a public musical life. Rather than perform publicly or record music to be consumed by a larger public, the hobbyists are beginning to privatize their music. The hobbyists, though drifting away from music, are in fact still planning to commit to music for the remainder of their lives. The only element that will change, a major shift no doubt, is the dwindled pursuit of building it into a career. They will still write music and continue to perform, albeit limited to the realm of their private life. This is art in its most genuine sense: something created for the purpose of creative vision itself, perhaps never to be shared outside of the performer's life.

Consequences to Life

Music's Function for Understanding the Self

Music had numerous consequences to musicians' lives, many of which were meaningful in terms of identity. For a vast majority of the musicians with whom I spoke, music was a critical component of understanding who they were, not even necessarily as musicians or artists, but as human beings making their way through the world. As the musicians spoke of the significance that music had to their lives and their growing older, they often, without much probing, also told stories that highlighted the ways music influenced their understandings of their selves and constructions of their identities.

The musicians emphasized that music allowed for the emergence (often framed as a discovery) of their identities and self-perceptions (Laughey 2006; MacDonald et al. 2002). Were it not for music, said many of the musicians, their "true" selves would have likely remained dormant, undiscovered, and buried for their lives' entirety. Some of them, as discussed in Chapter 1, were self-described outsiders who saw music as their salvation. Those moments were often key to their beginning to pry open their true selves, again due to their interest in and exploration of music.

Many musicians clearly remembered how discovering particular musical artists led to creating and redefining a new part of their selves. A more common pattern, however, was that investing oneself in the cultural production of music opened up possibilities of moving in new, uncharted directions in life. For instance, when I asked if music helped him understand anything about himself, Owen responded:

> Absolutely. It gave me focus and also helped my sense of self-worth. Being a good musician gives you something to hang your hat on, as far as how you think about yourself and that's not a small thing, especially for younger people, kids. I think that writing [music] really helps to focus people on who they are, but the purpose for art, to me, is to illuminate people's experience as human beings, [to] help them fundamentally understand what it means to be human. And that's why every Tom Waits song can turn me into a soggy-eyed mess and Motörhead can make me feel like each one of my balls weighs five pounds each and I could eat my way through a plate-glass window. It's all about connecting with that emotional experience. I had this experience and now you had this experience. I think all art should do that. You've got to be open to it. I think kids should be encouraged to do artistic and creative things because it informs their experiences. It informs them about how they feel about things, but also because it gives them a strong sense of who they are.

Some of the musicians, like Owen, believed that the true function of music or any art was to inform them of the human condition. Music and art is what makes us human, and consequently gives rise to understanding one's identity and sense of self (Bennett 2001). Music was the dynamic in his life that helped him understand the multifaceted workings of who he was: the emotionality, the aggression, and the numerous other minutiae of his identity that collectively comprised the totality of his self. Similarly, other musicians strongly believed that music urged them to discover the pieces of them that they initially did not know lie inside them. It was a key process that helped them unlock who they "really" were, something that many of the musicians realized was a difficult task to accomplish without the right tools. They suggested, as theorists and philosophers have suggested for some time, that one's purpose—be it in music or otherwise—is essentially a task to find oneself.

Music's Function in Enhancing the Self

Music was influential to musicians' senses of self in ways beyond prompting them to understand their "true" selves. Time and again, musicians discussed the other benefits music had to their lives. One of the most consistent benefits of participating in music culture they cited was the boost in confidence music generated (Finnegan 1989; Wagner 2015). Admittedly, most of the musicians said that their initial steps into public performance were nerve wracking, though most grew to revel being on stage. They still experienced nerves before the show, but they grew to genuinely enjoy performing in front of audiences. Along with the comfort of being on stage, many musicians also experienced a confidence boost, such as Roger: "It definitely gave me self-confidence, which is something that I had never had much in my life. It sounds so cliché, but after the first show where I played really well, and there were people there, it felt cool, you know? Like I felt for the first time in my life I felt comfortable. Living in Athens my whole life, I [was always] sort of huddled in the corner and I never talked to anyone. . . . The only other thing I was ever good at was school, and you don't do school in front of a crowd. [The experience of being in] a rock band [is] tailor made for filling up people's egos: put a group of people around to cheer your musical abilities. It's a big deal."

The boost musicians felt by virtue of performing in bands could not be replicated elsewhere, according to the musicians. Music is "tailor made" for soothing bruised identities. Though talents and skills outside of music could enhance one's identity, many of those skills are not necessarily prone to public display, such as academics. Those sorts of skills could of course be recognized and honored in other less-public settings and observances, but the musicians felt there was no other feeling in the world as being on stage with an attentive crowd waiting to hear songs birthed in the private realm of the musicians' minds and bedrooms.

Furthermore, their increased confidence was not limited to the stage only. In fact, most of the musicians appreciated the extent to which their newfound confidence in their band often transpired to nonmusic facets of life. The sense of accomplishment they gained in their bands trickled into their other jobs, college life, even their personal relationships. As discussed in Chapter 2, many of the musicians felt lost early in life, not knowing their exact purpose or calling in life. Music was their foray on to their true life path in many respects. The confidence and comfort they felt knowing they were on the right path, coupled with their increased comfort with their senses of self and boosted confidence, often led musicians to feel that they finally felt "comfortable in their own skin," or as if they were finally "home."

Music also was a tool by which the musicians developed character. Many of them were surprised with the extent to which their simple love of music eventually paved the way for them to grow as individuals, to come closer to their full potential as adult women and men (Wagner 2015). Surprisingly to the musicians, their leisure time spent in music contributed to their work ethic. They felt, for the first time in their lives, that they understood what devotion, hard work, and passion truly was. Roman, in discussing what he has taken away from music thus far, said: "It's actually taught me about personal work ethic more than anything. I've come to realize what kind of personal character I have. If I want something, I [now] know how much I have to put into it. It is a kind of self-discovery. . . . I think now I am more self-motivated, and it's because of [the band]."

Many of the musicians were consistent in coming to understand the value of a hard day's work. Of course, they had been employed in other taxing jobs before, but some had never quite put as much of themselves into anything in life as they did with their music. The economic payoff was negligible, but the intrinsic payoff in writing a great song or playing a great show was worth more than any club owner could ever pay them. It also taught them about job satisfaction, particularly the extent to which it outweighs normative measures of workplace success (Finnegan 1989). Collectively, the lessons they learned in the work ethic, persistence, and patience taught the musicians volumes about themselves.

Music's Connection to Mental Health

Part of the musicians' continued investment in music is about pleasurable leisure, but another important, though private, function seems attuned to social-psychological health. Music, many of the musicians suggested, had a special connection to mental health (Carr 2006). The experience of being in a band—the process of songwriting in particular—prodded musicians to understand and bare open their untapped selves. They often felt the emotional dimensions of their inner selves were once veiled, and only exposed through their musical experiences.

Writing helped musicians delve deeper into their psyches. They went places they didn't know they would and became self-aware in ways they didn't necessarily want nor intend to. Some of them described the process of writing as "self-therapy" or therapy without a practitioner. Some musicians, more so the men than women, relayed that the creative process of songwriting keyed them in to their needing to "unload" issues, tensions, and anxieties that they were evidently keeping at bay. Paul said: "With my solo stuff, writing songs, I will definitely put things in songs that are much more brutally honest than I might be able to admit in conversation. It's a way to express things, a way to be honest about yourself, at least in the songs I write. A way to be honest about things and not have to walk around saying it. I know things about myself because of my songs. It's a way to dig into those things about yourself that you maybe don't want to."

The musicians, again more so the men than women, suggested that music helped them work through difficulties in their private lives. Music was a conduit for men to feel more tightly connected to the world and themselves. It was similar to practices of "getting back to nature" to separate oneself from the stresses of everyday urban life. Men's mythopoetic movements frame their weekend retreats similarly: a ritual of returning to nature to regain one's inner, lost masculinity (Newton 2004; Schwalbe 1996). Music provided similar functions. It was a way for men to investigate their inner selves, lost to the contemporary world. For instance, most of the men were in jobs that, even when providing satisfaction, tended not to allow them to attend to their inner, true selves. Music, however, accomplished those things.

Music's greatest latent function was its therapeutic nature, as it contributed to a soothing balance in musicians' minds and mental health. The connections between mind, body, and spirit were enhanced by the special power of music. Musicians spoke of the zen-like quality of music, especially when performing live. Being on stage gave them personal satisfaction, but it also was a cathartic experience. Many musicians liked music to religious experiences. They felt "reborn" or "cleansed" on stage. All the stresses in their lives, the questions as to whether they were where they needed to be in life, all the prompts to abandon music—all of these stressors faded away when on stage because in those moments they felt at home.

JANE: Even though it's hard work, there's nothing else in the world that makes you feel that way like when you're in a club and it's just the loud music. And it doesn't even matter if there's any people there or not. Once I'm up there I just forget about everything, just kind of apart from the rest of the world and bills and cleaning the toilets.

BRANDON: When I play a really good show or have a really good practice, I get a feeling that I don't ever get anywhere else. It's really cool. I exorcise all my demons. It's almost like, for a religious person, a baptism. You come out, and you are clean. You've sweated everything out, you're tired. Like for an athlete, at the end of the game, you play so hard, you're done. At the end of it, you can't complain, you can't be upset, you're just worn out. You're satisfied.

They felt accomplished after their performances. Even when the sense of comfort and security they felt on stage faded after the show, they were nonetheless reminded as to why they continued down what was often a tedious and demanding life pathway in music. They did it because it brought them comfort, much like religion functions in the larger population. And similar to religion, the musicians had undying faith that their life choices in music were the right ones—they didn't always know precisely why or how long they would persist, but they felt secure in who they were as individuals, lessons they imagined they could only have learned via music.

Speculation on Alternate Life Paths

Up to this point, I have traced the actual lived experiences of musicians and the directions their lives have taken. All of the musicians' lives were indelibly marked by the influence music had left on their developmental trajectories. They easily spoke of the significance music had on their lives, the particular directions they felt it pulled them, and how it undeniably reshaped numerous facets of their identities. However, their discussions of music's influence did not end there. In discussing their present lives, the musicians often speculated as to what their lives would have been like without music. They all were easily able to peer into an alternate universe that held what their lives would have been like had they not discovered, explored, and developed an intense interest in music.

These imaginings, of course, are the musicians' speculations. However, they are more than that—their visions of their individual life outcomes absent of music illustrate the power they believe music has had on their lives. They can never know for sure precisely how their lives would have panned out without the influence of music, but they have internalized their beliefs on the power of music and act on the basis of those beliefs.[6] In a word, it has given their world structure—the musicians can easily make sense of their lives, their identities, and their decisions because they believe full well that music is the most powerful social factor that has brought them to where they are in life.

Likewise, the musicians, as is undoubtedly the case for people in other careers, make decisions in their lives that have a domino effect elsewhere (Settersten 1999). Their choices regarding music affect other aspects of their lives, particularly other potential career trajectories that they decided against. A few of them are direct in stating that they made clear, conscious decisions for music at the expense of other career goals they initially had. Some musicians unquestionably have had to decide between a "good, stable" job that would require less time for their bands and jobs that offered more flexibility but less pay, fewer benefits, and lower status. Many select the latter, clearly prioritizing music over building a traditional career. Some musicians, in contrast, decipher how their less dramatic, incremental decisions regarding pursuing music may affect their lives as well. For instance, Alicia's following comments illustrate how she only recently began considering how her band has impacted her life:

ALICIA: I was thinking actually about this interview before I came out here, and it's not really something that had occurred to me before, but when I started thinking about it, how different would my life be as a grown up if I wasn't playing music, if that wasn't important to me at all? What would I be doing? ... I hate to think that this would be the case, but probably if it wasn't important to me, I would have moved away from Athens, and I would have some soul-sucking job at X Corporation in Atlanta and live in the suburbs in some little house. I don't think that I would ever be happy doing something like that, and it's nice to think that having this thing that's important to me has maybe saved me from just falling into the normal, what-you-do-when-you're-done-with-college type of routine, you know, get a job and have kids.... I think, if I wasn't playing music and if it wasn't important to me at all, I would probably be somewhere else. I wouldn't be here.

MR: So was that an intentional decision once you graduated? To stay here?

ALICIA: Yeah. I didn't say, "I'm going to stay here and continue to play music because that's really important to me." But I think, were I not playing music and if that wasn't important to me, I probably would have moved away.... And it's really weird to think about it because ... when something like that is important to you, you don't necessarily consciously think, "This is going to make my life different in so many ways," but it really does.

Similar to Alicia, other musicians, particularly those who had recently graduated from college, imagine that they would likely be in a more traditional career were it not for their current band. Some of them envision they would have pursued teaching, medicine, or veterinary careers. These decisions that led them astray from professional careers never felt like particular turning points. Musicians such as Alicia never particularly felt forced to choose either music or a normative path. Instead, they made incremental decisions as they aged, all of which ultimately culminated in their finding themselves on musical trajectories. These musicians find themselves gently drifting towards musical commitments as they move through adulthood. These are "easier" choices with less pressure and less feelings of risk taking. As such, the musicians with an incremental drift toward music feel fewer pressures stemming from their atypical adulthoods.

Other musicians, however, took the long-term, definitive perspective in evaluating the influence of music. Many of them recognized how dramatically music was the major influence at every turn, major and minor, in their lives since childhood. The musicians often compared themselves to their peers, as did Andrew, who imagined that "just about everyone who graduated [college] with me, their path is probably very different." They felt music fundamentally set them on particular paths in their lives. Nate said: "I think when you're young, what music you listen to determines the kind of people that you hang out with and that determines your influences, what you think is important, especially at that age. It's not whether you like music or not, it's what *type* of music you like. If you like certain types of music, it seems like those people turned into certain types of people." Nate and others were attentive to music redirecting them onto entirely different pathways than they perhaps otherwise would have been on without its influence. They grew up and experienced a different world, as they became acquainted with people interested in music. They were informally socialized in ways distinct from their nonmusical peers. The arts became something they valued. Their interests and identities unfolded in new directions. Some of the musicians believed that music allowed them to leave their former selves behind for better, more evolved, and the more genuine, "real" selves they became. These two perspectives—music as prompting an incremental drift versus music as dramatically shifting one's life direction—contrast with one another, but also overlap in one important respect. They regard music as triggering an unheralded shift in a new direction in life.

When I asked them to consider their lives absent of music, the musicians believed they would be missing something that inspired the direction they needed in life, but also expected that they would have "gone stir crazy" or been "really frustrated" in not having found an adequate passion in life. A common cultural misconception about rock and roll suggests it to be the pathway to deviance for youth, particularly in the lives of young men (Bennett 2001; Straw 2000). The musicians suggested otherwise. Their experiences indicated that it was quite the inverse, as Charlie remembers music keeping him out of more trouble. Though not initially on the straightest of pathways, he later developed into a "sort of goody two-shoes kid" who avoided the pitfalls of adolescence after sparking an interest in rock music. Part of it was due to the time commitment that music required—spare time that Charlie would have otherwise spent doing other things, some of which may have been delinquent. It gave his adolescent life a degree of structure. Even at an early age, he developed a sense of regimen to his leisure hours. Had it not been for the music clique he fell into, he imagines he would have fallen victim to the typical pressures of adolescence.

Some of the musicians shared sentiments similar to Shane, who said, "It's scary to think about how life would have turned out" without music. A handful of men and women, though more of the former, believed that music saved their lives. Were it not for music, they imagine they would not have survived to adulthood. When asked to described his alternate life without his passion for music, Owen said: "Imagine a teakettle with a hole welded shut. I would probably have turned to drugs or firearms. I think a lot of people who are soulless, sociopathic, the kind of people who become killers or criminals are people whose abilities to express themselves has been thwarted in some way or another by their socialization. 'Men don't have those emotions.' 'You're not allowed to have those emotions.' I think they get all bent up inside. And broken. So yeah, I'd be broken had [music] not entered the picture. I'd be fucked up. I'd be insufferable."

Music was an outlet for their angst, for the frustrations they felt. True, these frustrations are shared by many youth as they come of age, but the discovery of music fortuitously acted as a solace to the men and women with whom I spoke.[7] Many of them realized how therapeutic music was immediately upon it entering their lives. For those musicians who had more harrowing traumas in life, music eased their suffering, though they typically did not realize it at the time. A few musicians experienced the death of family members early in life. Vincent, whose older brother took his life during his teenage years, found a private solace to assuage his pain. In the aftermath of his brother's death, who he credited as sparking his interest in music initially, Vincent said he "retreated into music." Music was a solace for personal pains, especially depression, that a few of the musicians faced. Four of the musicians in total imagined that they would not be alive today were it not for music. One musician believed: "I would be dead for sure. Yeah, because there was nothing [else]. Music was the only constant reliable thing that I had."

A greater proportion of musicians voiced similar, though less drastic sentiments, that music saved them from a mundane life experience.[8] A majority of the musicians thought that their explorations in music enhanced their lives and identities. Had they not been marked by these experiences, they imagine they "probably would be a lot more boring" and "probably be stuck in a cubicle somewhere," as two musicians stated. Music helped them break out of their shells and find themselves, sometimes to the surprise of their family and peers.

LILLY: [Without music] I'd probably be what people expect me to be. I think people expect me to be a librarian who goes home and has plants and a couple of dogs—which to some extent I do go home and have dogs—but some people look at me and think, "Oh, she's the quiet, mousey girl who is probably just very introverted and doesn't have much [in life] except her job." And I probably would be like that [if I had never become a musician]. Being

> in a band has made me be more social than I normally would be inclined to be.... Probably if I didn't have music, I would be the person who just sits there and deals with some inanimate object [at work] and then goes home and spends time with her dogs or cats.

A common reaction of some of the musicians' co-workers, like Lilly, was the shock of discovering their "shy, introverted" co-workers were rock musicians on the side. Musicians agreed that, absent of music, their lives likely would have been drab. Not only did music give them a colorful and rewarding way to spend their leisure time, but it also added depth to their identities, as they developed in ways only music could allow.

Were it not for their intense devotion to music, many believe they would have continued on the path set forth for them via their middle-class social-ization (Bozick et al. 2010; Kohn 1969). Though most of the musicians had high educational attainment, many imagined they would have extended their education beyond the undergraduate degree, like Roger: "I'm happy the way my life has gone. I mean, if I had gone to one of those [other] schools and not [moved to Athens], I would have fallen headfirst into academics, you know? I was already on that path. I would have dropped music completely and maybe continued to be a listener and a fan, but I would've focused more on my education. I'd be getting my PhD in English or something." He and other musicians imagined that had music not entered their lives to the extent it did, they would have ventured into normative and privileged pathways of attaining credentials for jobs in high-status professions. What's amusing in Roger's response is his reading of his alternate pathway—the "wrong" choice he could have made—was one that leads to the highest possible level of education. With more educational credentials come the opportunities for increased opportunities in the labor market, something Roger fully acknowl-edged. Clearly, advantages would accrue from that "other choice" he decided against, which Roger full well understood. However, the musicians' avoiding the pitfalls of continuing down the middle-class default pathway of advanced educational credentials also veered them away from the endpoints of those pathways: normative careers and professions. Musician after musician stressed their avoiding the start of professional careers in the normative busi-ness world as a saving grace of music entering their lives. For example, Nate said: "At the point that I really started getting into music, I think [that my life direction changed]. Had I not gotten into music, I would now be wearing khakis and selling insurance. I look back at all the people that I went to high school with, and there was a group of people that got into, not necessarily music, but art. And now they're all doing these really cool things. And all the other kids, the 'normal' kids, are all living back in [my hometown]. They're not really going out and making something of themselves."

Nate and other musicians cited instances of their peers making normative choices as forging successful careers in the business world. Those measures of success, however, were not tempting to any of the musicians. Instead, the musicians were pursuing lives of artisans of sorts. A major satisfaction in their lives was that they had a tangible product, one that was intrinsically satisfying, to show for their work—something that would be missing in other lines of work.

DEAN: With music, you don't necessarily have tangible results from it, but there are these accomplishments that you make. You practice and rehearse for a show, and then you play the show. That's something—it's like a feather in your cap. It's something that everybody works towards together, and you accomplish something, you know what I mean? And I think that's something that's missing from a lot of people's lives. I have always been envious of people like carpenters and stuff. When you frame a house, when you're done with your work, you've got a fucking house, man. Think about how many things in life that you could actually say that for—not very many. You go to your 9-to-5 job, and it's like, what do you have at the end of the day? Well, nothing, you've got another day at work under your belt. Congratulations, you sat in a fucking chair all day long! I've kinda come around to the idea that there can be a little bit of artistry in music. It's a way to be creative, I guess. That's where you can draw the parallel between say a painter or a sculptor and a musician. I think even the thing that has held true of all of the bands that I've ever been in, is that we've at least been creative. Maybe we haven't been good, but we've at least been creative.

As Dean and nearly all of the musicians made clear, their life's goal was not to climb the corporate ladder to generate economic success and live a posh life. In some ways, they failed their socialization to internalize the American Dream. They did not prize status or wealth, but yearned for a life with art, music, and the development of their artistry. The goals they hungered for—and attained—were attuned to those components. Like construction workers who pride themselves on the bridges and buildings they literally built, the musicians took pride in being able to walk down an aisle in a record store, pull out their band's records, and say they played a role in those recordings (Hodson 2001). They had little income to show for their work, and little social status perhaps, but were flooded with pride in showcasing the fruits of their artistic labor.

In sum, the normative trajectory of middle-class attainment was a safer, more comfortable alternative to pursuing careers in music, but it was also stifling. The musicians without doubt saw the advantages that accompanied higher educational credentials and lucrative professional careers, but they considered the other costs that were part and parcel of those lifestyle choices. Many of them wanted something more than security and to follow in their parents' and peers' footsteps into adulthood (Swartz et al. 2011). They were artists at heart who perceived those normative trajectories as a muffled existence that, were they to make those safe choices, would haunt them for the rest of their days. They instead ended up pursuing something much bigger than music: they achieved a life of experiences that most people never get a glimpse of. Isaac said: "I have luxuries that other people will never have. I can go off and play in bands and travel, and other people can't. They'll *never* have that ability. There's just not enough time in life, [given] the way that other people have structured their lives." A life without music, they surmised, would be one without passion. Granted, they would have in all probability succeeded in other lines of work, but music gave them deeper meaning in their place in the world, "a purpose for life, something to live for, a reason to get up." Their minds at times throughout life had attempted to convince them to rationally play the safer bet by choosing the life expected of them, but their hearts, at least for a time, persuaded them to take a chance and pursue their musical dreams.

The musicians' lives are far from perfect and often include struggles of economics, identity, and adulthood, among others. They are, however, uniform in seeing their lives as outweighing the alternatives they could have otherwise taken. They also recognize their lives as somewhat off-time, but simultaneously redefine their decisions as appropriate and in line with contemporary adulthood. Finally, they are grateful to music, their bandmates, their fans, and the countless people they had the privilege of meeting as they journeyed throughout the music world. They are forever changed because of music. And they have each left an indelible mark on the world themselves.

Conclusion

In this chapter, musicians discussed two interdependent issues: their commitment to music and their ideas on the directions their lives will take in the future. A portion of the musicians had an undying passion for and commitment to music. It was what they were driven to continue to pursue for the rest of their days. They sincerely imagined music would always be the centerpiece of their lives and careers, though one accompanied by struggle. Not all musicians, though, were necessarily devoted to a lifetime of musical pursuits. Some framed their musical participation as temporal. These musicians were often planning their exit, sometimes unbeknownst to their bandmates. They remained confident, however, that music had boosted their lives and that they intend to remain partially involved in music participation, though as "hobbyists."

Regardless of their level of commitment to music, all musicians agreed that music was a compelling force in their individual lives that propelled them in the best and necessary directions they needed in their development over time. Because of music, they were able to discover who they were and delve deeper into their psyches. Music functioned to key them in to aspects of their identity that would have otherwise remained dormant. Music also acted as a tool that allowed them to develop a sense of character as they grew into adulthood. They developed skills that would forever remain part of their future endeavors, even outside of the music world. Musical participation also advanced their emotional health, as they were able to deal with personal struggles and mental health issues via music. In their discussions of a lifetime of music, the musicians emphasized ways their lives have been marked by music in the context of other developmental issues.

Finally, the musicians commented on their imaginings of how their lives would have potentially unfolded had they not discovered and developed a deep investment in music. Again, some of the musicians felt that music warded off an alternate life that would have dead-ended in less-than-ideal outcomes. In many ways, the latent functions—the unintended consequences—of music were more powerful, meaningful, and influential than the pursuit of music in and of itself. It was only because they devoted themselves to music that they were able to see the world the way they did, to experience the world in the manner they did, and to walk away with a résumé of experiences and skills that few others have the privilege to achieve.

Conclusion

• •

Music is more than a leisure activity or a creative outlet. It is more than a string of notes or the lyrics that accompany those melodies. It is more than a calling for those who imagine a life devoted to it. Music, said the musicians, was the one constant anchor in their lives that gave them the drive and hope for a meaningful future. The musicians' lives are insightful, curious, and intriguing in and of themselves. In this chapter, however, I expand my focus beyond the lives of the musicians in this book to frame broader contributions to understanding four key sociological concerns: aging and the life course, gender, occupational outcomes, and identity. Ultimately, I illustrate the extent to which musicians' unique experiences over the life course are not all that unique in comparison to the lives of many young adults today. Though placed in the specific subcultural milieu of music, their lives reveal the recurring challenges encountered during the transition to adulthood today.

Aging and the Life Course

Age Norms, Socialization, and the Influence of Gender and Social Class

The women and men with whom I spoke indicate the life course for musicians, and many young adults today, to be far less standardized that it was for generations past (Settersten 2003). At the same time, young adults today continue to be bound to cultural life course expectations that hold little relevance for their lives, experiences, as well as the institutions and structures embedded in the world. The tensions experienced by the women and men in this book are not unique to musicians only, but indicative of broader tensions at play in the lives of many young adults today. Their pervasive sense of limbo is attributable

FIGURE 8   A view of the stage, as The Late B.P. Helium wraps up a performance (Photo by Mike White, deadlydesigns.com)

to the longer time it takes in today's time for young adults to discover, prepare for, and settle into their careers of choice, be they in the informal sector or not (Furstenberg et al. 2005; Hamilton and Hamilton 2006). Those working toward the attainment of credentials or building experience for their career of choice today find the training period to be lengthy. This was true of the musicians, as it took time to figure out the music world, find a band, compose original songs, rehearse, book shows, record albums, and of course network to spread their band's appeal. Such lengthy time spans for prepping one's career in the formal sector is similar: a prolonged sequence of training, education, internships, and networking to build a more lucrative experience in hopes of landing the job to which they aspire.

The musicians' lives also illustrate the extent to which the life course continues to be organized by gender even in seemingly open-ended careers in music. While many researchers have examined the more delineated structure of trajectories for normative careers, a long-held assumption is that informal careers instead have arbitrary, blurry organizations (Merton et al. 1957). The findings in this book show such is not the case. Quite to the contrary, informal careers appear to be bound to similarly structured constraints and expectations of normative lines of work. To be sure, informal careers, such as those in music, are open. Fewer hard credentials are necessary for entering and pursuing them. Fewer formal gatekeepers guard the threshold of these careers. However, informal careers are influenced nonetheless by a host of obstacles that mirror those in formal career paths. Formal occupational frameworks are increasingly used as the business model in the music world. Despite an allegiance to the DIY (do-it-yourself) ethos, the music industry gauges success on quantitative measures, namely, record sales, fan base breadth, and tour lengths and tenures. Likewise, as Bielby (2004) has speculated, rock culture, constructed outside of the regimented structure of formal organizations, inadvertently uses elements from them as a model in its construction. Barriers of gender, social class, and race thus remain firmly in place in music scenes.

Age takes on special meaning in the music world as well. Women and men attach different social meanings to age and use different guidelines to measure progress in life (Hagestad 1988). Individuals hold strong to age norms, the best age at which to make particular life choices, both big and small. Likewise, culture dictates prescriptive and proscriptive age norms, the idea that individuals should do certain things, but not others, at particular ages (Settersten and Mayer 1997). In the music world, there are more proscriptive norms for women than for men. Not only is it rare for women to play music, but it is also unbefitting for older (adult) women to persist in this line of work. As many musicians suggested, social aging is sped up in the music world, due in part to the members of this world being young (typically college-aged) and having a high turnover rate (with a recurrent batch of eighteen- to twenty-two-year-old students taking their place). From the perspective of life course theory, the musicians are clearly in the early adulthood period. However, within the world of indie rock, they recognize themselves as having reached old age in this occupation, sometimes before having attained the level of success they had desired. They thus face dilemmas that life course developmental theorists more commonly identify as the crises of middle age.

Social class bears a significant influence on the process of aging as well. The entrance to middle-class adulthood is characterized as a time of exploration. For instance, researchers have shown the ways in which college buys young adults additional time in which to explore options (while of course earning credentials) (Karp et al. 1998). Musical life course pathways are similarly marked by a middle-class status, as musicians similarly "buy" their way into a phase of life with the privilege of self-discovery within the music world. Furthermore, traversing through college buys musicians additional time to explore music. For the musicians in this book who were college bound, those years were critical to opening up avenues into the music world. Of course, pursuing music does not require a college student status, but it does no doubt provide cover for doing so.

Additionally, middle-class socialization early in life prompted experiences that opened possible pathways onto musical trajectories. The typical musician remembered a childhood in which music was built into family life. They were exposed to music and the arts at an early age and, more importantly, prodded to learn instruments to become well-rounded middle-class youth. All of the musicians cited early music experiences as paving the way for their interest and skill acquisition in rock music later in life. The middle-class experience also allowed for greater resources to acquire instruments and/or private lessons during childhood. Children were granted ample opportunity to explore more seriously musical participation early in life, something that snowballed into advantage later in life.

The parents, in general, demonstrated a general appreciation for the arts. They valued their children's dabbling in various activities, music or otherwise. The children were granted wide opportunity to explore extracurricular and other leisure activities from childhood through adolescence. The latent function of such appreciation was the flourishing of artistic expression and the consideration of nontraditional careers in music performance in the years to come. Concerted cultivation did not necessarily promote pursuing music, but it did grant generous freedom in exploring a range of interests (Lareau 2003). From the perspective of some parents, middle-class socialization partially "backfired." In encouraging their children to explore a variety of interests to find their best and ideal fit, the parents did not expect children to ultimately select informal careers in the arts, threatening their middle-class status. They granted their children freedom, but assumed their ultimate career choice would be aligned with normative, professional careers. While parents were generally supportive, keeping their children's happiness and autonomy in mind, many were visibly disappointed, pressuring them to shift to a "better career [choice] before it was too late."

Music scenes the world over are not interchangeable, but instead are arranged to allow distinct opportunities for and life cycles of musicians' lives therein. Pathways for middle-class musicians in independent rock are almost certainly distinct from musicians in other scenes and social class backgrounds. For instance, the working-class settings of country and punk scenes would likely play out differently than did the experiences of the largely middle-class musicians in the college music town examined in this book. The musicians with whom I spoke of course acted with agency in resolving their life directions, but they did have the benefit and security of middle-class backgrounds, resources, socialization, and parents with similar visions of adulthood. Middle-class adulthood is a lengthier road with more time to explore career prospects. Securing possibilities in music is one such exploration that they were partially granted (though they did eventually reach their limits, as discussed in Chapter 2). Working-class musicians may have a different experience: perhaps more weightily critiqued as off-track in pursuing music in lieu of "real" work. Not having the resources at their disposal to

combat such sanctions, they may experience difficulty in securing commitment to music. Indeed, music may be a more grueling life course pathway for
the working class to board to begin with. Many musicians in this book did
so while in college—and with relative ease. Working-class men and women
have lower rates of college attendance and hence may not be able to "sneak"
music exploration into the early part of adulthood as easily as college students can. Living in a college music town, in and of itself, no doubt makes
access to musical possibilities more plausible as well. The context itself opens
up pathways for greater numbers of women and men to consider, test out,
and commit to music. The number of venues provided ample opportunity
for musicians to test out music—they could book shows, albeit on weekday
nights with smaller crowds, with greater success than would likely be the case
for musicians outside of college music contexts. The locale was saturated with
other musicians with similar demographic backgrounds, easing opportunities to expand networks to advantage their musical possibilities. All in all, the
advantages of locale, context, and demographics may be factors that synergistically converge to hearten middle-class musicians to persist. Would-be musicians in working-class contexts, in contrast, may consequently have a more
challenging experience in securing music possibilities.

Contemporary Adulthood

US culture invokes adolescence as a time of pastiche—picking and choosing
activities, social cliques, interests—in a word, forging identities and pasting
them together to construct one's lifelong and seemingly permanent identity.
Classic scholars such as Erikson (1950), among a host of others, argued adolescence to be the time in life during which the young discovered their identities
and explored who they "really" were. Adolescence is of course a time a discovery, as the musicians' histories clearly illustrate, but the explorations that have
come to characterize the introductory adulthood period are far more influential and potentially life altering than are the adolescent years. As a result, the
early adult years are presumably replacing adolescence as the most critical time
in development over the life course.

The musicians illustrate the dynamic change that accompanies the emerging adult years. They typically embarked on adulthood with fuzzy plans that
became fuzzier over time, not due to lack of commitment or distraction, but
instead because of the augmentation of attractive alternatives. Many musicians
entered adulthood with college and standardized professional careers on the
horizon, only to shift their aspirations upon gaining more experience in the
music world. While their parents may have felt such shifts were less than ideal,
the musicians treated them as serious career endeavors. Coupled with this shift
is a second change at play in the larger population: the transition to adulthood has become an increasingly complex, arduous task for contemporary

generations. The life course for today's young adults in the United States is far less "standardized" than it was for previous generations (Shanahan 2000). There is no single "right" or straightforward pathway to adulthood (the assumption that it ever was is faulty at best, and classist at worst). Meanings of adulthood are open ended and variable by social locations, such as social class, gender, generation, place, and historical time. Markers of adulthood have shifted too. The historical criteria of adulthood resting on starting a family and setting off a career are quickly becoming obsolete in the real world (Arnett 2004; Aronson 2008; Shanahan et al. 2005). These markers are organized by social class and gender and are far too confining in terms of the lived experience of age transitions in the United States. Though musicians are often critiqued as being pseudo-adults or having failed to launch into an appropriate adulthood, they are meeting—and in some cases exceeding—the criteria of adulthood. With rare exception, the musicians are residentially and financially independent of their parents, and demonstrate individualistic criteria of adulthood such as demonstrating responsibility and independent decision making. Their lives were not characterized by a drift into adulthood (Kimmel 2008), but instead by purpose. Musicians, as other scholars would likely agree, demonstrate an exceptional alignment with meeting the core components of adulthood (Shanahan et al. 2005). Like other young adults today, the musicians in this book reconstruct the meaning of adulthood, applying subjective criteria used by generations of late (Arnett 2004). And finally, music is a tool men and women use as they age, acting as a bridge from one life stage to the next (Kotarba 2013). The primary latent function of music is the possibility of securing a stable, music-centered self throughout life.

My findings also illustrate the extent to which subcultural participation in music allows for a more fluid experience in life. Musical life course trajectories are more open ended, variable, and less rigidly structured than those of standardized careers. My data suggest that the transition to adulthood among musicians takes place within a looser age structure than is typical among those in traditional careers. Such open-endedness does not prescribe complete freedom from stress or anxiety, however, and these life course pathways are not without their challenges. Musicians' pathways to adulthood are more convoluted in comparison to those of their nonmusical peers. Persistence in informal musical careers requires creativity, but more effort to align with a conceivable adulthood.

Finally, this book illustrates the increasing choice available to contemporary generations. Our culture grants a wider range of choices today than in the past, in both mundane, everyday aspects of life, such as TV channels and smart phones, as well as in more pressing, and seemingly permanent decisions, such as mate selection and career options. The unintended consequences of choice are many. Increased choice is freedom, but it can be paralyzing. Schwartz (2004) suggests too many choices can lead to anxiety, regret, and an overall dissatisfaction in life. The musicians exhibited stress—mounting with every passing year—but none expressed regret with their choices, nor dissatisfaction with the "big choices" in life. All believed music improved their lives more than it hurt them, that it bolstered their identities more than it truncated them, and that it ultimately was the right choice even when not a permanent one. The unintended consequences of choice complicate the progression through the life course, though they do of course allow for the potential for a greater maximization of life satisfaction.

Gender in the Context of Music

Men and Masculinities

As shown in Chapter 4, men's experiences with music were bound to issues of masculinity. For one, the musicians' histories clearly illustrate the extent to which men's life course pathways more directly lead to musical aspirations and commitments than do women's. Multiple factors converge that prompts men's life courses to be considerably more aligned with music. Rock music culture, as a simple leisure or a serious occupational endeavor, is more congruent with men and masculinity (Cohen 1997; Frith and McRobbie 1990; Leonard 2007; Walser 1993). Peer culture at play throughout the early part of the life course similarly provides a push for men to develop interests in rock music and invest in learning those instruments. The men were in social circles, composed predominantly of other boys and men, who provoked deeper interest and serious contemplation of music. By virtue of socializing with others in their peer groups who themselves had fascinations in music, the boys had these interests sometimes "rub off" on them. Their peers also introduced them to music, and much of their leisure time was spent listening to those bands, all of which slowly led to the development of musical dreams for the boys. The family, as discussed in Chapter 1, played a role in developing musical interests in both boys and girls. Again, for boys, family socialization with music was more direct than in comparison to girls. Fathers introducing their sons to rock music (sometimes outside the company of mothers and sisters) was a typical bonding experience during childhood, and one that men regularly evoked as they reminisced about their fathers. Similar to the development of boys' interests in sports, fathers were often at the helm of their sons' musical introductions (Coakley 2006). Finally, the constructions of masculinity in US culture overlap with workings of rock music. Boys spoke of easily identifying with rock culture—its bands, specific musicians, and even the themes in rock songs. Music was an agent of socialization that invited them to inhabit particular masculinities.

Musical participation also worked to enhance the men's masculinities, particularly early in the life course. Upon learning instruments and starting bands in adolescence, the men found an attractive masculinity, experienced a widening of their peer group, and witnessed a boost in their social standing. It provided a rare alternative to a valued masculinity in high school that was outside of the "jock" masculine formula.[1] This appeal was also apparent in the college years. Men who otherwise would have been lost in an anonymous sea of college students saw boosts in their visibility by being members of bands. Though they were not necessarily "famous" or even "almost famous," they were recognizable to the devout crowd of music fans in town and gained respect among their peers in other bands.

Identities centered on music only became a cost to masculinity when the men began exiting emerging adulthood for young adulthood. The appeal of music did not fade in the musicians' lives themselves, but instead consequences in their lives gave them pause. Primarily, the status of being a "struggling musician" took an economic toll on their lives. Though they could successfully manage their bills and maintain independence (through juggling multiple jobs and seeking creative living arrangements), the stress came from their economically vulnerable positions that posed a threat to their masculinities. The archaic provider role continues to influence men's lives, job choices, and commitments to their passions. Such was true of the musicians, and similar trends are likely at play in the lives of men outside the world of music. Masculinity, despite the changes in our economic and gendered landscape of the United States, continues to be measured by one's pay.

In terms of the social-psychological masculine identities, music demonstrated a dramatic influence in men's lives. In general, music provided a "both/and" quality to men's constructions of their masculinities. Via their participation in music, they embodied both normative *and* innovative constructions of masculinities. The archetypical man in music was regarded as a jack of all trades—a veritable Everyman—who conducted business with a DIY ethic that again harbored masculine undertones. These men were autonomous workers, go-getters who relied on no outsiders to perform the variety of tasks associated with their working lives as musicians. Finally, they also credited their aggressiveness and determination as factors that led to their unrelenting pursuit of music, all of which implicitly paints their work, not to mention themselves, in masculine hues. At the same time, men were quick to point out the ways in which music marked them with nontraditional masculinities. Many of the men regarded themselves and other men in rock as embodying softer, more emotional, "heart on my sleeve" masculinities. The craft in which they worked made them vulnerable. Sharing original compositions, often focused on private, lived, emotional issues in their lives, made their masculinities a proverbial open book. Participation in nonnormative work, particularly one that bears on expressiveness and creativity such as art and music, allowed for new masculinities to emerge.

Certainly, music is a site of gender resistance for men. Most suggested their identities comprised a combination of both normative and inventive masculinities. They also suggested their identities to be marked by a clear yet subtle feminization of masculinity, as is the case in other music worlds (Peters 2010; Ryalls 2013). However, though they challenged hegemonic conceptions of masculinity via their gender enactments, they ultimately reified its hegemony at the same time (Ryalls 2013). They, of course, could pick and choose what aspects of masculinity to highlight at will. In instances in which their masculinities were threatened (often due to financial insecurity or emotional vulnerability), they would redirect their identities by focusing on the cultural status, sexual benefits, and rock-and-roll lifestyle that was a part (though often minor, if that) of their lives. They undeniably made certain to emphasize how they were "real" men more than they challenged hegemonic masculinity. Their incorporation of strategic elements of femininity illustrates a restabilization of gender and power in the context of music scenes, not an overhaul in which it is permanently challenged. All in all, the music world exalts elements of the feminine to grant further status to a group with privilege already in place: men.

The musicians in this book suggest that, despite the unique configuration of their work world of music, their experiences may not be too distinct from those of men in normative careers today. The workplace continues to shape how men construct their masculinities, as well as the way they are regarded by outsiders. Our culture has witnessed a reorganization of the workplace in recent years. More men are pursuing nontraditional careers once marked as "women's" work. These men are adept are configuring their work to be fully masculine (Williams 1995). Greater proportions of men today are taking longer to forge careers due to the extension of education and/or are part of the contingent workforce, threatening a fully secure masculinity as well. And, of course, most jobs today in our postindustrial world, especially those in the white-collar and service sector, do not as easily imbue masculinity in its workers in comparison to heavily masculine lines of work such as manual labor or the military.

Women and Femininities

Music is a space for women to perform gender in ways unavailable in the everyday world (Butler 1990; Halberstam 2005; Taylor 2012). It is a site of rebellion for some women, while others framed it as a site of revision. Women overwhelmingly agreed that they and other women musicians embody femininities far different from those in mainstream, nonmusical culture. They did not suggest that performing in a band would de facto alter one's femininity, just as they imagined entering any alternative occupation would not directly change those women's femininities either. However, they resolve that participation in an informal career requiring drive, persistence, and "tough skin" would inevitably influence women's constructions and display of their femininities.

During their tenure in music, women produce new forms of femininities—what Halberstam (1998) details as "female masculinities"—as they reimagine masculinities as relevant and pertinent to their lives and circumstances. They distinguish women musicians as enacting more masculine-coded characteristics, such as aggression, courage, and confidence. Since rock culture is imbued with such masculinity, women were prone to adopt masculine characteristics (sometimes inadvertently) to enter and succeed in this arena. In effect, women musicians create new forms of femininity to transgress the gender divide in traditional conception of music as a "man's world." Others regarded the artistic thread of the music world as contributing to women's novel femininities. Participation in the "male" culture of rock allowed women to release the inner workings of one's identity deemed transgressive, even inappropriate, in normative culture (Halberstam 1998).

The musicians are witnessing and participating in the frontier of change in the gendered world of music. They largely feel at odds as to whether women in music challenge gender or are merely a part of music's contemporary landscape. Their apprehension in reading women as a challenge to the world of music is part of the larger arc of the shift they have witnessed for some time. They could easily look to the token women in music, both nationally and regionally, as evidence that women have made it. There still were instances, however, that made it difficult for them to discount the cultural significance gender retained in their lives. For one, women musicians' experiences in music parallel those of women in more professional, male-dominated careers. Women in music often have unwarranted reputations of being "bitchy" or having inflated egos. Women who have "made it" in music are recounted as being too demanding, too assertive, and too inflexible. Of course, as many others have documented, many women in prestigious, high-status positions in the normative workplace are often regarded similarly (Harris and Giuffre 2015; Kanter 1977; Ridgeway 2011). There are consequences, however, to women's adhering to the male worker prototype (Acker 1990). Many a man in music who has demanded his band's compensation from a problematic club owner is regarded as an advocate for the band and the general population of musicians. Men are doing it for the greater good. Women who acted in similar fashions, in contrast, are difficult, catty, and not cut out for the business. Women musicians often have no choice but to conform to masculine ideal types in the music world, the cost of which is their being sanctioned as difficult individuals with whom to work.

One final aspect of women's straddling the traditional/transgressive femininity divide hinged on their alignment with (or distance from) feminism. Not all the women identified as feminist. Those who did, however, tended to conceptualize their alignment with third wave feminism. Women often cited the idea that although gender was an influence in their (and other women's) lives, equally important were the identity markers of social class, race and ethnicity, and sexuality, among others. Consistent with other women of their generation, they also seemed to embody a "pick and choose" conceptualization of feminism, selecting the aspects, beliefs, and attitudes that resonated most readily with their lives and experiences. To be sure, many of the women adhered to aspects of feminism, yet did not see it as an anchor of their identity. Rather, it was an important artifact in history that helped lead them to where they and other women were today. They did not discount or minimize the work, efforts, nor advocacy of women musicians past, but they did generally see women as having "made it." The gender imbalance that unfortunately remains in the music world (among other institutions) was due to socialization and other individualistic factors that prompted few women to actively choose music. They tended not to recognize the structural components of the rock world—often due to its informality—as a major influence to women's limited presence.

Without a doubt, women did find themselves in a precarious position in the music world. They were empowered and at times considered "just one of the guys," yet they often were short-changed in a world that largely remained male dominated. In contrast to other studies, however, women encountered far fewer instances of discrimination, harassment, and exclusion than did women in music scenes from long ago (Leblanc 1999; Reddington 2004; Walser 1993). Women in past scenes are characterized with an assertive and confrontational resistance (Leblanc 1999; Reddington 2004). The women with whom I spoke tended to behave differently, due not to their being less confrontation or headstrong, but instead due to the muted inequality in their music worlds. In the rare instances in which men discriminated against or harassed women, they typically responded with confrontation, similar to that of punk women in earlier time periods (Leblanc 1999). They were assertive in their demands for appropriate treatment and status recognition as band members.

Rare was the case, however, in which other musicians told women they did not belong or were not "good enough" to make it, illustrating a substantial change in the music world: women's participation is almost never questioned. Women today are more firmly embedded in the central network of the music scene, generally securing an insider status rather than attempting to find a space with other women in music, as was the case in past scenes (Leblanc 1999). And because their presence was so "ordinary," women (and men bandmates) were hesitant to describe women musicians as feminist, political, or transgressive. Though women were still not necessarily the norm in music, they were likewise not regarded as token torchbearers of activism and social change.

The push for social change by women (and men) from days gone by has indisputably shifted the culture of music to be more inclusive for the women examined in the 2000s. Part of the "ease" with which they entered the music world was due to the work of women musicians in previous times. However, subtle discrimination and inequality that persist today are frequently more insidious. There was "no one to blame" for women's comparative absence in music. As a result, some music participants would fault women themselves. Others, however, cited the culture of rock as the primary culprit. Likewise, they began to recognize the influence of socialization, not as fate, but as a factor that would put some individuals (namely, men) on musical pathways more readily than others (namely, women). Of course, discrimination, subtle or overt, stems from the same root origin: gendered division of power. Women have less status, abbreviated histories, and constitute smaller populations in the male bastion of music, all of which grants them limited power to claim a space in music. The culture of the indie rock world, however, was more similar to the alternative rock scene examined by Schippers (2002) in which participants engaged in "gender maneuvering" to change the culture and expectations of gender within. At the micro level, the culture of music has shifted. It is one that is more inclusive, accepting, and less blatantly sexist. There is clear and genuine change taking place. However, the macro level of the cultural production of music, as well as the structure of the life course, remains one in which men are advantaged and afforded more direct pathways to futures that include musical participation. By underscoring the "going rate" of sexism from times long ago or other more sexist genres, musicians (often men, but at times women as well) render contemporary scenes as more open and equal, while ignoring the continued dimensions that continue to privilege men (Mullaney 2007).

The Social Organization of Informal Careers in Music

In clear contrast to other theoretical perspectives framing musical endeavors as "serious leisure" (Stebbins 2009), the musicians were adamant that their participation in music was not leisure in the slightest. The women and men in this book instead framed it as an informal career. The musicians, especially the lifers, did not characterize music as enjoyable in the traditional, hobbyist sense. It was work—excruciating, demanding, tiresome, and stressful. They did of course gain some intrinsic satisfaction from music performance, but music had by and large lost its pleasure. This was not necessarily a negative, so suggested the musicians, but instead part and parcel of the demands of the informal career. It was, in fact, seen as a matter of maturity and occupational commitment.

While informal careers provide only a loose structure for musical careers, they do visibly influence life course pathways to the musician identity. There are clear patterns to pursuing musical careers, but these transitions are less distinctive than for people in other traditional careers. For instance, there are no timed transitions that are tied to age in the music world. While individuals in the business world may have a somewhat rigid "timeline for success" for moving up the corporate ladder, such age- and time-graded meters are less clear in the music world. While gauges for musical success are more fluid, they are not entirely absent.

Informal careers in music were taxing to both women and men, though the former faced a number of unique challenges. To be sure, women's patterns were generally consistent with men's, but particular aspects of their life courses marked their decisions more sharply. First, musical careers, despite their informality, are clearly organized by gender. Career timelines are different for women and men musicians. Women have shorter timelines for success in comparison to men. The women not only started later but they also have shorter self-imposed time periods in which they expected to achieve success. Women expect to reach a suitable level of success by a particular age, while men's expectations are more ambiguous. If women do not meet their expectations by a particular time frame (corresponding to their reaching their thirties, most often), they are likely to define this as the appropriate time to disengage from the music world. Women in other competitive careers may exhibit similar experiences. Other research has shown men to persist longer in lucrative, "long shot" careers in comparison to women (Fiorentine and Cole 1992; Hancock et al. 2013). Partly an issue of masculinity, men may have boosted confidence prompting them to shoot for the moon while women are "more realistic." Even more critical, perhaps, is the extent to which familial support (or lack thereof) may truncate women's aspirations. Those who initially have interests in lucrative careers and "dream big" may pare down those aspirations to something safer, more appropriate, and pragmatic.

Second, gender queues in music remain persistent (Reskin and Roos 1990). Women rarely played the guitar. When they did, they were often the lead singers of their band. The few women who held the dual (and highly visible) roles of lead singer and guitarist were always the "founders" of those bands, thus illustrating that the primary mechanism for women avoiding cursory roles was by starting bands themselves. However, women were not relegated to "invisible" roles in the backgrounds of bands. They were often front and center both on stage and musically. The bands, said their bandmates, would not exist were it not for the women's contributions stylistically. They were regarded as irreplaceable, yet remained in the secondary queue, seemingly at the hands of the gatekeepers to recruit them in to bands, thus bringing them into the foyer of the music world. In this sense, women musicians paralleled women in the historical workplace, treated as a reserve army of sorts, a population with the talent, qualifications, and interest in entering the work world, yet powerless and thus waiting for the invite to join the proverbial boys' club.

Third, musicians, like individuals in other lines of work, recruited mentors to informally coach them for musical life. Musicians' mentoring relationships, as evidenced by their narratives, are tightly organized by gender. Men engaged in little footwork to harness their mentors. Typically, they passively recruited them through their social networks. Many times, their mentors were their friends, bandmates, or others with whom they were already acquainted in another social realm of their lives. Men were hesitant to use the term *mentor* to describe the relationship with the individual who assisted them. For some, this was due to the covert nature of the mentoring relationship.[2] Men musicians rarely forthright asked for assistance in these relationships, instead they surreptitiously emerged early in the men's careers. The issue of power may have been at hand too. Men often prided themselves as individualists venturing into the world of music on their own. To suggest they were aided by mentors dilutes their rugged individualism and hence their masculinities. This trend may very well be relevant to the experiences of men in other lines of work. While women today are more vocal about the role of mentoring in their lives, men the world over may pride themselves in embarking and staking successes in their work lives seemingly on their own.

Women's mentors came from the same pool as men's, but the ways in which they evolved were unique. Two issues stand out as most distinct in women's mentorships. Overwhelmingly, women's mentors were men, due primarily to the pool of potential mentors from which they had to choose. The music scene was dominated by men, thus those with the most experience to guide women into their careers would be those same men. Furthermore, women repeatedly stated that men to whom they were already connected— boyfriends and men family members—were the ones most likely to take on those roles. Women were somewhat outside the music world, thus it was difficult for them to forge relationships, mentoring or otherwise, with men already established in the scene.

The occupational structure of musical careers has implications to musicians' lives, one of which being its factoring into an undulating testimony of job satisfaction. On one hand, the musicians consistently proclaimed self-actualization in their work. Their focus on art and creating music for personal satisfaction was what was often most valued in their lives. It was highly satisfying to see the fruits of their musical labor via new songs, successful public performances, and the eventual recording and release of their albums. Many of them felt they were leaving behind a legacy of sorts: music that would survive beyond them, marking their contribution to the music world and to Athens in particular.

On the other hand, the musicians did feel a subtle, yet recurring, alienation. Unlike many traditional lines of work, the musicians did not feel stifled. They experienced a high degree of autonomy in their working lives in the music world. The creative component to their work boosted their satisfaction. However, they were bound to other undying pressures. When music is promoted from leisure to work, the musicians suggested it lost its romance. Part of this hazard was due to their treating music seriously, much like they imagined the work of artists, writers, or actors would similarly downshift in its "pure" enjoyment. This was the most bittersweet work hazard they mentioned. The one aspect that initially drew them to music—the drive to create—became tinged with the pressures of work. They felt increased (self-)pressure to succeed, be more prolific, more creative, and stamp their music with their sound. Some of the musicians felt guilty when they had fun—on tour, no less, as they were traveling and exploring the country. What should have been a highlight of their career (and, no doubt, was) became shaded with hues of a sober gravity. Such is likely the case with other nonstandard careers in the arts. The structure of informal careers grants freedom for work to be purely fun, alternately serious, or something in between. The musicians in this book, because they were devoted to music, treated it as the most serious of professions, and hence self-prophesized the ennui of work to emerge in their day-to-day lives. These pressures, again often self-induced, eventually led some to surrender their commitments to music.

Musical careers in college music scenes seemingly know no boundaries. They are open playing fields in which anyone with the intention can participate or, at the very least, attempt to do so. Informal careers, such as those in music, presumably have fewer constraints that prevent men and women from pursuing them. Informal careers are certainly less standardized and work within a more informal social organization, but the loose organization of these occupations may not necessarily be purged of all constraints entirely. Instead, new barriers and constraints, many of which may not be found in the formal sector, infiltrate the informal social world of music, impeding people's success.

Identity

Examining the musicians' life courses show there are no clear markers, events, or rites of initiation that grant one's legitimacy as a musician. Musicians do not undergo occupational socialization that individuals in more traditional career paths do (Hermanowicz 1998; Mortimer and Simmons 1978). Their informal training and preparation for the music world—largely devoid of educational institutions—is not accompanied by a normative set of expectations as to how to succeed, how to become the "right" type of musician, and so on.

Instead, constructions of musician identities hinge on two mutually reinforcing factors: authenticity and attempts at the professionalization of informal careers. First, authenticity is a project of the self (Kotarba 2013; Vannini and Williams 2009). Expectations of authenticity guide (and may inevitably self-prohibit) the adoption of musician identities, and those who attain the subjective claim of authenticity more easily self-situate themselves in the music world. Other genres—blues, hiphop, heavy metal, and country, for instance—are bound by tropes of authenticity (Grazian 2003; Harrison 2008; Larsson 2013; Mullaney 2012). In independent rock, however, there are few criteria for authenticity. Musicians did emphasize the DIY ethic as one center point of the indie rock identity, but not much else. They have a "proletarian" approach to musicianhood—anyone could presumably claim the identity— due to the limited criteria for inclusion. Safer to err on the other side, however, musicians instead tend to opt to not strongly identify as a true musician. All musicians, as described in my criteria for inclusion in the Introduction, did have extensive experience in music: lengthy tenures in their bands, vast experience performing publicly, touring the country, and recording and releasing albums. Despite their breadth of experience, their staking claims of musicianhood were cautious at best. Unsuccessfully securing authentic musician identities was a considerable prompt that culminated in their exiting music for other ventures.

Second, attempts at the professionalization of informal careers worked to reinforce authentic musician identities. The musicians who were more comfortable self-describing themselves as "real" musicians sometimes had other factors at play in their lives. They framed their work in their bands as "just like any other business" and thus were likely to internalize the musician identity. These musicians placed their work identities on the "work" rather than "leisure" side of the music continuum. They treated music as a serious endeavor that overlapped with normative lines of work. Furthermore, they were often more deeply embedded in the music world due to their dual statuses as musicians and employees in another (often more formal) realm of the music industry. Men, in particular, who worked as audio engineers, promoters, or ran their own recording studios felt a boost in their musician identity, not to mention their professional identity in the music sector.

The musicians consistently agreed that their participation in music had fundamentally shaped their identities, not simply as cultural producers, but more generally as men and women making their way through the world. Musical participation also led them to uncover and develop aspects of their identities that were long dormant. Were it not for music, many of them imagined they would not have had the opportunity to discover their true selves. Others, in contrast, felt that their realized identities were not necessarily dormant, but altogether reshaped by music. In this sense, music propelled them to develop into entirely new individuals.

Finally, the musicians in this book illustrate the ways in which participation in music marks them for the rest of their lives, whether they persist or move on to something new. Regardless of their anticipated commitment to music in the future, all of the musicians felt fortunate to have had the chance to discover new aspects of their identities that would have remained undeveloped were it not for their time in the music world. Looking back on his lifelong devotion to music, Owen captured its significance in his life:

You make these fantastic friendships [with people all over the country] and see them every now and then. You watch their lives progress and their heartbreaks and triumphs and children and jobs. It's almost embarrassing how lucky you are to know so many people who live for music and love art and nurture that part of their lives. You just end up with this tribe of poets and artists and madmen that you are connected with. I could name thirty people off the top of my head that I haven't seen in ten years who I'd be [curious] in knowing what they're up to. Those friendships, that's worth the price right there. People are like, "It's too bad [the band] never made it." I'm like, "Man, we *made* it." We made it in a way that bands who go straight from being the A&R guy's nephew's band in a basement to being on the cover of *Rolling Stone* will never experience. They don't stay at people's houses. They don't break bread with them, eat meals with them, sleep on their couches and have to deal with their fucking dog. If you're gonna do the Jack Kerouac thing, pick up a guitar. If you want to see the country, if you want to know the difference between jambalaya in New Orleans and Thai food in San Francisco, or what it's like to swim in the beaches in Northern California versus the Kill Devil Hills on the East Coast, join a band. You'll travel more, you'll see more, you'll experience more. . . . It was the best experience.

The musicians' stories and lives illustrate the importance of the cultural production of music over the life course, emphasizing that this book's focus on one small, nontraditional population represents recurring challenges that many contemporary young adults face as they move into adulthood today. The musicians in this book, like many other young adults in other contexts, do not typify an arrested development, nor a series of false starts. Instead, they illustrate the precarious and newfound challenges of navigating adulthood in a world that has not existed before.

Finally, the musicians were convinced music was the reason for which they were put on this earth. They believed their fate was to create art, to leave something behind, to make a mark on the world, to do something great. While many musicians in this book felt "destined" for music, I have attempted to illustrate that they, like most individuals in other careers, ultimately arrive on particular life course pathways due more so to gender, social class, race, and a range of contextual, social, and temporal factors than due to matters of destiny and fate. The musicians were also consistent in the power music has had in shaping their lives in one fashion or another. Regardless of their speculations of roads not taken, they consistently recognize the blessed experience in music that has shaped their lives—what they regard as the ultimate takeaway from their time in the music world. That, said the musicians, was the true and most fundamental power of music.

Acknowledgments

Like all the important things in life, writing this book was a lot harder than I imagined it would be. I am lucky to have had an army of support behind me as I completed this project. I would like to thank all of the educators who shaped my mind and interests throughout my life. Ms. Linda Shasberger and Ms. Bettye Albright were the first to grant me freedom to write in my own voice at an early age. Mindy Stombler was key to putting me on my sociological pathway as an undergrad. The sociological light bulb she ignited in me burns to this day. During my grad school years at the University of Georgia, Linda Grant was my constant advocate, pushing me to be brave and take chances when I didn't think I could. Her mentorship is a gift I will value forever. Concetta Kirschner is a treasured mentor who I am beyond fortunate to have worked with on this book and the larger project of life.

The friendships I built during my time in Athens will always remain special. Liz Cherry, I thank you for our special friendship, our weekly excursions to the dog park, and the wonderful vegan food you shared with me. Nicole Pallotta, Stephanie McClure, Anita Winfrey, Lorraine Evans, Eric Griffith, and Wendy Moore are among my dearest of friends from my time in Athens as well. I am beyond grateful to have met and befriended Kim Cox (and Pica) during the chaos of graduate school. And a very special thank you to Beth Montemurro who was critical to making this book a reality. I am also grateful for the advice I received from Patricia Richards, Marybeth Stalp, and Reuben A. Buford May as I began writing this book.

I am grateful to my colleagues at Texas A&M University–Corpus Christi for their encouragement during this project, especially Pam Meyer, Isabel Araiza, Bilaye Benibo, and Jennifer Epley. A most sincere thank you is in order for the ever-wise and ever-entertaining Eric Moore. I am happy that your office is just steps away from mine. The diversions we have each week are valuable to me. I appreciate the encouragement I received from my department chairs over the years, especially Joe Jozwiak and Pam Brouillard. I am grateful to Katie Reese for her efficient work when I dropped the ball on a few critical tasks while completing this book. Many thanks to the members of my academic band, Ded Sledge: Mark Hartlaub, Steve Seidel, Jack Gron, and Greg Reuter. I appreciate the invitation you extended to me many years ago to begin playing music with you. I look forward to many more rehearsals and shows in the future.

The brawniest of thank yous to Coach Vonkiel Advincula and the staff at CrossFit Iron Addicts for the many times I needed to give my brain a break and get my body active. I am lucky to have developed friendships with everyone at the box, especially Emma Hanley, Angelica Sanders, Kim and Robert Cirilo, Stephanie and Aaron DeVictoria, Ernest Valdez, Shandele Smith, Heather Cardona, Francis Torres, and Jennifer Abeto.

My feeling is this book was destined for Rutgers University Press. My editor, Peter Mickulas, was a godsend. I am thankful for his undying support and encouragement of my work. I sometimes felt like I was stumbling through this process, but he always shined a light for me. Thanks also to the staff at Rutgers and BookComp for their assistance in editing, formatting, and finalizing this book, especially Jennifer Blanc-Tal and Nicholle Robertson. I am particularly indebted to Ross Haenfler and Joe Kotarba for their thoughtful and meticulous reviews of early versions of this manuscript. This book is considerably improved due to their insight and suggestions. I have long admired your work, and having you both review mine was humbling.

I am grateful to the Miriam Wagenschein Fellowship for providing me time and resources to devote to this book. I never had the pleasure to meet Dr. Wagenschein, but I hope she would be happy with my work in this book. Thanks to Sage Publications for allowing portions of my previously published work to appear in this book. Some elements of Chapter 2 are based on my 2013 article "'You Start Feeling Old': Rock Musicians Reconciling the Dilemmas of Adulthood," *Journal of Adolescent Research* 28: 299–324. Sections of Chapter 4 are based on my 2012 article, "Performing Gender through Performing Music: Constructions of Masculinities in a College Music Scene," *Journal of Men's Studies* 20: 108–124.

Mike White at Deadly Designs is among the best humans on this earth, and I am grateful his photographs contribute to the narrative in this book. Thanks to Don Chambers a hundred times over for allowing me the use of his haunting and beautiful lyrics. I am delighted that this book is a space where our words linger together.

And, of course, the most loving appreciation to my family. Mom and Dad have always been supportive of my dreams, even when they were not yet fully developed. I do much of this for them. Yvonne, who will always be the coolest sister in the world, is among my closest of friends and confidants. Sheila and Blade, the most loveable of all canine companions, were by my side as I started this project. I miss you, Blade, every day. Sheila, you are essentially my co-author, as you were literally beside me as I wrote and edited this book. I love our daily walks that clear my mind and remind me to enjoy every moment I get to spend with you.

My most tender thank you to my partner, Ashley, and to my daughter, Brianna Renee. Writing this book was probably a lonelier process for Ashley than it was for me. I spent many nights locked in my office working on and revising these chapters, when we otherwise could have been watching horror movies and wrestling. Her love, patience, and impassioned encouragement motivates me to do work that matters and inspires me to be the best person I can be. If everyone had someone like Ashley in their lives, this world would be a much more joyful place. Brianna, you are my world. I want to make this world better, safer, and more loving so that it will one day be deserving of you. I celebrate every day I have with you and your mother.

Finally, a very warm thank you to the musicians who participated in the interviews that are the heart of this book. There were many times I was equal parts fascinated, excited, and amused to have the opportunity to sit down with each of you and talk about your lives. I was a consummate music lover long before starting this project, but hearing the impact music had on each of you forced me to recognize the special power of music. Thank you for your candidness, and thank you for shaping Athens, and all of us who have had the privilege to live there, with the gift of your music.

Notes

Introduction

1 The Census Bureau does not track men's rates of changing their last names after marriage. However, limited data suggest that support for such decisions may be increasing, though few men anticipate adopting their wives' last names upon marriage (Hamilton et al. 2011; Scheuble and Johnson 1993).

2 Sociologists use the terms *sex* and *gender* to distinguish two distinct, though related, aspects of the social world. Sex refers to the biological criteria of being female, male, or intersex. Gender, in contrast, emphasizes the social construction of behaviors, norms, and expectations culturally associated with being feminine and/or masculine. Gender influences microlevel interactions, including individual identities and behaviors, as well as macrolevel structures, such as the gendered social order of the economy, family, and other institutions. Gender is a cluster of learned attitudes and social expectations that may feel "natural" but is rooted in culture and socialization. While these concepts are constructed in relation to each other and may in fact influence one another, they are distinct in their meanings and usage. Throughout this book, I attempt to consistently use the terms *sex* and *gender* to address the distinct functions, influences, and consequences of each concept. See Lorber (2012) and Gerson (2010) for further discussion of these and other relevant concepts.

3 While many events culminated to the birth of rock music, two events stand out as particularly central. The seminal song, "Rocket 88," performed by Jackie Brenston and his Delta Cats (Ike Turner's alias) was released in 1951. It is considered by many to be the first rock and roll record. The following year, Leo Fender and Doc Kaufman designed the first-ever mass-produced electric guitar. The inexpensive model of this guitar would allow far more would-be musicians to pick up the instrument, thus propelling the cultural production of rock and roll to the masses.

4 This chronology is by no means exhaustive, nor does it necessarily include all musicians who influenced the musicians in this project, though many of them were cited in the stories told by the musicians with whom I spoke. Rather, it is a brief account of the musical flavors and directions rock has taken, due at least partially to those described here. What's more, music history has largely defined each of them as cultural icons deeply influential to the musical landscape of rock.

5 As others have noted, however, in an age of increasingly complex musical landscapes, the popularity of rock has declined over time. Nevertheless, rock remains a powerful force in the life course today (Kortaba 2013). More than other genres, rock triggers an early interest in music and, as will be shown in later chapters, is the impetus for youth learning instruments, writing songs, and developing musical dreams. At the same time, it is also more than a cornerstone of youth culture. Rock is increasingly multigenerational, as many adults have come of age within the context of rock music and inscribe it as a key feature of adult culture (Bennett and Hodkinson 2012). The cultural shift in the social experience of aging allows for a continued engagement with rock well into adulthood. As the preeminent form of popular music, rock is particularly social in its organization and influence throughout the entirety of the life course (Kotarba 2013).

6 Music sales data generally show similar rates of music consumption by gender. Women are slightly more likely than men to be "music consumers" (RIAA 2015). While there are gender differences in rates of purchasing music, downloading music, streaming music, and subscribing to satellite music services, women and men generally consume music at similar rates (RIAA 2015). There is far more variation by age, race, and ethnicity than by gender.

7 The divide between "fan" and "musician" is largely a false one, especially for the men and women in this book. Musicians of course begin as consummate fans before transitioning to musicians themselves, and they remain fans as they move along their musical pathways. However, they generally spoke of their musician and fan identities as distinct, albeit overlapping, identities.

8 Gendered enactments of fandom may be tied to the gender composition of the bands themselves. If a majority of bands are composed of men, girls and women may participate in heteronormative scripts in their desires to be romantically linked to the musicians, as well as a means by which they explore their sexuality (Walser 1993; Wise 1990).

9 The "objective" weight of turning points, whether they are actual shifts or simply *perceived* as significant, is not of central concern, since the perception of a shift in and of itself creates new possibilities and the potential for new identities (Clausen 1993).

10 Social class and gender influence one's "feel" age, as those from lower socioeconomic statuses tend to perceive the onset of old age occurring earlier than for higher classes (Barrett 2003). Likewise, women tend to have more youthful identities than men (Barrett 2005).

11 Some worked part-time jobs, often due to their concurrent status as college students.

12 Tallies exceed the sample size due to some musicians taking on multiple roles in bands, such as singers sharing guitar responsibilities or some musicians switching between the bass and keyboards in their bands.

13 See Ramirez (2014) for an expanded analysis of my identity and its methodological implications in the field.

1. First Hearing the Sounds

1 Life course scholars have long used retrospective data to understand life outcomes, much to the chagrin of life-span theorists who prefer a more "objective" measure of key events over life. As human animals, our memories are unquestionably faulty. What's more, the moments we highlight as being critical turning points in the course of life may perhaps be of little influence, unlike Bob Dylan's recollection of

hearing Elvis during his adolescence. The reality is that individuals can never be confident that what they self-perceive and remember as a turning point is a bona fide *categorical* turning point. We can never know how life would have unfolded had particular events not transpired (or not at that particular moment in that particular context that we deem as setting the course for our future life course). Nevertheless, such recollections are the only issues that matter as we think back on moments that shaped our life outcomes. The factors, events, and turning points that we cite as the defining moments in the paths we take in life are quite real in our recollections of our life experiences. A basic tenet of symbolic interaction stems from the Thomas Theorem: "If people define situations as real, they are real in their consequences" (Thomas and Thomas 1928:57). In this sense, meaningful events that individuals "file away" in their memories are presumably important enough to be "real" in their consequences.

2 Music often acts as an anchor for early life memories, typically within the context of the family (DeNora 2000).

3 Christenson et al. (1985) find similar starting points for musical interests among cohorts who came of age in the 1980s.

4 During the childhood and especially the adolescent years, the introduction to a range of extracurricular activities forges stronger, deeper, and more emotional connections between parents and children. Sports, in particular, are often the key conduit by which fathers bond more readily and intensely develop deeper bonds with their sons (Messner 1990). Likewise, music builds familial bonds similarly, though perhaps with a muted gender dimension in comparison to sports (Bennett 2000 and 2013; Kotarba 2013).

5 In her study of women bass players, Clawson (1999) finds that women with whom she spoke similarly selected the bass due to their assumptions of the instrument's lower level of rigor for mastery.

6 This is consistent with Green's (1997) work suggesting girls to be more interested in and successful in vocal performance over instrumentation.

7 Today, girlhood is characterized by participation in worlds once the exclusive field of boys, such as sports, and their participation in them often allows for an increase in social status. The tomboy status, once a disparaged term (and often associated with the threat of being marked as lesbian), now allows for a boost in status (Heywood and Dworkin 2003). Some women suggested their interests in rock music during the early years of the life course often worked in tandem with their other masculine pursuits as marking them as tomboys (Halberstam 1998).

8 Though difficult to decipher which music world is more callous, Wagner's (2015) study of young virtuosos clearly illustrates the classical music world to be an incredibly competitive one in which very few ultimately succeed.

2. First Making the Sounds

1 Rodger Lyle Brown's (1991) *Party Out of Bounds* is considered the premier documentation of the history of 1980s-era Athens, a book that a few musicians referenced during (or after) interviews. Though their experience was twenty-plus years after the Athens that Brown documented, many of them suggested the culture of the town continued to act as a foundation for the contemporary music scene.

2 Davis's (2006) work illustrates the conflict punks negotiate as they come to terms with aging within their music subculture. While some successfully remain committed to punk well into adulthood, many ultimately reject the scene.

3 Other studies show the sense of liminality to be a standardized experience in the emerging adulthood years (Karp et al. 1998).

4 Bennett's (2013) volume notes the varied and multidimensional complications that aging brings to various music worlds, as participants consistently struggle with squaring their aging identities with their roles in music.

5 Particular settings and contexts can allow for the emergence of more secure adult identities, as young people often feel more like adults while at work (Settersten 2011; Shanahan et al. 2005).

6 Recent surveys of young adults show that they regard individualistic criteria, such as personal responsibility, as paramount to securing an adult status today (Arnett 1998, 2006).

3. I Feel It in My Bones

1 Classic theorists, such as Erikson (1950), suggest identity to be a prime task of adolescence.

2 The tenuous construction of "authenticity" is similarly obscure in other musical genres, such as punk, heavy metal, and country, among others (Eastman 2012; Fox 1987; Hebdige 1979; Larsson 2013).

3 Bayton (1990) found women musicians to be less likely than men to self-identify as musicians, even when they had lengthy and formal training on instruments. Their lack of self-confidence made them prone to criticism, both from themselves as well as from other (men) musicians.

4 The only musicians who did not work for pay were two who were currently enrolled in college and the one who was a stay-at-home parent. Every other musician worked either full time in a single job or juggled multiple jobs (often in the service sector). The musicians were most likely to be employed in white-collar, professional work. Twenty-two musicians held such jobs, working in offices and professional settings either at the university or with local businesses. Fifteen musicians worked in the service sector, most often in the food industry as servers, cooks, or bartenders. Another six musicians had jobs in the music sector, working for recording studios, record labels, or music promotion companies. Very few musicians (2 of 48) worked in manual labor jobs.

4. Men and Masculinities in a Musical World

1 Ad-Rock is married to Kathleen Hannah, the founder and singer/guitarist of Bikini Kill, who is revered as the mother of the riot grrrl movement spawned in the 1990s.

2 Older siblings bear a significant influence on younger siblings in a range of outcomes, both positive and negative, including generating an interest in sports and/or art, peer competence, and educational attainment, as well as increased risky behaviors and the onset of sexual activity (Hauser and Wong 1989; Whiteman et al. 2007; Widmer 1997).

3 The musical style that Presley supposedly "invented" was of course borrowed, some would say co-opted, from black music culture, but this too is a genre similarly dominated by men.

4 Women icons, such as Janis Joplin, Joan Jett, Chrissie Hynde, Kim Gordon, and Liz Phair, to name a few, have of course been commended by critics, music historians, and contemporary musicians, including those in this book, for their contribution

to rock. However, they are rarely cited by men as an inspiration for pursuing music careers. The role of these and other women is complex for women musicians. While they do cite them as role models of sorts, many of them did not necessarily develop an interest in rock music because of women musicians, but instead were most often "bit by the music bug" from men in rock.

5 Researchers in this vein have typically focused on formal mentoring among musicians in training in college institutions and conservatories (Creech et al. 2008; Gaunt et al. 2012).

6 Other research has demonstrated one partner in the potential mentoring relationship is often unlikely to recognize the relationship as a mentoring one (Welsh et al. 2012).

7 Sexual identity is not only mutable, but also socially constructed. Scholars have addressed the multiple ways in which men and women situate their sexualities. As many scholars have noted, the sexual practices in which one engages in (and with whom they do so) do not necessarily align with self-identifications (Almaguer 1993; Fausto-Sterling 2003).

5. Women and the Challenges of Musical Life Course Trajectories

1 Gadbois and Bowker (2007) suggest nonathletic extracurricular activities may contribute to girls' self-esteem and development more significantly than athletics, whereas athletics are more critical to boys' positive development.

2 Research has suggested that other styles of music are more accessible to girls that are not as strictly male dominated as rock (Frith and Goodwin 1990; Shepherd and Devine 2015; Whiteley 1997). Pop music in particular has been a strong pathway into girls' musical development. While other genres outside of rock have generated alternative interests in music to girls, the women with whom I spoke suggested a lifelong interest in rock music in particular despite its barriers. They were certainly fans of pop bands during their childhoods. While these early musical interests may have presumably influenced their music making in rock later in life, they did not necessarily nor directly make such connections.

3 Research on mentoring in normative occupations in the public sector suggests that women's mentoring relationships and experiences do not differ drastically from men's, nor are they more problematic (Feeney 2006; Feeney and Bozeman 2008).

4 Numerous studies suggest, however, that the transition to work is becoming increasingly precarious for many, regardless of their level of education and career aspirations (Heinz 2002, 2003; Lowe 2001).

5 Feelings of inadequacy and an outsider status are not limited to nontraditional occupations, nor are they necessarily exclusive to male-dominated lines of work. Women and people of color similarly experience the "impostor syndrome" in a range of occupations, from banking to education to STEM fields (Dancy and Brown 2011; Sealy 2010).

6 Numerous studies illustrate the stronger influence family life, particularly children, has on women's work lives (Chodorow 1978; Hochschild 1989; Reskin and Padavic 2002). When men become fathers, in contrast, their work lives and contributions to domestic work typically change very little (Coltrane 2000).

7 These trends are consistent with other research illustrating gendered musical instrumentation in school-structured settings. Boys prefer larger, heavier, and more rock-oriented instruments, while girls have consistently shown preferences for smaller and high-pitched instruments (Hallam et al. 2008; Sheldon and Price 2005).

8 Wald (1998) suggests that the inclusion of women in music culture signifies a legitimate shift in the gendered organization in music, but simultaneously reifies the appropriate femininity as based on appearance and sexuality.

6. The Great Beyond

1 Rapuano (2009) has noted the complications that arise when the leisure-work divide is blurred among musicians working for pay. Theoretically, work and leisure are separate endeavors (Haworth and Veal 2005). When they begin to overlap, as in the case of musicians, enjoyment diminishes from the once pleasurable activity that is music making (Haney and Kline 2010).

2 Contemporary young adults increasingly prioritize meaningful work over lucrative careers with high pay (Swartz et al. 2011).

3 Others, J. Brown (1991) in particular, have found that individuals use nontraditional (or deviant) histories as a conduit in which they transition to conventional lives and careers.

4 Other music worlds appear to work similarly, as many classical musicians shift to nonmusical careers after years of investment (Wagner 2015).

5 The remaining eight musicians describe music as both a career *and* a hobby. They are not at a point in their lives in which they are certain what direction their lives may take. As such, they believe their musical futures could do either way: a possible career in music or perhaps something else entirely.

6 The fundamental insight of the symbolic interactionist perspective of the life course is that people actively assign meaning to the life course. It is a lifelong project of integrating accounts to explain one's life and life outcomes (Gubrium et al. 1994; Holstein and Gubrium 2003).

7 Scholars theorize the tension-release effect of media, including music, to be a motive for and positive consequence of media consumption (Rubin 2009).

8 While Cohen (1997) found musicians to cite musical trajectories as a decisive decision to intentionally avoid unfulfilling work options elsewhere, the musicians with whom I spoke framed the positive consequences of pursuing music as unintentional. They did not actively select music to avoid mundane options, but instead in hindsight recognized the monotonous lives they imagined they otherwise would have lived had they made the more "rational" choices of pursuing normative occupations.

Conclusion

1 Kinney (1993) suggests the transition to high school enables more opportunities for adolescents to develop and salvage identities. He is more attentive to school-structured activities, overlooking the influence of informal activities such as the participation in rock music culture.

2 A similar strategy to perhaps preserve one's masculinity, men's friendships are often characterized by a "covert intimacy" in which the relationship is valued, but of assumed significance (Swain 1989).

References

Acker, Joan. 1990. "Hierarchies, Jobs, Bodies: A Theory of Gendered Organizations." *Gender & Society* 4: 139–158.

Almaguer, Tomas. 1993. "Chicano Men: A Cartography of Homosexual Identity and Behavior." In *The Lesbian and Gay Studies Reader*, edited by Henry Abelove, Michele Aina Barale, and David M. Halperin, 255–273. New York: Routledge.

Arnett, Jeffrey Jensen. 1997. "Young People's Conceptions of the Transition to Adulthood." *Youth & Society* 29: 1–23.

Arnett, Jeffrey Jensen. 1998. "Learning to Stand Alone: The Contemporary American Transition to Adulthood in Cultural and Historical Context." *Human Development* 41: 295–315.

Arnett, Jeffrey Jensen. 2000. "Emerging Adulthood: A Theory of Development from the Late Teens through the Twenties." *American Psychologist* 55: 469–480.

Arnett, Jeffrey Jensen. 2001. "Conceptions of the Transition to Adulthood among Emerging Adults in American Ethnic Groups." *Journal of Adult Development* 8: 133–143.

Arnett, Jeffrey Jensen. 2004. *Emerging Adulthood: The Winding Road from Late Teens through the Twenties*. New York: Oxford University Press.

Arnett, Jeffrey Jensen. 2006. "Emerging Adulthood: Understanding the New Way of Coming of Age." In *Emerging Adults in America: Coming of Age in the 21st Century*, edited by Jeffrey Jensen Arnett and Jennifer Lynn Tanner, 3–19. Washington, DC: American Psychological Association.

Aronson, Pamela. 2008. "The Markers and Meanings of Growing Up: Contemporary Young Women's Transition from Adolescence to Adulthood." *Gender & Society* 22: 56–82.

Arthur, Michael B. 1994. "The Boundaryless Career: A New Perspective for Organizational Inquiry." *Journal of Organizational Behavior* 15: 295–306.

Ashley, Martin. 2011. "The Perpetuation of Hegemonic Male Power and the Loss of Boyhood Innocence: Case Studies from the Music Industry." *Journal of Youth Studies* 14: 59–76.

Bannister, Matthew. 2006. *White Boys, White Noise: Masculinities and 1980s Indie Guitar Rock*. Burlington, VT: Ashgate.

Barrett, Anne. 2003. "Socioeconomic Status and Age Identity: The Role of Dimensions of Health in the Subjective Construction of Age Identity." *Journal of Gerontology* 58: S101–110.

Barrett, Anne. 2005. "Gendered Experiences in Midlife: Implications for Age Identity." *Journal of Aging Studies* 19: 163–183.

Bayton, Mavis. 1990. "How Women Become Musicians." In *On Record: Rock, Pop and the Written Word*, edited by Simon Frith and Andrew Goodwin, 238–257. New York: Routledge.

Bayton, Mavis. 1997. "Women and the Electric Guitar." In *Sexing the Groove: Popular Music and Gender*, edited by Sheila Whiteley, 37–50. New York: Routledge.

Becker, Howard S. 1982. *Art Worlds*. Berkeley: University of California Press.

Bennett, Andy. 2000. *Popular Music and Youth Culture: Music, Identity and Place*. London: Macmillan.

Bennett, Andy. 2001. *Cultures of Popular Music*. Philadelphia: Open University Press.

Bennett, Andy. 2013. *Music, Aging and Style: Growing Old Disgracefully? Popular Music, Ageing and Lifestyle*. Philadelphia: Temple University Press.

Bennett, Andy, and Paul Hodkinson. 2012. *Ageing and Youth Cultures: Music, Style and Identity*. New York: Berg.

Bennett, Dawn. 2009. "Academy and the Real World: Developing Realistic Notions of Career in the Performing Arts." *Arts and Humanities in Higher Education* 8: 309–327.

Bielby, William T. 2004. "Rock in a Hard Place: Grassroots Cultural Production." *American Sociological Review* 69: 1–13.

Bourdieu, Pierre. 1984. *Distinction: A Social Critique of the Judgement of Taste*. Cambridge, MA: Harvard University Press.

Bozick, Robert, Karl Alexander, Doris Entwisle, Susan Dauber, and Kerri Kerr. 2010. "Framing the Future: Revisiting the Place of Educational Expectations in Status Attainment." *Social Forces* 88: 2027–2052.

Brandtstädter, Jochen. 2006. "Action Perspectives on Human Development." In *Handbook of Child Psychology*, edited by W. Damon and R. M. Lerner, 516–568. New York: John Wiley.

Briscoe, Jon T., and Douglas P. Hall. 2006. "The Interplay of Boundaryless and Protean Careers: Combinations and Implications." *Journal of Vocational Behavior* 69: 4–18.

Brooks, Matthew. 2006. "Man-to-Man. A Body Talk Between Male Friends." *Qualitative Inquiry* 11: 185–207.

Brown, J. David. 1991. "The Professional Ex-: An Alternative for Exiting the Deviant Career." *Sociological Quarterly* 32: 219–230.

Brown, Rodger Lyle. 1991. *Party out of Bounds: The B-52's, R.E.M., and the Kids Who Rocked Athens, Georgia*. Atlanta: Everthemore Books.

Burland, Karen, and Jane W. Davidson. 2002. "Training the Talented." *Music Education Research* 4: 121–140.

Butler, Judith. 1990. *Gender Trouble: Feminism and the Subversion of Identity*. New York: Routledge.

Byrd, Samuel K. 2015. *The Sounds of Latinidad: Immigrants Making Music and Creating Culture in a Southern City*. New York: New York University Press.

Cahn, Susan K. 1993. "From the 'Muscle Moll' to the 'Butch' Ballplayer: Mannishness, Lesbianism, and Homophobia in U.S. Women's Sport." *Feminist Studies* 19: 343–368.

Calasanti, Toni M., and Kathleen F. Slevin 2001. *Gender, Social Inequalities, and Aging*. New York: Alta Mira.

Cancian, Francesca M. "The Feminization of Love." *Signs* 11: 692–709.

Carr, Dawn C. 2006. "Music, Socializing, Performance, and the Web of Social Ties." *Activities, Adaptation and Aging* 30: 1–24.

Chao, Georgia T. 2007. "Mentoring and Organizational Socialization: Networks for Work Adjustment." *The Handbook of Mentoring at Work*, edited by Belle Rose Ragins and Kathy E. Kram, 179–196. Thousand Oaks, CA: Sage.

Chodorow, Nancy. 1978. *The Reproduction of Mothering: Psychoanalysis and the Sociology of Gender*. Berkeley: University of California Press.

Christenson, Peter G., Peter Debenedittis, and Thomas R. Lindlof. 1985. "Children's Use of Audio Media." *Communication Research* 12: 327–343.

Christenson, Peter G., and Donald F. Roberts. 1998. *It's Not Only Rock & Roll: Popular Music in the Lives of Adolescents*. Cresskill, NJ: Hampton.

Clausen, John A. 1986. *The Life Course: A Sociological Perspective*. Upper Saddle River, NJ: Prentice-Hall.

Clausen, John A. 1993. *American Lives: Looking Back at the Children of the Great Depression*. Berkeley: University of California Press.

Clawson, Mary Ann. 1999. "When Women Play the Bass: Instrument Specialization and Gender Interpretation in Alternative Rock Music." *Gender & Society* 13: 193–210.

Coakley, Jay. 2006. "The Good Father: Parental Expectations and Youth Sports." *Leisure Studies* 25: 153–163.

Coates, Norma. 1997. "(R)evolution Now." In *Sexing the Groove: Popular Music and Gender*, edited by Sheila Whiteley, 50–64. New York: Routledge.

Cohen, Sara. 1997. "Men Making a Scene: Rock Music and the Production of Gender." In *Sexing the Groove: Popular Music and Gender*, edited by Sheila Whiteley, 17–36. New York: Routledge.

Collins, Patricia Hill. 1986. "Learning from the Outsider Within: The Sociological Significance of Black Feminist Thought." *Social Problems* 33: 14–32.

Coltrane, Scott. 2000. *Gender and Families*. New York: Rowman & Littlefield.

Connell, R.W. 1987. *Gender and Power*. Stanford, CA: Stanford University Press.

Connell, R.W. 1990. "An Iron Man: The Body and Some Contradictions of Hegemonic Masculinity." In *Sport, Men and the Gender Order: Critical Feminist Perspectives*, edited by M. Messner & D. Sabo, 83–95. Champaign, IL: Human Kinetics.

Connell, R.W. 1995. *Masculinities*. Berkeley: University of California Press.

Cooley, Charles Horton. 1909. *Social Organization: A Study of the Large Mind*. New York: Scribner.

Coser, Lewis A. 1974. *Greedy Institutions. Patterns of Undivided Commitment*. New York: Free Press.

Craig, Maxine Leeds. 2014. *Sorry I Don't Dance: Why Men Refuse to Dance*. New York: Oxford University Press.

Creech, Andrea, Ioulia Papageorgi, Celia Duffy, Frances Morton, Elizabeth Haddon, John Potter, Christophe de Bezenac, Tony Whyton, Evangelos Himonides, and Graham Welch. 2008. "From Music Student to Professional: The Process of Transition." *British Journal of Music* 25: 315–331.

Csikszentmihalyi, Mihaly, and Barbara Schneider. 2000. *Becoming Adult: How Teenagers Prepare for the World of Work*. New York: Basic Books.

Dagaz, Mari C. 2012. "Learning from the Band: Trust, Acceptance, and Self-Confidence." *Journal of Contemporary Ethnography* 41: 432–461.

Dancy, Elon T., and Christopher M. Brown. 2011. "The Mentoring and Induction of Educators of Color: Addressing the Impostor Syndrome in Academe." *Journal of School Leadership* 21: 607–634.

Davis, Joanna R. 2006. "Growing up Punk: Negotiating Aging Identity in a Local Music Scene." *Symbolic Interaction* 29: 63–69.

DeNora, Tia. 2000. *Music in Everyday Life*. Cambridge: Cambridge University Press.

DeVault, Marjorie L. 1991. *Feeding the Family: The Social Organization of Caring as Gendered Work*. Chicago: University of Chicago Press.

DiMaggio, Paul, and Michael Useem. 1978. "Social Class and Arts Consumption: The Origins and Consequences of Class Differences in Exposure to Arts in America." *Theory and Society* 5: 141–161.

DeMichele, Kimberly A. 2009. "Memories of Suffering: Exploring the Life Story Narratives of Twice-Widowed Elderly Women." *Journal of Aging Studies* 23: 103–113.

Dobrow, Shoshana R., and Monica C. Higgins. 2005. "Developmental Networks and Professional Identity: A Longitudinal Study." *Career Development International* 10: 567–583.

Drummond, John D. 1990. "The Characteristics of Amateur and Professional." *International Journal of Music Education* 75: 3–8.

Durkheim, Emile. 1893. *The Division of Labour in Society*. New York: Free Press.

Eastman, Jason T. 2012. "Rebel Manhood: The Hegemonic Masculinity of the Southern Rock Music Revival." *Journal of Contemporary Ethnography* 41: 189–219.

Eccles, Jacquelynne S., and Bonnie L. Barber. 1999. "Student Council, Volunteering, Basketball, or Marching Band?: What Kind of Extracurricular Involvement Matters?" *Journal of Adolescent Research* 14: 10–43.

Eccles, Jacquelynne S., Bonnie L. Barber, Margaret Stone, and James Hunt. 2003. "Extracurricular Activities and Adolescent Development." *Journal of Social Issues* 59: 865–889.

Elder, Glen H. Jr. 1975. "Age Differentiation and the Life Course." *Annual Review of Sociology* 1: 165–190.

Elder, Glen H. Jr. 1985. "Perspectives on the Life Course." In *Life Course Dynamics: Trajectories and Transitions, 1968–1980*, edited by Glen H. Elder Jr., 23–49. Ithaca, NY: Cornell University Press.

Elder, Glen H. Jr., Monica Kirkpatrick Johnson, and Robert Crosnoe. 2003. "The Emergence and Development of Life Course Theory." In *Handbook of the Life Course*, edited by Jeylan T. Mortimer and Michael J. Shanahan, 3–19. New York: Springer.

Erikson, Erik H. 1950. *Childhood and Society*. New York: W. W. Norton.

Evetts, Julia. 1996. *Gender and Career in Science and Engineering*. Bristol, PA: Taylor & Francis.

Ezzell, Matthew B. 2009. "'Barbie Dolls' on the Pitch: Identity Work, Defensive Othering, and Inequality in Women's Rugby." *Social Problems* 56: 111–131.

Fausto-Sterling, Anne. 2003. *Sexing the Body: Gender Politics and the Construction of Sexuality*. New York: Basic Books.

Feeney, Mary Kathleen. 2006. "Mentoring Women in the Public Sector: Expectations and Realities." *International Journal of Learning and Change* 1: 381–406.

Feeney, Mary K., and Barry Bozeman. 2008. "Mentoring and Network Ties." *Human Relations* 61: 1651–1676.

Finnegan, Ruth. 1989. *The Hidden Musicians: Music-Making in an English Town*. Cambridge: Cambridge University Press.

Fiorentine, Robert, and Stephen Cole. 1992. "Why Fewer Women Become Physicians: Explaining the Premed Persistence Gap." *Sociological Forum* 7: 469–496.

Fornäs, Johan, Ulf Sernhade, and Ove Sernhade. 1995. *In Garageland: Rock, Youth, and Modernity*. New York: Routledge.

Foschi, Martha. 1996. "Double Standards in the Evaluations of Men and Women." *Social Psychology Quarterly* 59: 237–254.

Fournet, Adele. 2010. "Women Rockers and the Strategies of a Minority Position." *Music and Arts in Action* 3, no. 1: 20–47.

Fox, Kathryn J. 1987. "Real Punks and Pretenders: The Social Organization of a Counterculture." *Journal of Contemporary Ethnography* 16: 344–370.

Frith, Simon. 1981. *Sound Effects: Youth, Leisure, and the Politics of Rock 'n' Roll*. New York: Pantheon.

Frith, Simon, and Andrew Goodwin. 1990. *On Record: Rock, Pop, and the Written Word*. New York: Routledge.

Frith, Simon, and Angela McRobbie. 1990. "Rock and Sexuality." In *On Record: Rock, Pop and the Written Word*, edited by Simon Frith and Andrew Goodwin, 317–332. New York: Routledge.

Furstenberg, Frank F. Jr., Rubén G. Rumbaut, and Richard A. Settersten Jr. 2005. "On the Frontier of Adulthood: Emerging Themes and New Directions." In *On the Frontier of Adulthood: Theory, Research, and Public Policy*, edited by Richard A. Settersten Jr., Frank F. Furstenburg Jr., and Rubén G. Rumbaut, 3–25. Chicago: University of Chicago Press.

Fussell, Elizabeth, and Frank F. Furstenberg, Jr. 2005. "The Transition to Adulthood During the Twentieth Century." In *On the Frontier of Adulthood: Theory, Research, and Public Policy*, edited by Richard A. Settersten Jr., Frank F. Furstenburg Jr., and Rubén G. Rumbaut, 29–75. Chicago: University of Chicago Press.

Gadbois, Shannon, and Anne Bowker. 2007. "Gender Differences in the Relationships between Extracurricular Activities Participation, Self-Description, and Domain-Specific and General Self-Esteem." *Sex Roles* 56: 675–689.

Garratt, Sheryl. 1990. "Teenage Dreams." In *On Record: Rock, Pop, and the Written Word*, edited by Simon Frith and Andrew Goodwin, 399–409. New York: Routledge.

Gaunt, Helena, Andrea Creech, Marion Long, and Susan Hallam. 2012. "Supporting Conservatoire Students Towards Professional Integration: One-to-One Tuition and the Potential of Mentoring." *Music Education Research* 14: 25–43.

Gerson, Kathleen. 1985. *Hard Choices: How Women Decide about Work, Career, and Motherhood*. Berkeley: University of California Press.

Gerson, Kathleen. 2010. *The Unfinished Revolution: How a New Generation is Reshaping Family, Work, and Gender in America*. New York: Oxford University Press.

Giffort, Danielle M. 2011. "Show or Tell? Feminist Dilemmas and Implicit Feminism at Girls' Rock Camp." *Gender & Society* 25: 545–568.

Gillespie, Rosemary. 2003. "Childfree and Feminine: Understanding the Gender Identity of Voluntarily Childless Women." *Gender & Society* 17: 122–136.

Goffman, Erving. 1959. *The Presentation of Self in Everyday Life*. New York: Doubleday.

Golden, Lonnie. 2001. "Flexible Work Schedules: Which Workers Get Them?" *American Behavioral Scientist* 44: 1157–1178.

Gould, Robert. 1974. "Measuring Masculinity by the Size of a Paycheck." In *Men and Masculinity*, edited by Joseph H. Pleck and Jack Sawyer, 96–100. Englewood Cliffs, NJ: Prentice-Hall.

Grazian, David. 2003. *Blue Chicago: The Search for Authenticity in Urban Blues Clubs*. Chicago: University of Chicago Press.

Green, Lucy. 1997. *Music, Gender and Education*. New York: Cambridge University Press.

Groce, Stephen B., and Margaret Cooper. 1990. "Just Me and the Boys?: Women in Local-Level Rock and Roll." *Gender & Society* 4: 220–229.

Gubrium, Jaber F., James A. Holstein, and David R. Buckholdt. 1994. *Constructing the Life Course*. Dix Hills, NY: General Hall.

Guest, Andrew, and Barbara Schneider. 2003. "Adolescents' Extracurricular Participation in Context: The Mediating Effects of Schools, Communities, and Identity." *Sociology of Education* 76: 89–109.

Hajdu, David. May 23, 2011. "Forever Young? In Some Ways, Yes." *New York Times.*

Haenfler, Ross. 2006. *Straight Edge: Hardcore Punk, Clean-Living Youth, and Social Change.* New Brunswick, NJ: Rutgers University Press

Hagestad, Gunhild O. 1990. "Social Perspectives on the Life Course." In *Handbook of Aging and the Social Sciences,* edited by Robert H. Binstock and Linda K. George, 151–168. San Diego, CA: Academic Press.

Halberstam, Judith. 1998. *Female Masculinity.* Durham, NC: Duke University Press.

Halberstam, Judith. 2005. *In a Queer Time and Place: Transgender Bodies, Subcultural Lives.* New York: New York University Press.

Hallam, Susan, Lynne Rogers, and Andrea Creech. 2008. "Gender Differences in Musical Instrument Choice." *International Journal of Music Education* 26: 7–19.

Hamilton, Laura, Claudia Geist, and Brian Powell. 2011. "Marital Name Change as a Window into Gender Attitudes." *Gender & Society* 25: 145–175.

Hamilton, Stephen F., and Mary Agnes Hamilton. 2006. "School, Work, and Emerging Adulthood." In *Emerging Adults in America: Coming of Age in the 21st Century,* edited by J. J. Arnett and J. L. Tanner, 257–277. Washington, DC: American Psychological Association.

Hancock, Kathleen J., Matthew A. Baum, and Marijke Breuning. 2013. "Women and Pre-Tenure Scholarly Productivity in International Studies: An Investigation into the Leaky Career Pipeline." *International Studies Perspectives* 14: 507–527.

Haney, Mitchell R., and A. David Kline. 2010. *The Value of Time and Leisure in a World of Work.* Lanham, MD: Lexington.

Hargrove, Byron K., Maureen G. Creagh, and Brian L. Burgess. 2002. "Family Interaction Patterns as Predictors of Vocational Identity and Career Decision-Making Self-Efficacy." *Journal of Vocational Behavior* 61: 185–201.

Harris, Deborah A., and Patti Giuffre. 2015. *Taking the Heat: Women Chefs and Gender Inequality in the Professional Kitchen.* New Brunswick, NJ: Rutgers University Press.

Harrison, Anthony K. 2008. "Racial Authenticity in Rap Music and Hip Hop." *Sociology Compass* 2: 1783–1800.

Hauge, Mona-Iren, and Hanne Haavind. 2011. "Boys' Bodies and the Constitution of Adolescent Masculinities." *Sport, Education, and Society* 16: 1–16.

Hauser, Robert M., and Raymond S. Wong. 1989. "Sibling Resemblance and Intersibling Effects in Educational Attainment." *Sociology of Education* 62: 149–171.

Haworth, John T., and Anthony J. Veal. 2005. *Work and Leisure.* New York: Routledge.

Hebdige, Dick. 1979. *Subculture: The Meaning of Style.* New York: Routledge.

Heckman, James J. 1994. "Is Job Training Oversold?" *The Public Interest* 115: 91–115.

Heinz, Walter R. 2002. "Transition Discontinuities and the Biographical Shaping of Early Work Careers." *Journal of Vocational Behavior* 60: 220–240.

Heinz, Walter R. 2003. "From Work Trajectories to Negotiated Careers: The Contingent Work Life Course." In *Handbook of the Life Course,* edited by Jeylan T. Mortimer and Michael J. Shanahan, 185–204. New York: Springer.

Hermanowicz, Joseph C. 1998. *The Stars Are Not Enough: Scientists—Their Passions and Professions.* Chicago: University of Chicago Press.

Heywood, Leslie, and Shari L. Dworkin. 2003. *Built to Win: The Female Athlete as Cultural Icon.* Minneapolis: University of Minnesota Press.

Hochschild, Arlie Russel. 1989. *The Second Shift: Working Parents and the Revolution at Home.* New York: Viking Penguin.

Hodkinson, Phil, and Andrew C. Sparkes. 1997. "Careership: A Sociological Theory of Career Decision Making." *British Journal of Sociology of Education* 18: 29–44.

Hodson, Randy. 2001. *Dignity at Work*. Cambridge: Cambridge University Press.

Holstein, James A., and Jaber F. Gubrium. 2003. "The Life Course." In *Handbook of Symbolic Interactionism*, edited by Larry T. Reynolds and Nancy J. Herman-Kinney, 835–855. Walnut Creek, CA: AltaMira.

Hymowitz, Kay S. 1999. *Ready or Not: What Happens When We Treat Children as Small Adults*. San Francisco: Encounter.

Johnson, Mary C., and Paul Hager. 2008. "Navigating the Wilderness of Becoming Professional." *Journal of Workplace Learning* 20: 526–536.

Johnson, Monica Kirkpatrick, Justin Allen Berg, and Toni Sirotzki. 2007. "Differentiation in Self-Perceived Adulthood: Extending the Confluence Model of Subjective Age Identity." *Social Psychology Quarterly* 70: 243–261.

Kanter, Rosabeth Moss. 1977. *Men and Women of the Corporation*. New York: Basic Books.

Karp, David A., Lynda Lytle Homstrom, and Paul S. Gray. 1998. "Leaving Home for College: Expectations for Selective Reconstruction of Self." *Symbolic Interaction* 21, no. 3: 253–276.

Kay, Fiona M., John Hagan, and Patricia Parker. 2009. "Principals in Practice: The Importance of Mentorship in the Early Stages of Career Development." *Law & Policy* 31: 69–110.

Kimmel, Michael. 2008. *Guyland: The Perilous World Where Boys Become Men*. New York: Harper Collins.

Kimmel, Michael. 2011. *Manhood in America*, 3rd ed. New York: Oxford University Press.

Kinney, David. 1993. "From Nerds to Normals: The Recovery of Identity among Adolescents from Middle School to High School." *Sociology of Education* 66: 21–40.

Kins, Evie, and Wim Beyers. 2010. "Failure to Launch, Failure to Achieve Criteria for Adulthood?" *Journal of Adolescent Research* 25: 743–777.

Kohn, Melvin. 1969. *Class and Conformity*. Homewood, IL: Dorsey.

Kotarba, Joseph. 2013. *Baby Boomer Rock 'n' Roll Fans: The Music Never Ends*. Lanham, MD: Scarecrow.

Lareau, Annette 2003. *Unequal Childhoods: Class, Race, and Family Life*. Berkeley: University of California Press.

LaRocco, Susan A. 2007. "A Grounded Theory Study of Socializing Men into Nursing." *Journal of Men's Studies* 15: 120–129.

Larsson, Susanna. 2013. "'I Bang My Head, Therefore I Am': Constructing Individual and Social Authenticity in the Heavy Metal Subculture." *Young* 21: 95–110.

Laughey, Dan. 2006. *Music and Youth Culture*. Edinburgh: Edinburgh University Press.

Laz, Cheryl. 1998. "Act Your Age." *Sociological Forum* 13: 85–113.

Leblanc, Lauraine. 1999. *Pretty in Punk: Girls' Gender Resistance in a Boys' Subculture*. New Brunswick, NJ: Rutgers University Press.

Leonard, Marion. 2007. *Gender in the Music Industry*. Burlington, VT: Ashgate.

Lever, Janet. 1976. "Sex Differences in the Games Children Play." *Social Problems* 23: 478–487.

Levinson, Daniel J. 1978. *The Seasons of a Man's Life*. New York: Knopf.

Lorber, Judith. 2012. *Gender Inequality: Feminist Theories and Politics, Fifth Edition*. New York: Oxford University Press.

Lowe, Graham S. 2001. "Youth, Transitions, and the New World of Work." In *Restructuring Work and the Life Course*, edited by Victor W. Marshall, Walter R. Heinz, Hegla Kruger, and Anil Verma, 29–44. Toronto: University of Toronto Press.

MacDonald, Raymond, David Hargreaves, and Dorothy Miell. 2002. *Musical Identities*. Oxford: Oxford University Press.

Marsden, Peter V., John Shelton Reed, Michael D. Kennedy, and Kandi M. Stinson. 1982. "American Regional Cultures and Differences in Leisure Time Activities." *Social Forces* 60: 1023–49.

Maslow, A.H. 1943. "A Theory of Human Motivation." *Psychological Review* 50: 370–396.

Maume, David J., Anthony R. Bardo, and Rachel A. Sebastian. 2009. "Gender Differences in Sleep Disruption among Retail Food Workers." *American Sociological Review* 74: 989–1007.

Maume, David J., and Marcia L. Bellas. 2001. "The Overworked American or the Time Bind? Assessing Competing Explanations for Time Spent in Paid Labor." *American Behavioral Scientist* 44: 1137–1156.

McDonald, Steve, Lance D. Erickson, Monica K. Johnson, and Glen H. Elder. 2007. "Informal Mentoring and Young Adult Employment." *Social Science Research* 36: 1328–1347.

McHale, Susan M., Ann C. Crouter, and Shawn D. Whiteman. 2003. "The Family Contexts of Gender Development in Childhood and Adolescence." *Social Development* 12: 125–148.

Meltzer, Andrea L., and James K. McNulty. 2011. "Contrast Effects of Stereotypes." *Journal of Men's Studies* 19: 57–64.

Merton, Robert K., George G. Reader, and Patricia Kendall. 1957. *The Student Physician: Introductory Studies in the Sociology of Medical Education*. Cambridge, MA: Harvard University Press.

Messner, Michael. 1990. "Boyhood, Organized Sports, and the Construction of Masculinities." *Journal of Contemporary Ethnography* 18: 416–444.

Messner, Michael. 1992. *Power at Play: Sports and the Problem of Masculinity*. Boston: Beacon.

Mollenkopf, John H., Mary Waters, Jennifer Holdaway, and Philip Kasinitz. 2005. "The Ever-Winding Path: Ethnic and Racial Diversity in the Transition to Adulthood." In *On the Frontier of Adulthood: Theory, Research, and Public Policy*, edited by Richard A. Settersten Jr., Frank F. Furstenburg Jr., and Rubén G. Rumbaut, 454–497. Chicago: University of Chicago Press.

Monem, Nadine. 2007. *Riot Grrrl: Revolution Grrrl Style Now!* London: Black Dog.

Mortimer, Jeylan T., and Roberta G. Simmons. 1978. "Adult Socialization." *Annual Review of Sociology* 4: 421–454.

Mortimer, Jeylan T., Melanie J. Zimmer-Gembeck, Mikki Holmes, and Michael J. Shanahan. 2002. "The Process of Occupational Decision Making: Patterns During the Transition to Adulthood." *Journal of Vocational Behavior* 61: 439–465.

Mullaney, Jamie L. 2007. "'Unity Admirable but Not Necessarily Heeded': Going Rates and Gender Boundaries in the Straight Edge Hardcore Music Scene." *Gender & Society* 21: 384–408.

Mullaney, Jamie L. 2012. "All in Time: Age and the Temporality of Authenticity in the Straight-Edge Music Scene." *Journal of Contemporary Ethnography* 41: 611–635.

Nelson, Larry J., and Carolyn McNamara Barry. 2005. "Distinguishing Features of Emerging Adulthood: The Role of Self-Classification as an Adult." *Journal of Adolescent Research* 20: 242–262.

Neugarten, Bernice L., Joan W. Moore, and John C. Lowe. 1965. "Age Norms, Age Constraints, and Adult Socialization." *American Journal of Sociology* 70: 710–717.

Newton, Judith. 2004. *From Panthers to Promise Keepers: Rethinking the Men's Movement.* Lanham, MD: Rowman and Littlefield.

Nippert-Eng, Christena E. 1996. *Home and Work: Negotiating Boundaries through Everyday Life.* Chicago: University of Chicago Press.

O'Connor, Alan. 2004. "Punk and Globalization: Spain and Mexico." *International Journal of Cultural Studies* 7: 175–195.

Osgood, D. Wayne, Gretchen Ruth, Jacquelynne S. Eccles, Janis E. Jacobs, and Bonnie L. Barber. 2005. "Six Paths to Adulthood." In *On the Frontier of Adulthood: Theory,*

Research, and Public Policy, edited by Richard A. Settersten Jr., Frank F. Furstenburg Jr., and Rubén G. Rumbaut, 320–347. Chicago: University of Chicago Press.

Peters, Brian M. 2010. "Emo Gay Boys and Subcultures: Postpunk Queer Youth and (Re)thinking Images of Masculinity." *Journal of LGBT Youth* 7: 129–146.

Peterson, Richard A. 1992. "Understanding Audience Segmentation: From Elite and Mass to Omnivore and Univore." *Poetics* 21: 243–258.

Peterson, Richard A. 2005. "In Search of Authenticity." *Journal of Management Studies* 42: 1083–1098.

Peterson, Richard A., and Albert Simkus. 1992. "How Musical Tastes Mark Occupation Status Groups." In *Cultivating Differences. Symbolic Boundaries and the Making of Inequality*, edited by M. Lamont and M. Fournier, 152–186. Chicago: University of Chicago Press.

Philip, Kate, and Leo B. Hendry. 1996. "Young People and Mentoring—Towards a Typology?" *Journal of Adolescence* 19: 189–201.

Philip, Kate, and Leo B. Hendry. 2000. "Making Sense of Mentoring or Mentoring Making Sense? Reflections on the Mentoring Process by Adult Mentors with Young People." *Journal of Community & Applied Social Psychology* 10: 211–223.

Phinney, Jean S. 2006. "Ethnic Identity in Emerging Adulthood." In *Emerging Adults in America: Coming of Age in the 21st Century*, edited by Jeffrey Jensen Arnett and Jennifer Lynn Tanner, 117–134. Washington, DC: American Psychological Association.

Pickett, Susan A., James R. Greenley, and Jan S. Greenberg. 1995. "Off-Timedness as a Contributor to Subjective Burdens for Parents of Offspring with Severe Mental Illness." *Family Relations* 44: 195–201.

Ramirez, Michael. 2012. "Performing Gender through Performing Music: Constructions of Masculinities in a College Music Scene." *Journal of Men's Studies* 20: 108–124.

Ramirez, Michael. 2013. "'You Start Feeling Old': Rock Musicians Reconciling the Dilemmas of Adulthood." *Journal of Adolescent Research* 28: 299–324.

Ramirez, Michael. 2014. "'I'm Not a Musician, But . . .': Negotiating the Research Process in Examining the Lives of Musicians." *Qualitative Sociology Review* 10: 80–93.

Rapuano, Deborah. 2009. "Working at Fun: Conceptualizing Leisurework." *Current Sociology* 57: 617–636.

Ravert, Russell D. 2009. "'You're Only Young Once': Things College Students Report Doing Now Before It Is Too Late." *Journal of Adolescent Research* 24: 376–396.

Reddington, Helen. 2004. "The Forgotten Revolution of Female Punk Musicians in the 1970s." *Peace Review* 16: 439–444.

Reskin, Barbara, and Irene Padavic. 2002. *Women and Men at Work*. Thousand Oaks, CA: Pine Forge.

Reskin, Barbara F., and Patricia A. Roos. 1990. *Job Queues, Gender Queues: Explaining Women's Inroads into Male Occupations*. Philadelphia: Temple University Press.

Reynolds, Simon, and Joy Press. 1995. *The Sex Revolts: Gender, Rebellion, and Rock 'n' Roll*. Cambridge, MA: Harvard University Press.

RIAA (Recording Industry Association of America). 2015. "Music Consumer Profile—2015." Accessed July 28, 2017 from https://www.riaa.com/wp-content/uploads/2016/08/MusicWatch-Music-Consumer-Profile-2015.pdf

Ridgeway, Cecilia. 2011. *Framed by Gender: How Gender Inequality Persists in the Modern World*. Oxford: Oxford University Press.

Roberts, Donald F., and Peter G. Christenson. 2000. "Popular Music in Childhood and Adolescence." In *Handbook of Children and the Media*, edited by Dorothy G. Singer and Jerome L. Singer, 395–413. Thousand Oaks, CA: Sage.

Roberts, Donald F., Peter G. Christenson, and Douglas A. Gentile. 2003. "The Effects of Violent Music on Children and Adolescents." In *Media Violence and Children: A Complete Guide for Parents and Professionals*, edited by Douglas A. Gentile, 153–170. Westport, CT: Praeger.

Robinson, Victoria, Alexandra Hall, and Jenny Hockey. 2011. "Masculinities, Sexualities, and the Limits of Subversion: Being a Man in Hairdressing." *Men and Masculinities* 14: 31–50.

Roth, Louise Marie. 2011. *Selling Women Short: Gender and Money on Wall Street*. Princeton, NJ: Princeton University Press.

Rothman, Robert A. 1998. *Working: Sociological Perspectives, Second Edition*. Upper Saddle River, NJ: Prentice Hall.

Rubin, Alan M. 2009. "Uses and Gratifications: An Evolving Perspective of Media Effects." In *The Sage Handbook of Media Processes and Effects*, edited by Robin L. Nabi and Mary Beth Oliver, 147–159. Thousand Oaks, CA: Sage.

Ryalls, Emily. 2013. "Emo Angst, Masochism, and Masculinity in Crisis." *Text and Performance Quarterly* 33: 83–97.

Ryff, Carol D. 1985. "The Subjective Experience of Life-Span Transitions." In *Gender and the Life Course*, edited by Alice S. Rossi, 97–113. New York: Aldine.

Sackman, Reinhold, and Matthias Wingens. 2003. "From Transitions to Trajectories: Sequence Types." In *Social Dynamics of the Life Course: Transitions, Institutions, and Interrelations*, by W. R. Heinz and V. W. Marshall, 93–115. New York: de Gruyter.

Sandefur, Gary D., Jennifer Eggerling-Boeck, and Hyunjoon Park. 2005. "Off to a Good Start? Postsecondary Education and Early Adult Life." In *On the Frontier of Adulthood: Theory, Research, and Public Policy*, edited by Richard A. Settersten Jr., Frank F. Furstenburg Jr., and Rubén G. Rumbaut, 292–319. Chicago: University of Chicago Press.

Scheuble, Laurie K., and David R. Johnson. 1993. "Marital Name Change: Plans and Attitudes of College Students." *Journal of Marriage and Family* 55: 747–54.

Schieman, Scott, Paul Glavin, and Melissa A. Milkie. 2009. "When Work Interferes with Life: Work-Nonwork Interference and the Influence of Work-Related Demands and Resources." *American Sociological Review* 74: 966–988.

Schieman, Scott, and Marisa Young. 2010. "The Demands of Creative Work: Implications for Stress in the Work-Family Interface." *Social Science Research* 39: 246–259.

Schilt, Kristen, and Danielle Giffort. 2012. "'Strong Riot Women' and the Continuity of Feminist Subcultural Participation." In *Ageing and Youth Cultures: Music, Style, and Identity*, edited by Andy Bennett and Paul Hodkinson, 146–158. New York: Berg.

Schilt, Kristen, and Ekle Zobl. 2008. "Connecting the Dots: Riot Grrrls, Ladyfests, and the International Grrrl Zine Network." In *Next Wave Cultures: Feminism, Subcultures, and Activism*, edited by Anita Harris, 171–192. New York: Routledge.

Schippers, Mimi. 2000. "The Social Organization of Sexuality and Gender in Alternative Hard Rock: An Analysis of Intersectionality." *Gender & Society* 14: 747–764.

Schippers, Mimi. 2002. *Rockin' out of the Box: Gender Maneuvering in Alternative Hard Rock*. New Brunswick, NJ: Rutgers University Press.

Schneider, Barbara, and David Stevenson. 1999. *The Ambitious Generation: America's Teenagers, Motivated But Directionless*. New Haven, CT: Yale University Press.

Schoon, Ingrid, and Samantha Parsons. 2002. "Teenage Aspirations for Future Careers and Occupational Outcomes." *Journal of Vocational Behavior* 60: 262–288.

Schudson, Michael. 1989. "How Culture Works: Perspectives from Media Studies and the Efficacy of Symbols." *Theory and Society* 18: 153–180.

Schwalbe, Michael. 1996. *Unlocking the Iron Cage: The Men's Movement, Gender Politics, and American Culture*. New York: Oxford University Press.

Schwartz, Barry. 2004. *The Paradox of Choice: Why More Is Less*. New York: Harper Collins.

Sealy, Ruth. 2010. "Changing Perceptions of Meritocracy in Senior Women's Careers." *Gender in Management* 25: 184–197.

Settersten, Richard A. 1999. *Lives in Time and Place: The Problems and Promises of Developmental Science*. Amityville, NY: Baywood.

Settersten, Richard A. 2003. "Age Structuring and the Rhythm of the Life Course." In *Handbook of the Life Course*, edited by J. T. Mortimer & M. J. Shanahan, 81–98. New York: Springer.

Settersten, Richard A. 2011. "Becoming Adult: Meanings and Markers for Young Americans." In *Coming of Age in America: The Transition to Adulthood in the Twenty-First Century*, edited by Mary C. Waters, Patrick J. Carr, Maria J. Kefalas, and Jennifer Holdaway, 169–190. Berkeley: University of California Press.

Settersten, Richard, and Gunhild Hagestad. 1996. "What's the Latest?: Cultural Age Deadlines for Family Transitions." *Gerontologist* 36: 178–188.

Settersten, Richard A., and Karl Ulrich Mayer. 1997. "The Measurement of Age, Age Structuring, and the Life Course." *Annual Review of Sociology* 23: 233–261.

Sewell, William H., and Robert M. Hauser. 1975. *Education, Occupation and Earnings: Achievement in the Early Career*. New York: Academic Press.

Shanahan, Michael J. 2000. "Pathways to Adulthood in Changing Societies: Variability and Mechanisms in Life Course Perspective." *Annual Review of Sociology* 26: 667–692.

Shanahan, Michael J., Erik J. Porfeli, Jeylan T. Mortimer, and Lance D. Erickson. 2005. "Subjective Age Identity and the Transition to Adulthood: When Do Adolescents Become Adults?" In *On the Frontier of Adulthood: Theory, Research, and Public Policy*, by Richard A. Settersten Jr., Frank F. Furstenburg Jr., and Rubén G. Rumbaut, 225–255. Chicago: University of Chicago Press.

Shank, Barry. 1994. *Dissonant Identities: The Rock'n'Roll Scene in Austin, Texas*. Hanover, NH: Wesleyan University Press.

Sheldon, Deborah A., and Harry E. Price. 2005. "Gender and Instrumentation Distribution in an International Cross-Section of Wind and Percussion Ensembles." *Bulletin of the Council for Research in Music Education* 163: 43–51.

Shepherd, John, and Kyle Devine. 2015. *The Routledge Reader on the Sociology of Music*. New York: Routledge.

Smith, Tom. W. 2005. "Generation Gaps in Attitudes and Values from the 1970s to the 1990s." In *On the Frontier of Adulthood: Theory, Research, and Public Policy*, edited by Richard A. Settersten Jr., Frank F. Furstenburg Jr., and Rubén G. Rumbaut, 177–221. Chicago: University of Chicago Press.

Stalp, Marybeth C. 2006. "Creating an Artistic Self: Amateur Quilters and Subjective Careers." *Sociological Focus* 39: 193–216.

Stebbins, Robert A. 1970. "Career: The Subjective Approach." *Sociological Quarterly* 11: 32–49.

Stebbins, Robert A. 1976. "Music among Friends: The Social Networks of Amateur Musicians." *International Review of Sociology* 12: 52–73.

Stebbins, Robert A. 1979. *Amateurs: On the Margin Between Work and Leisure*. Beverly Hills, CA: Sage.

Stebbins, Robert A. 1992. *Amateurs, Professionals and Serious Leisure*. Montreal: McGill-Queen's University Press.

Stebbins, Robert A. 1997. "Casual Leisure: A Conceptual Statement." *Leisure Studies* 16: 17–25.

Stebbins, Robert. 2009. "Serious Leisure and Work." *Sociology Compass* 10: 764–775.

Stets, Jan E., and Peter J. Burke. 2000. "Identity Theory and Social Identity Theory." *Social Psychology Quarterly* 63: 224–237.

Straw, Will. 2000. "Characterizing Rock Music Culture: The Case of Heavy Metal." In *On Record: Rock, Pop, and the Written Word*, edited by Simon Frith and Andrew Goodwin, 97–110. New York: Routledge.

Stuij, Mirjam. 2015. "Habitus and Social Class: A Case Study on Socialisation into Sports and Exercise." *Sport, Education and Society* 20: 780–798.

Sullivan, Sherry E. 1999. "The Changing Nature of Careers: A Review and Research Agenda." *Journal of Management* 25: 457–484.

Swain, Jon. 2003. "How Young Schoolboys Become Somebody: The Role of the Body in the Construction of Masculinity." *British Journal of Sociology of Education* 24: 299–314.

Swain, Jon. 2006. "The Role of Sport in the Construction of Masculinities in an English Independent Junior School." *Sport, Education, and Society* 11: 317–334.

Swain, Scott. 1989. "Covert Intimacy: Closeness in Men's Friendships." In *Gender in Intimate Relationships: A Microstructural Approach*, edited by Barbara Risman and Pepper Schwartz, 71–86. Belmont, CA: Wadsworth.

Swartz, Teresa Toguchi, Douglas Hartmann, and Jeylan T. Mortimer. 2011. "Transitions to Adulthood in the Land of Lake Wobegon." In *Coming of Age in America: The Transition to Adulthood in the Twenty-First Century*, edited by Mary C. Waters, Patrick J. Carr, Maria J. Kefalas, and Jennifer Holdaway, 59–105. Berkeley: University of California Press.

Taylor, Jodie. 2012. *Playing It Queer: Popular Music, Identity, and Queer World-Making*. New York: Peter Lang.

Thomas, William I., and Dorothy Thomas. 1928. *The Child in America: Behavior Problems and Programs*. New York: Knopf.

Thorne, Barrie. 1993. *Gender Play: Girls and Boys in School*. New Brunswick, NJ: Rutgers University Press.

Townsend, Nicholas W. 2002. *The Package Deal: Marriage, Work and Fatherhood in Men's Lives*. Philadelphia: Temple University Press.

Vannini, Phillip, and J. Patrick Williams. 2009. *Authenticity in Culture, Self, and Society*. New York: Routledge.

Wagner, Izabela. 2015. *Producing Excellence: The Making of Virtuosos*. New Brunswick, NJ: Rutgers University Press.

Wald, Gayle. 1998. "Just a Girl?: Rock Music, Feminism, and the Cultural Construction of Female Youth." *Signs* 23: 585–610.

Walser, Robert. 1993. *Running with the Devil: Power, Gender, and Madness in Heavy Metal Music*. Middletown, CT: Wesleyan University Press.

Welsh, Elizabeth Torney, Devasheesh Bhave, and Kyoung Yong Kim. 2012. "Are You My Mentor? Informal Mentoring Mutual Identification." *Career Development International* 17: 137–148.

Whiteley, Sheila. 1997. *Sexing the Groove: Popular Music and Gender*. New York: Routledge.

Whiteman, Shawn D., Susan M. McHale, and Ann C. Crouter. 2007. "Explaining Sibling Similarities: Perceptions of Sibling Influences." *Journal of Youth and Adolescence* 36: 963–972.

Widmer, Eric D. 1997. "Influence of Older Siblings on Initiation of Sexual Intercourse." *Journal of Marriage and the Family* 59: 928–938.

Williams, Christine. 1995. *Still a Man's World: Men Who Do "Women's Work"*. Berkeley: University of California Press.

Williams, Joan. 2000. *Unbending Gender: Why Family & Work Conflict and What to Do About It*. New York: Oxford University Press.

Wilson, Stephan M., Gary W. Peterson, and Patricia Wilson. 1993. "The Process of Educational and Occupational Attainment of Adolescent Females from Low-Income, Rural Families." *Journal of Marriage and the Family* 55: 158–175.

Wise, Sue. 1990. "Sexing Elvis." In *On Record: Rock, Pop, and the Written Word*, edited by Simon Frith and Andrew Goodwin, 390–398. New York: Routledge.

Wynn, Jonathan R. 2015. *Music/City: American Festivals and Placemaking in Austin, Nashville, and Newport*. Chicago: University of Chicago Press.

Index

Ad-Rock, 104, 105, 210n1
adulthood, contemporary, 189–191
adulthood, young, 62, 75–76; among young adults, 72; and internalized adulthood, 62–63; maturity as a recurring concern and the tensions of aging, 65–67; and tensions with parents, 62–65. *See also* adulthood, young, reconciling the dilemmas of
adulthood, young, reconciling the dilemmas of, 67; the adult "alter ego" and alternative versions of adulthood, 73–75; and deemphasizing of the musician status, 69–70; leaving music behind (disengagement from music), 67–69; and persistence in musical careers, 70–71; and the reconciliation of aging, 71–72; and redefining music as a business, 72–73
aging: age norms, socialization, and the influence of gender and social class, 185–189, 208n10; and the changing criteria of adulthood, 13–15; influence of social class on the aging process, 187; life course perspective and the social construction of aging, 11–13; and music, 3–6; special meaning of in the music world, 187; tensions of in young adulthood, 65–67
Athens, Georgia, 209n1; availability of musicians in, 92–93; as an iconic college music town, 17; influence of on musicians' identities, 91–95; opportunities for musicians in, 93–95; reasons that aspiring musicians move to Athens, 54–58

authenticity: and the "moving target" of authenticity, 83; of musician identity, 43, 78, 79, 90–91, 199–200, 210n2

bass guitar, 7, 17, 38, 47, 138, 209n5; as easier to learn and less prestigious than lead guitar, 139–140
Bayton, Mavis, 210n3
Beastie Boys, 104–105
Beatles, The, 3, 153
Berry, Chuck, 3
B-52s, The, 17
Bielby, William T., 109
Black, Jack, 50
Bolan, Marc, 111
Bones of What You Believe, The, 131
Boucher, Claire, 131, 132
Bowie, David, 3, 73, 110, 111, 112, 122, 124; and the blending of the feminine with the masculine, 4, 122–123
Brenston, Jackie, 207n3
Brown, Rodger Lyle, 209n1
Byrne, David, 111

Churches, 131
Clark, Annie. *See* St. Vincent
Clash, The, 3, 109
Clawson, Mary Ann, 209n5
Colbert, Stephen, 78
Collins, Patricia Hill, 146
Cooper, Alice, and the blending of the feminine with the masculine, 122–123

About the Author

MICHAEL RAMIREZ is an associate professor of sociology at Texas A&M University–Corpus Christi.

Printed in the United States
By Bookmasters